what is
anarchism ?

Alexander Berkman

AK PRESS: EDINBURGH • LONDON • OAKLAND

Library of Congress
Cataloging-in-Publication Control Number
2003108752

The production of this book was made possible in part by a
generous donation from the Anarchist Archives Project.
For more information, please contact
The Anarchist Archives Project
P.O. Box 383123
Cambridge, MA 02238-1323
Printed in Canada

interior layout and design by c.nelson
cover design: Enamel Media

AK Press   AK Press
PO Box 12766   674A 23rd St.
Edinburgh   Oakland, CA 94612
Scotland EH89YE   www.akpress.org
www.akuk.com   akpress@akpress.org
ak@akedin.demon.uk   (510) 208.1700
(0131) 555.5165

INTRODUCTION

Alexander Berkman was born Ovsej Berkman in 1870 into a middle class Jewish family in Lithuania. Berkman's uncle, Mark Natanson, was a founder of the Chaikovsky Circle and the Zemlya I Volya (Land and Liberty) Society, the largest Russian Populist group in the 1870s. In February 1888 Berkman emigrated to the United States, and there joined the Jewish anarchist group Pionire der Frayhayt (Pioneers of Liberty) which had been formed in 1886 to fight for the release of the imprisoned Haymarket anarchists. He worked as a cigar maker and as a tailor before learning typesetting. Berkman then worked for a time on Johann Most's paper, *Freiheit*. Gradually Berkman distanced himself ideologically from Most and *Freiheit*, gravitating towards the anarchism of Josef Peukert and the Autonomie group, associated with the anarchist communist newspaper *Die Autonomie*, a paper in the tradition of George Engel and Adolph Fischer, two of the Haymarket Martyrs.

Berkman met Emma Goldman on 15 August 1889 in New York, and within a short time they began living communally with Modest Stein (called Fedya in Goldman's *Living My Life*) and Anna and Helene Minkin (who later would become the partner of Johann Most). After living in Connecticut and Massachusetts, Goldman, Berkman and Stein returned to New York in an effort to work out support for the striking and locked out steel workers at the Carnegie Steel Company in Homestead, Pennsylvania. They were especially incensed by the attempts of 300 strike breaking Pinkerton Detective Agency men to enter the factory on 6 July 1892. In the ensuing gun battle, three detectives and seven workers were killed. Berkman, Goldman, Stein, probably Claus Timmerman (later editor of the German anarchist papers *Die Brandfackel* and *Sturmvogel*) and others decided to kill Henry Clay Frick, the steel company's managing director whom they held accountable for deaths of the strikers by bringing Pinkerton men on to the site.

Berkman traveled to Pittsburgh on 13 July and on 23 July he made an unsuccessful attempt on the life of Frick. He was sentenced to 22 years in prison (later reduced to fourteen). From prison he sent correspondence to several anarchist papers and edited the secret journal *Prison Blossoms* with imprisoned anarchists Henry Bauer and Carl Nold. In it he wrote "it was my aim first and last, to express, by my deed, my sentiments towards the existing system of legal oppression and industrial despotism; to attack the institution of wage-slavery in the person of one of its most prominent representatives, to give it a blow—rather morally than physically—this was the real purpose and significance of my act" (ca 1893–1894). Berkman's prison years are described in gripping and powerful detail in his *Prison Memoirs of an Anarchist* (New York: Mother Earth Publishing Association, 1912).

Released from prison to the workhouse in 1905, he was finally released from imprisonment in May 1906. He suffered terribly from depression, began a short lived printing business and from March 1907 began editing *Mother Earth*. He remained editor until his political and personal split from Goldman around the end of 1914 and his move to California in 1915. During this period he played a leading role in the anarchist movement in New York and throughout the country. He helped organize the Anarchist Federation of America in 1908 and was arrested several times for a variety of offenses connected with anarchist activity. In 1910 and 1911, he helped organize and run the Ferrer School in New York. After the October 1910 bombing of the anti-union *Los Angeles Times* building by the McNamara brothers as part of the California-wide campaign against the open shop, Berkman helped craft a manifesto of solidarity with California workers embroiled in labor disputes there. He was instrumental in organizing the New York Unemployed in the harsh winter of 1913–1914, took part in protests against calls for war with Mexico in 1914 and following the Ludlow Massacre, in which the Colorado National Guard volleyed machine gun fire into the striking miners tent village in Ludlow, Colorado on April 20, 1914, killing five miners, two women and twelve children, he founded the Anti-Militarist League to support the striking miners with "men, arms and ammunition" and to protest against Colorado Fuel and Iron owner, John D. Rockefeller's apparent lack of sympathy for the dead. The Anti-Militarist League's activities lead to the Tarrytown protests in front of Rockefeller's home in New Jersey and Berkman was the probable organizer of the planned bomb attack on Rockefeller's house, which ended in tragedy on 4 July 1914 when the bomb exploded killing three militants whose apartment it was in, and a young woman who lived there.

In late 1914 he left *Mother Earth* on a lecture tour to gain support for the imprisoned David Caplan and Matthew Schmidt, two anarchists accused of aiding the McNamara's in their bombing of the *LA Times*. He moved to San Francisco and together with M. Eleanor Fitzgerald

(Fitzie) published *The Blast* (15 January 1916–1 June 1917) still one of the most powerful, astute and challenging of American anarchist newspapers. After the 22 July 1916 Preparedness Day bomb in San Francisco, he took an active role through the International Workers Defense League in organizing for the defense of Tom Mooney, Warren Billings and others accused of the act.

In early 1917 he left the office of *The Blast* in the care of Fitzie and traveled to the East Coast to raise support and funds for Tom Mooney's defense. When Fitzgerald arrived in New York he continued to edit *The Blast*, now from New York. With Goldman and other comrades, he founded the No Conscription League in May 1917 in response to America's drive towards entering World War One. Together with Goldman and other militants, he spoke on a number of occasions against the new draft law. The two were arrested in June 1917 for their anti-conscription work and attempts were then made to extradite Berkman to California on the charge of conspiracy in the Preparedness Day bombing. Although this attempt was defeated, his conviction for conspiracy to violate the Selective Service Act of May 1918 was upheld by the Supreme Court and he spent two years in federal prison in Atlanta. He was released in October 1919 (Goldman was released at the same time after serving a similar sentence in Missouri). The two were eventually deported from America to Russia in December 1919 under the Immigration Act of 1918 along with many members of the anarcho-syndicalist Union of Russian Workers.

The experience of Russia was pivotal in Berkman's (and Goldman's) life. It's hard for us to sense the excitement of possibility that Russia offered at this time. Here was a new world in the making. The country they both felt was their spiritual home, the country that had provided them with their revolutionary heroes and heroines was creating the type of society they had always dreamed of and fought for. Neither Berkman nor Goldman yet shared other anarchists' fears about the Bolsheviks. Once there, both found some difficulty in adjusting to life after America, though Berkman's belief in the creative possibilities of Russia lasted longer than Goldman's. They traveled widely together collecting material for the Museum of the Revolution in Petrograd. All around them anarchist meetings were being suppressed, anarchists were being arrested, in some cases shot, anarchist newspapers were suppressed, the Soviets had become no more than Bolshevik appendages and Makhno's army with all its rich contributions to anarchism was under constant attack. The suppression of the Kronstadt uprising in March 1921 provided the final straw. At the end of 1921 Berkman and Goldman, along with anarchist Alexander Schapiro, left Russia. Berkman wrote in *The Bolshevik Myth*, "The Revolution is dead; its spirit cries in the wilderness…I have decided to leave Russia." *The Bolshevik Myth* (1925) and Goldman's *My Disillusionment in Russia* (1923) were two of the most pertinent, chilling and harrowing critiques of Bolshevism in Russia. The ideas expressed in them helped contribute to Berkman's and Goldman's physical and intellectual exile—without a home and shunned by many former friends and supporters for their critique of Bolshevik tactics and methodology.

Berkman spent most of the remaining years of his life in France living on little money and the insecurity of a Nansen passport, liable to deportation at any time. In 1926 he was invited by the Jewish Anarchist Federation of New York to write an introduction to anarchism. He was reluctant at first, and indeed found the whole task very difficult and never felt at ease with it. In a letter to Goldman he writes, "I think I have to accept it. First because such a book is needed, secondly because it would enable me to live about 6 months." (Berkman to Goldman, 11 February 1927) The driving force behind the book was his recognition that the experiences of the anarchists in the Russian Revolution meant that much about anarchism needed to be re-evaluated. "The Russian Revolution has opened problems which the theories have never earnestly considered before and certainly never solved." (Berkman to Goldman 24 February 1927) Like Goldman, the experiences of Russia led him to intermittent feelings of despair coupled with an awareness of how, suddenly, the events in Russia had challenged the very core of his beliefs, "there are many problems that are not solved and they are not easy to solve…the old generalizations, etc will not do." (Berkman to Goldman 24 February 1927)

He was aware of the publication of the Organizational Platform of the Libertarian Communists written by Piotr Arshinov, Nestor Makhno, Ida Mett and others and recognized it as another attempt to reconfigure anarchist practice and organization in the light of the Russian experience. He saw in it the germs of Bolshevism ("their Platform is Bolshevik in spirit if not in words," May 1927) and was also influenced by what he saw as the unprincipled treatment of Volin by Makhno and others. He calls Makhno a "skunk" and suggests that the treatment of Volin by some of the Russian anarchist exiles in Paris grouped around the Platform "does not encourage one about the character of AN[archists] and their possibilities of building a new life." (Berkman to Goldman 24 February 1927)

Another major influence on Berkman was his desire to write something that the ordinary man and woman would understand and yet offer something new to those comrades already in the movement. To do this he adopted a plain and straightforward style similar to Malatesta in his pamphlet, *A Talk Between Two Workers*.

Goldman was in Canada throughout 1927 and Berkman's correspondence with her reflects the difficulty he had in writing what he and Goldman began to describe as an ABC of Anarchism. Indeed, by July 1927 Berkman had decided to abandon the book as impossible for him to write. He returned to it later the same year and by November 1927 had struggled to ten chapters, but could still say to Goldman in a letter of 1 December 1927, "I can't say I get any joy out of this book." Much of his frustration and sadness was his feeling as he wrote to Goldman that "there is no field in the world for the propaganda of AN[archist] ideas; at least not just now," and such a sense of sadness permeates sections of his writing.

At the same time that Berkman was struggling with the book, he and Goldman had decided to call a conference of leading anarchist militants "to see whether we could not come to some agreement on the need of a new literature, for instance, dealing with our ideas in the light of modern events" (Goldman to Rudolf Rocker, April 1928), Alexander Schapiro, Volin, Sabastien Faure, Marie Goldsmith, Luigi Fabbri, Luigi Bertonini and Max Nettlau were all contacted. Plans were made to meet in Paris in May 1928 and release a Manifesto, but the event fell through. However Berkman's ideas for the book benefited from the discussion of ideas preceding the abortive meeting. He especially, it would appear, took to heart Alexander Schapiro's suggestion in a letter to Goldman that "the center of gravity of the new literature is to be in the solution of problems and not in the exposition of a new theory." (Schapiro to Goldman, 19 April 1928) Indeed his book attempted to do just that. Writing in everyday language, using examples from everyday life, it examines the recent political events to create an interlocking and comprehensive assessment of what anarchism is and how we might get there. It's a mixture of moral and practical argument that, despite its pedantic style at times, and some archaic language, sadly has not been surpassed. It was the first attempt of an anarchist to present his ideas in a thorough and cohesive way, ideas distilled from nearly forty years of activism. He examines how change comes about—and, just as importantly for him, why it doesn't. Perhaps in a book filled with thoughtful and contentious points, the most salient discussion is why people continue to accept capitalism and all its institutions that oppress and repress individual freedom. For Berkman, human evolution was instinctively predicated on mutual aid and justice was a kind of instinctive sympathy that can only be hindered or corrupted by government. We start from there.

Alexander Berkman died on 28 June 1926, three weeks before the Spanish Revolution broke out. He had been an outstanding militant, lucid thinker, harsh self-critic and warm and loyal comrade and the fact that his writings and thoughts are relevant today is a sad comment on how ordinary people have yet been prevented from creating a free and equitable society. The re-publication of this book, I hope, may contribute in however small a way to that end. As Berkman writes of his ideal, "life will not consist in functioning, but in living…freedom in joy."

—Barry Pateman, curator of *Emma Goldman Archive and Kate Sharpley Library*

§ § § §

Berkman gave his book the title, *Now and After: The ABC of Anarchism*. Extracts of the work were initially published in *Freie Arbeiter Stimme*, the Yiddish anarchist newspaper, before the Vanguard Press and the Jewish Anarchist Federation published it in book form in May 1929. Vanguard also printed a cheaper edition at the same time entitled, *What is Communist Anarchism?* this edition was later reprinted by Dover Press Publications, (New York, 1972) and Phoenix Press (London, 1989). *Freie Arbeiter Stimme* republished *Now and After* in 1937 (with an introduction by Emma Goldman) and *Freedom Press* in London published an abridged version with the title, *The ABC of Anarchism*, during 1942. This has since been reprinted many times by the same publisher. Haskell House Publishers, New York published another edition in 1977. This edition is a reprint of *What is Communist Anarchism*, with the preface by Emma Goldman first published in the 1937 edition of *Now and After* published by *Freie Arbeiter Stimme*.

PREFACE TO THE 1937 REPRINT EDITION

The superior quality of Anarchist literature as compared with the writings of other social schools is its simplicity of style. Michael Bakunin, Elisée Reclus, Peter Kropotkin, Enrico Malatesta and others wrote in a way as to make their ideas easily understood by the workers. Especially is this true of Kropotkin and Malatesta. Yet it would be true to say that even they hardly had in mind the average man—the average man of Anglo-Saxon mentality. There is no getting away from the fact that there is a vast difference between the mind of the Latin worker and that of his brother in the United States and in England: the former has been steeped in the revolutionary traditions and struggles for freedom and other causes, while the latter has been brought up on the "blessings" of parliamentarianism. A different approach was therefore essential, if the Anglo-Saxon mind was to be reached at all.

It was this factor which decided Alexander Berkman to write his book *The ABC of Communist Anarchism*, and to write it in simple conversational style, a style that would appeal to the man-in-the-street whose knowledge and use of the English language does not exceed far the elementary stage. This was all the more imperative as it is just the man-in-the-street who is saturated with the most fantastic notions about Anarchism. The daily press has seen to that: day in and day out they fill their readers with bloodcurdling stories of bombs, dagger's, plots of killing presidents and other lurid descriptions of those awful criminals, the Anarchists, bent on murder and destruction!

Neither would it be true to assume that it is only the ignorant masses of humanity that are imbued with such silly notions about Communist Anarchism. There are considerable numbers among the so-called educated classes who have not escaped the baneful influence exercised by the capitalist press and are not much wiser as regards the meaning of Communist Anarchism. Even though they no longer see bombs and dagger's in the air, they still cling to the belief that Anarchists are crack-brained individuals and Anarchism an utterly absurd idea, and that only when human beings would become angels could it be possible to put Anarchism into practice.

All such people need a primer of Anarchism—an ABC, as it were, that would teach them the rudimentary principles of Communist Anarchism and whet their appetites for something more profound. *The ABC of Communist Anarchism* was intended to serve this purpose. That it has fulfilled its purpose no one who has read this little book will deny.

There was, moreover, another motive which impelled Alexander Berkman to undertake the work. It was the urgent need for a new orientation of revolutionary tactics, called forth by the experience of the Russian Revolution. Anarchists as well as all Social Revolutionists had been steeped in the romantic glamour of the French Revolution. We all believed (I do not exclude myself) that the Social Revolution had magic power, not merely to destroy the old decayed order, but that it could, by its own terrific force, build up the new social edifice. The Russian Revolution demolished this romantic dream. It proved that, while it can rouse the masses to the very zenith of revolutionary fervor, it cannot maintain them in that height for very long. The very fact that Lenin and his comrades succeeded in a very brief space of time to alienate the Russian masses from the Revolution, and Stalin was able to emasculate the latter altogether, proved that mere revolutionary fervor is not enough. More was needed to safeguard the Revolution from the political State design of the new masters of Russia. The will to constructive work, the economic and social preparation were needed in order to direct the Revolution into channels where it was meant to go.

None of the post-revolutionary Anarchist writings had attempted to deal with the new orientation. It was left to Alexander Berkman to carry out his difficult, yet most important, task. And who was there so eminently qualified, so able and with so penetrating an intellect to do justice to such a subject? Not in his wildest fancies did Alexander Berkman anticipate that the lesson from the Russian Revolution, discussed by him so ably in this volume, would become a living factor within six short years of its creation. The Spanish Revolution of July 19, 1936 and the part played in it by the Anarcho-Syndicalists and Anarchists imbue with much deeper meaning the ideas presented in the present volume of Alexander Berkman's *The ABC of Communist Anarchism* than its author ever dared to hope for. From the very first moment of the 19th of July, the National Confederation of Labor (the CNT) and the Anarchist Federation of Iberia (the FAI)—the most dominant, most ardent and daring organizations—were the forces that drove back the Fascist hordes from Catalonia. Their marvelous achievement is the first of its kind in any revolution. It merely bears out the truism asserted by Alexander Berkman regarding the imperative need for constructive preparedness, if the Social Revolution is not to repeat the errors of the past.

How my old pal and comrade would have gloried in the Spanish Revolution, in the heroic determination of the people to fight unto the last man against Fascism! Above all, how gratifying it would have been to him to see the Spanish people evince such profound feeling and understanding of *Communismo Libertario*—how that would have rejuvenated our comrade and given him new strength, new hope! If only he had lived a little longer! But the many years in exile, the unbelievable humiliations to which he was subjected, having to beg the right to breathe from creepy officials, the enervating and exhausting struggle for existence, and his severe illness combined to make life intolerable. Alexander Berkman hated dependence; he hated to become a burden to those he loved, and so he did what he had always said he would do: he hastened his end by his own hand.

Alexander Berkman was devoted to his ideal and served it single-mindedly, to the exclusion of any thought of self. Had he remotely anticipated the advent of the Spanish Revolution, he would have made an effort to continue living despite his shattered physique and the many other handicaps. The chance to serve our Spanish comrades in their gallant fight would have strengthened his hold on life, but the political sky of Europe in June 1936 was so clouded as to show no ray of revolutionary hope, and so life held out no incentive to him.

Alexander Berkman lies buried in a simple grave in Nice. But his ideal was re-born in Spain on the 19th of July, 1936.

EMMA GOLDMAN

London, July, 1937.

AUTHOR'S FOREWORD

I consider Anarchism the most rational and practical conception of a social life in freedom and harmony. I am convinced that its realization is a certainty in the course of human development.

The time of that realization will depend on two factors: first, on how soon existing conditions will grow physically and spiritually unbearable to considerable portions of mankind, particularly to the laboring classes; and, secondly, on the degree in which Anarchist views will become understood and accepted.

Our social institutions are founded on certain ideas; as long as the latter are generally believed, the institutions built on them are safe. Government remains strong because people think political authority and legal compulsion necessary. Capitalism will continue as long as such an economic system is considered adequate and just. The weakening of the ideas which support the evil and oppressive present day conditions means the ultimate breakdown of government and capitalism. Progress consists in abolishing what man has outlived and substituting in its place a more suitable environment.

It must be evident even to the casual observer that society is undergoing a radical change in its fundamental conceptions. The World War and the Russian Revolution are the main causes of it. The war has unmasked the vicious character of capitalist competition and the murderous incompetency of governments to settle quarrels among nations, or rather among the ruling financial cliques. It is because the people are losing faith in the old methods that the Great Powers are now compelled to discuss limitation of armaments and even the outlawing of war. It is not so long ago that the very suggestion of such a possibility met with utmost scorn and ridicule.

Similarly is breaking down the belief in other established institutions. Capitalism still "works" but doubt about its expediency and justice is gnawing at the heart of ever-widening social circles. The Russian Revolution has broadcasted ideas and feelings that are undermining capitalist society, particularly its economic bases and the sanctity of private ownership of the means of social existence. For not only in Russia did the October change take place: it has influenced the masses throughout the world. The cherished superstition that what exists is permanent has been shaken beyond recovery.

The war, the Russian Revolution, and the post-war developments have combined also to disillusion vast numbers about Socialism. It is literally true that, like Christianity, Socialism has conquered the world by defeating itself. The Socialist parties now run or help to run most of the European governments, but the people do not believe any more that they are different from other bourgeois regimes. They feel that Socialism has failed and is bankrupt.

In like manner have the Bolsheviki proven that Marxian dogma and Leninist principles can lead only to dictatorship and reaction.

To the Anarchists there is nothing surprising in all this. They have always claimed that the State is destructive to individual liberty and social harmony, and that only the abolition of coercive authority and material inequality can solve our political, economic, and national problems. But their arguments, though based on the age-long experience of man, seemed mere theory to the present generation, until the events of the last two decades have demonstrated in actual life the truth of the Anarchist position.

The breakdown of Socialism and of Bolshevism has cleared the way for Anarchism.

There is considerable literature on Anarchism, but most of its larger works were written before the World War. The experience of the recent past has been vital and has made certain revisions necessary in the Anarchist attitude and argumentation. Though the basic propositions remain the same, some modifications of practical application are dictated by the facts of current history. The lessons of the Russian Revolution in particular call for a new approach to various important problems, chief among them the character and activities of the social revolution.

Furthermore, Anarchist books, with few exceptions, are not accessible to the understanding of the average reader. It is the common failing of most works dealing with social questions that they are written on the assumption that the reader is already familiar to a considerable extent with the subject, which is generally not the case at all. As a result there are very few books treating of social problems in a sufficiently simple and intelligible manner.

For the above reason I consider a restatement of the Anarchist position very much needed at this time—a restatement in the plainest and clearest terms which can be understood by every one. That is, an ABC of Anarchism.

With that object in view the following pages have been written.

Paris, 1928.

INTRODUCTION

I want to tell you about Anarchism.

I want to tell you what Anarchism is, because I think it is well you should know it. Also because so little is known about it, and what is known is generally hearsay and mostly false.

I want to tell you about it, because I believe that Anarchism is the finest and biggest thing man has ever thought of; the only thing that can give you liberty and well-being and bring peace and joy to the world.

I want to tell you about it in such plain and simple language that there will be no misunderstanding it. Big words and high-sounding phrases serve only to confuse. Straight thinking means plain speaking.

But before I tell you what Anarchism is, I want to tell you what it *is not*.

That is necessary because so much falsehood has been spread about Anarchism. Even intelligent persons often have entirely wrong notions about it. Some people talk about Anarchism without knowing a thing about it. And some lie about Anarchism, because they don't want you to know the truth about it.

Anarchism has many enemies; they won't tell you the truth about it. Why Anarchism has enemies and who they are, you will see later, in the course of this story. Just now I can tell you that neither your political boss nor your employer, neither the capitalist nor the policeman will speak to you honestly about Anarchism. Most of them know nothing about it, and all of them hate it. Their newspapers and publications—the capitalist press—are also against it.

Even most Socialists and Bolsheviki misrepresent Anarchism. True, the majority of them don't know any better. But those who do know better also often lie about Anarchism and speak of it as "disorder and chaos." You can see for yourself how dishonest they are in this: the greatest teachers of Socialism—Karl Marx and Friedrich Engels—had taught that Anarchism would come from Socialism. They said that we must first have Socialism, but that after Socialism there will be Anarchism, and that it would be a freer and more beautiful condition of society to live in than Socialism. Yet the Socialists, who swear by Marx and Engels, insist on calling Anarchism "chaos and disorder," which shows you how ignorant or dishonest they are.

The Bolsheviki do the same, although their greatest teacher, Lenin, had said that Anarchism would follow Bolshevism, and that then it will be better and freer to live.

Therefore I must tell you, first of all, what Anarchism *is not.*

It is *not* bombs, disorder, or chaos.

It is *not* robbery and murder.

It is *not* a war of each against all.

It is *not* a return to barbarism or to the wild state of man.

Anarchism is the very opposite of all that.

Anarchism means that you should be free; that no one should enslave you, boss you, rob you, or impose upon you.

It means that you should be free to do the things you want to do; and that you should not be compelled to do what you don't want to do.

It means that you should have a chance to choose the kind of a life you want to live, and live it without anybody interfering.

It means that the next fellow should have the same freedom as you, that every one should have the same rights and liberties.

It means that all men are brothers, and that they should live like brothers, in peace and harmony.

That is to say, that there should be no war, no violence used by one set of men against another, no monopoly and no poverty, no oppression, no taking advantage of your fellow man.

In short, Anarchism means a condition or society where all men and women are free, and where all enjoy equally the benefits of an ordered and sensible life.

"Can that be?" you ask; "and how?"

"Not before we all become angels," your friend remarks.

Well, let us talk it over. Maybe I can show you that we can be decent and live as decent folks even without growing wings.

Christianity has conquered the world by defeating Christ. The churches preach to you a Christian life but make it impossible for you to live it. You would be declared a criminal or a lunatic if you tried to follow the precepts of the Nazarene, even for a single day. Christianity the greatest hypocrisy: it justifies and upholds everything that Jesus condemned. Other churches do the same.

Both want to change you by law. They call you bad, but they won't give you a chance to be good. How conditions compel people to act badly. Crime and punishment. Can the law reform the criminal and prevent crime? Why our prisons are filled. When wrong is lawful and when unlawful. Legal crime profitable. Punishing illegal crime a lucrative business. What the law is about. Capitalism takes the joy out of life: it needs government to help it do it. Our slave morality. The difference between olden times and now: formerly the robber baron hired armed bands to compel people to pay him tribute. Nowadays ruling is an easier job: the slaves are "educated" to imagine themselves free and sovereign. It pays the master class to keep you fooled with the game of politics.

Union means strength. Labor organizations legally prohibited in the past. Now other methods used by the masters. They do their utmost to keep the workers divided and weak. Why the boss is afraid of a strong labor union. The "identity of interests" fake. How you fall for it. Labor leaders helping to double cross the workers. Serving the interests of the masters. The "dignity of labor." Why strikes are lost.

What is real strength? The "power" of government and of the capitalist class. Your masters strong only because of your stupidity. What would happen if you would refuse to serve them? The difference between actual and alleged power. They who feed the world have the real power. The economic might of labor.

What part is the government playing in your life? Does it help you
live? Law and order the worst disorder. No government necessary
for our welfare. Man a social being: his wants and inclinations make
for association and mutual effort. Anarchism the expression of an
ancient and innate need of man. Most evils result from oppression
and inequality. Crime the legitimate offspring of coercive authority.
Government is itself the greatest crime. How Anarchy would treat
criminals. Justice and fair play: their role in individual and social life.

The character of equal opportunity. Anarchy would abolish government
and coercive authority. Social ownership and participation. The justice
and practicability of economic equality. Laziness implies the right man
in the wrong place. Interest needed in your work. Equality in freedom is
not leveling. Man's inborn tendency to variation and originality. The
deadening effect of invasive authority and compulsion. Social taboos
and legal imperatives. Freedom means diversification; it would make
life more interesting and richer.

Brief outline of non-Communist Anarchist theories: Mutualism and
Individualist Anarchism.

PART THREE — THE SOCIAL REVOLUTION

Man's rise from savagery has been a struggle against the inimical
forces of nature. In the degree that he learned to associate and cooperate with his fellow men, he conquered those forces and put them to
his service. We are still barbarians in that nations keep on fighting
each other instead of making common cause. We'll become civilized
only when the struggle of the classes within the nations will be ended.
Progress consists in developing mutual aid and joint effort instead of
enmity and strife. The masters of life determined to preserve their
mastery. Why revolution is unavoidable.

PART ONE —

NOW

CHAPTER I
WHAT DO YOU WANT
OUT OF LIFE?

What is it that every one wants most in life? What do you want most?

After all, we are all the same under our skins. Whoever you be — man or woman, rich or poor, aristocrat or tramp, white, yellow, red or black, of whatever land, nationality, or religion—we are all alike in feeling cold and hunger, love and hate; we all fear disaster and disease, and try to keep away from harm and death.

What you most want out of life, what you fear most, that also is true, in the main, of your neighbor.

Learned men have written big books, many of them, on sociology, psychology, and many other "ologies," to tell you what you want, but no two of those books ever agree. And yet I think that you know very well without them what you want.

They have studied and written and speculated so much about this, for them so difficult a question, that you, the individual, have become entirely lost in their philosophies. And they have at last come to the conclusion that you, my friend, don't count at all. What's important, they say, is not you, but "the whole," all the people together. This "whole" they call "society," "the commonwealth," or "the State," and the wise-acres have actually decided that it makes no difference if you, the individual, are miserable so long as "society" is all right. Somehow they forget to explain how "society" or "the whole" can be all right if the single members of it are wretched.

So they go on spinning their philosophic webs and producing thick volumes to find out where you really enter in the scheme of things called life, and what you really want.

But you yourself know very well what you want, and so does your neighbor.

You want to be well and healthy; you want to be free, to serve no master, to crawl and humiliate yourself before no man; you want to have well-being for yourself, your family, and those near and dear to you. And not to be harassed and worried by the fear of tomorrow.

You may feel sure that every one else wants the same. So the whole matter seems to stand this way:

You want health, liberty, and well-being.

Every one is like yourself in this respect.

Therefore we all seek the same thing in life.

Then why should we not all seek it together, by joint effort, helping each other in it?

Why should we cheat and rob, kill and murder each other, if we all seek the same thing? Aren't you entitled to the things you want as well as the next man?

Or is it that we can secure our health, liberty, and well-being better by fighting and slaughtering each other?

Or because there is no other way?

Let us look into this.

Does it not stand to reason that if we all want the same thing in life, if we have the same aim, then our *interests* must also be the same? In that case we should live like brothers, in peace and friendship; we should be good to each other, and help each other all we can.

But you know that it is not at all that way in life. You know that we do not live like brothers. You know that the world is full of strife and war, of misery, injustice, and wrong, of crime, poverty, and oppression.

Why is it that way then?

It is because, though we all have the same aim in life, our *interests are different*. It is this that makes all the trouble in the world.

Just think it over yourself.

Suppose you want to get a pair of shoes or a hat. You go into the store and you try to buy what you need as reasonably and cheaply as you can. That is your interest. But the storekeeper's interest is to sell it to you as dearly as he can, because then his *profit* will be greater. That is because everything in the life we live is built on making a profit, one way or another. We live in a *system of profit-making*.

Now, it is plain that if we have to make profits out of each other, then our interests cannot be the same. They must be different and often even opposed to each other.

In every country you will find people who live by making a profit out of others. Those who make the biggest profits are rich. Those who cannot make profits are poor. The only people who cannot make any profits are the workers. You can therefore understand that the interests of the workers cannot be the same as the interests of the other people. That is why you will find in every country several classes of people with entirely different interests.

Everywhere you will find:

(*1*) a comparatively small class of persons who make big profits and who are very rich, such as bankers, great manufacturers and land owners—people who have much capital and who are therefore called capitalists. These belong to *the capitalistic class*;

(*2*) a class of more or less well-to-do people, consisting of business men and their agents, real estate men, speculators, and professional men, such as doctors, lawyers, inventors, and so on. This is the middle class or *the bourgeoisie*;

(*3*) great numbers of workingmen employed in various industries—in mills and mines, in factories and shops, in transport and on the land. This is the working class, also called *the proletariat*.

The bourgeoisie and the capitalists really belong to the same capitalistic class, because they have about the same interests, and therefore the people of the bourgeoisie also generally side with the capitalist class as against the working class.

You will find that the working class is always the poorest class, in every country. Maybe you yourself belong to the workers, to the proletariat. Then you know that your wages will never make you rich.

Why are the workers the poorest class? Surely they labor more than the other classes, and harder. Is it because the workers are not very important in the life of society? Perhaps we can even do without them?

Let us see. What do we need to live? We need food, clothing, and shelter; schools for our children; street cars and trains for travel, and a thousand and one other things.

Can you look about you and point out a single thing that was made without labor? Why, the shoes you stand in, and the streets you walk on, are the result of labor. Without labor there would be nothing but the bare earth, and human life would be entirely impossible.

So it means that labor has created everything we have—all the wealth of the world. It is all the *product of labor* applied to the earth and its natural resources.

But if all the wealth is the product of labor, then why does it not belong to labor? That is, to those who have worked with their hands or with their heads to create it—the manual worker and the brain worker.

Everybody agrees that a person has a right to own the thing that he himself has made.

But *no one* person has made or can make anything all by himself. It takes many men, of different trades and professions, to create something. The carpenter, for instance, cannot make a simple chair or bench all by himself; not even if he should cut down a tree and prepare the lumber himself. He needs a saw and a hammer, nails and tools, which he cannot make himself. And even if he should make these himself, he would first have to have the raw materials—steel and iron—which other men would have to supply.

Or take another example—let us say a civil engineer. He could do nothing without paper and pencil and measuring tools, and these things other people have to make for him. Not to mention that first he has to learn his profession and spend many years in study, while others enable him to live in the meantime. This applies to every human being in the world today.

You can see then that no person can by his own efforts alone make the things he needs to exist. In early times the primitive man who lived in a cave could hammer a hatchet out of stone or make himself a bow and arrow, and live by that. But those days are gone. Today no man can live by his own work: he must be helped by the labor of others. Therefore all that we have, all wealth, is the product of the labor of many people, even of many generations. That is to say: *all labor and the products of labor are social*, made by society as a whole.

But if all the wealth we have is social, then it stands to reason that it should belong to society, to the people as a whole. How does it happen, then, that the wealth of the world is owned by some individuals and not by the people? Why does it not belong to those who have toiled to create it— the masses who work with hand or brain, the working class as a whole?

You know very well that it is the capitalistic class which owns the greatest part of the world's wealth. Must we therefore not conclude that the working people have lost the wealth they created, or that somehow it was taken away from them?

They did not lose it, for they never owned it. Then it must be that it was taken away from them.

This is beginning to look serious. Because if you say that the wealth they created has been taken away from the people who created it, then it means that it has been stolen from them, that they have been robbed, for surely no one has ever willingly consented to have his wealth taken away from him.

It is a terrible charge, but it is true. The wealth the workers have created, as a class, has indeed been stolen from them. And they are being robbed in the same way every day of their lives, even at this very moment. That is why one of the greatest thinkers, the French philosopher Proudhon, said that the possessions of the rich are stolen property.

You can readily understand how important it is that every honest man should know about this. And you may be sure that if the workers knew about it, they would not stand for it.

Let us see then *how* they are robbed and by *whom*.

CHAPTER II
THE WAGE SYSTEM

Do you ever stop to ask yourself this question: why were you born from *your* parents and not from some others?

You understand, of course, what I am driving at. I mean that *your consent was not asked.* You were simply born; you did not have a chance to select the place of your birth or to choose your parents. It was just chance.

So it happened that you were not born rich. Maybe your people are of the middle class; more likely, though, they belong to the workers, and so you are one of those millions, the masses, who have to work for a living.

The man who has money can put it into some business or industry. He invests it and lives *on the profits.* But you have no money. You have only your ability to work, your *labor power.*

There was a time when every workingman worked for himself. There were no factories then and no big industries. The laborer had his own tools and his own little workshop, and he even bought himself the raw materials he needed. He worked for himself, and he was called an artisan or craftsman.

Then came the factory and the large workshop. Little by little they crowded out the independent workman, the artisan, because he could not make things as cheaply as the factory—he could not compete with the big manufacturer. So the artisan had to give up his little workshop and go to the factory to work.

In the factories and large plants things are produced on a big scale. Such big-scale production is called *industrialism.* It has made the employers and manufacturers very rich, so that the lords of industry and commerce have accumulated much money, much capital. Therefore that system is called *capitalism.* We all live today in the capitalist system.

In the capitalist system the workingman cannot work for himself, as in the old days. He cannot compete with the big manufacturers. So, if you are a workman, you must find an employer. You work for him; that is, you give him your labor for so and so many hours a day or week, and he pays you for it. You sell him your labor power and he pays you *wages.*

In the capitalist system the whole working class sells its labor power to the employing class. The workers build factories, make machinery and tools, and produce goods. The employers keep the factories, the machinery, tools and the goods for themselves as *their profit*. The workers get only wages.

This arrangement is called the *wage system*.

Learned men have figured out that the worker receives as his wage only about *one-tenth* of what he produces. The other *nine-tenths* are divided among the landlord, the manufacturer, the railroad company, the wholesaler, the jobber, and other middlemen.

It means this:

Though the workers, as a class, have built the factories, a slice of their daily labor is taken from them for the privilege of *using* those factories. That's the landlord's profit.

Though the workers have made the tools and the machinery, another slice of their daily labor is taken from them for the privilege of *using* those tools and machinery. That's the manufacturer's profit.

Though the workers built the railroads and are running them, another slice of their daily labor is taken from them for the transportation of the goods they make. That's the railroad's profit.

And so on, including the banker who lends the manufacturer other people's money, the wholesaler, the jobber, and other middlemen, all of whom get their slice of the worker's toil.

What is left then—one tenth of the real worth of the worker's labor— is *his* share, his wage.

Can you guess now why the wisdom of Proudhon said that *the possessions of the rich are stolen property?* Stolen form the producer, the worker.

§ § § §

It seems strange, doesn't it, that such a thing should be permitted?

Yes, indeed, it is strange; and the strangest thing of all is that the whole world looks on and doesn't do a thing about it. Worse yet, the workers themselves don't do anything about it. Why, most of them think that everything is all right, and that the capitalist system is good.

It is because the workers don't see what is happening to them. They don't understand that they are being robbed. The rest of the world also understands very little about it, and when some honest man tries to tell them, they shout, "anarchist!" at him, and they shut him up or put him in prison.

Of course, the capitalists are very much satisfied with the capitalist system. Why shouldn't they be? They get rich by it. So you can't expect *them* to say it's no good.

The middle classes are the helpers of the capitalists and they also live off the labor of the working class, so why should they object? Of course, here and there you will find some man or woman in the middle class stand up and speak the truth about the whole matter. But such persons are quickly silenced and cried down as "enemies of the people," as crazy disturbers and anarchists.

But you would think that the workers would be the first to object to the capitalist system, for it is *they* who are robbed and suffer most from it.

Yes, so it should be. But, it isn't so, which is very sad.

The workers know that the shoe pinches somewhere. They know that they toil hard all their lives and that they get just enough to exist on, and sometimes not even enough.

They see that their employers can ride about in fine automobiles and live in the greatest luxury, with their wives decked out in expensive clothes and diamonds, while the worker's wife can hardly afford a new calico dress. So the workers seek to improve their condition by trying to get better wages. It is the same as if I woke up at night in my house and found that a burglar had collected all my things and is about to get away with them. Suppose that instead of stopping him, I should say to him: "Please, Mr. Burglar, leave me at least one suit of clothes so I can have something to put on," and then thank him if he gives me back a tenth part of the things he has stolen from me.

But I am getting ahead of my story. We shall return to the worker and see how he tries to improve his condition and how little he succeeds. Just now I want to tell you why the worker does not take the burglar by the neck and kick him out; that is, why he begs the capitalist for a little more bread or wages, and why he does not throw him off his back, altogether.

It is because the worker, like the rest of the world, has been made to believe that everything is all right and must remain as it is; and that if a few things are not quite as they should be, then it is because "people are bad," and everything will right itself in the end, anyhow.

Just see if that is not true of yourself. At home, when you were a child, and when you asked so many questions, you were told that "it is right so," that "it must be so," that "God made it so," and that everything was all right.

And you believed your father and mother, as they had believed their fathers and mothers, and that is why you now think just as your grandfather did.

Later, in school, you were told the same things. You were taught that God had made the world and that all is well; that there must be rich and poor, and that you should respect the rich and be content with your lot. You were told that your country stands for justice, and that you must obey the law. The teacher, the priest, and the preacher all impressed it upon you that your life is ordained by God and that "His will be done." And when you saw a poor man dragged off to prison, they told you that he was bad because he had stolen something, and that it was a great crime.

But neither at home, nor in school, nor anywhere else were you ever told that it is a crime for the rich man to steal the product of the worker's labor, or that the capitalists are rich because they have possessed themselves of the wealth which labor created.

No, you were never told that, nor did any one else ever hear it in school or church. How can you then expect the workers to know it?

On the contrary, your mind—when you were a child and later on, too—has been stuffed so full of false ideas that when you hear the plain truth you wonder if it is really possible.

Perhaps you can see now why the workers do not understand that the wealth they have created has been stolen from them and is being stolen every day.

"But the law," you ask, "the government—does it permit such robbery? Is not theft forbidden by law?"

CHAPTER III
LAW AND GOVERNMENT

Yes, you are right: the law forbids theft.

If I should steal something from you, you can call a policeman and have me arrested. The law will punish the thief, and the government will return to you the stolen property, if possible, because the law forbids stealing. It says that no one has a right to take anything from you without your consent.

But your employer takes from you what you produce. The whole wealth produced by labor is taken by the capitalists and kept by them as their property.

The law says that your employer does not steal anything from you, because it is done with your consent. You have agreed to work for your boss for certain pay, he to have all that you produce. Because you *consented* to it, the law says that he does not steal anything from you.

But did you really consent?

When the highwayman holds his gun to your head, you turn your valuables over to him. You "consent" all right, but you do so because you cannot help yourself, because you are *compelled* by his gun.

Are you not *compelled* to work for an employer? Your need compels you, just as the highwayman's gun. You must live, and so must your wife and children. You can't work for yourself; under the capitalist industrial system you must work for an employer. The factories, machinery, and tools belong to the employing class, so you *must* hire yourself out to that class in order to work and live. Whatever you work at, whoever your employer may be, it always comes to the same: you must work for *him*. You can't help yourself. You are *compelled*.

In this way the whole working class is compelled to work for the capitalist class. In this manner the workers are compelled to give up all the wealth they produce. The employers keep that wealth as their profit, while the worker gets only a wage, just enough to live on, so he can go on producing more wealth for his employer. Is that not cheating, robbery?

The law says it is a "free agreement." Just as well might the highwayman say that you "agreed" to give up your valuables. The only difference is that the highwayman's way is called stealing and robbery, and is forbidden by law. While the capitalist way is called business, industry, profit making, and is protected by law.

But whether it is done in the highwayman's way or in the capitalist way, you know that you are *robbed*.

The whole capitalist system rests on such robbery.

The whole system of law and government upholds and justifies this robbery.

That's the order of things called capitalism, and law and government are there to protect this order of things.

Do you wonder that the capitalist and employer, and all those who profit by this order of things, are strong for "law and order"?

But where do you come in? What benefit have you from that kind of "law and order"? Don't you see that this "law and order" only robs you, fools you, and just *enslaves* you?

"Enslave me?" you wonder. "Why, I am a free citizen!"

Are you free, really? Free to do what? To live as you please? To do what you please?

Let's see. How do you live? What does your freedom amount to?

You *depend* on your employer for your wages or your salary, don't you? And your wages determine your way of living, don't they? The conditions of your life, even what you eat and drink, where you go and with whom you associate all of it *depends on your wages*.

No, you are not a free man. You are *dependent* on your employer and on your wages. You are really a wage slave. The whole working class, under the capitalist system, is dependent on the capitalist class. The workers are wage slaves.

So, what becomes of your freedom? What can you do with it? Can you do more with it than your wages permit?

Can't you see that your wage—your salary or income—is all the freedom that you have? Your freedom, your liberty, don't go a step further than the wages you get.

The freedom that is given you on paper, that is written down in law books and constitutions, does not do you a bit of good. Such freedom only means that you have the *right* to do a certain thing. But it doesn't mean that you *can* do it. To be able to do it, you must have the chance, the opportunity. You have a *right* to eat three fine meals a day, but if you haven't the means, the *opportunity* to get those meals, then what good is that right to you?

So freedom really means opportunity to satisfy your needs and wants. If your freedom does not give you that opportunity, then it does you no good. Real freedom means opportunity and well-being. If it does not mean that, it means nothing.

You see, then, that the whole situation comes to this:

Capitalism robs you and makes a wage slave of you.

The law upholds and protects that robbery.

The government fools you into believing that you are independent and free.

In this way you are fooled and duped every day of your life.

But how does it happen that you didn't think of it before? How is it that most other people don't see it, either?

It is because you and every one else are lied to about this all the time, from your earliest childhood.

You are told to be honest, while you are being robbed all your life.

You are commanded to respect the law, while the law protects the capitalist who is robbing you.

You are taught that killing is wrong, while the government hangs and electrocutes people and slaughters them in war.

You are told to obey the law and government, though law and government stand for robbery and murder.

Thus all through life you are lied to, fooled, and deceived, so that it will be easier to make profits out of you, to *exploit* you.

Because it is not only the employer and the capitalist who make profits out of you. The government, the church, and the school—they all live on your labor. You support them all. That is why all of them teach you to be content with your lot and behave yourself.

"Is it really true that I support them all?" you ask in amazement.

Let us see. They eat and drink and are clothed, not to speak of the luxuries they enjoy. Do *they* make the things they use and consume, do *they* do the planting and sowing and building and so on?

"But they pay for those things," your friend objects.

Yes, they pay. Suppose a fellow stole fifty dollars from you and then went and bought with it a suit of clothes for himself. Is that suit by right his? Didn't he pay for it? Well, just so the people who don't produce anything or do no useful work pay for things. Their money is the profits they or their parents before them squeezed out of you, out of the workers.

"Then it is not my boss who supports me, but I him?"

Of course. He gives you a job; that is, permission to work in the factory or mill which was not built by him but by other workers like yourself. And for that permission you help to support him for the rest of your life or as long as you work for him. You support him so generously that he can afford a mansion in the city and a home in the country, even several of them, and servants to attend to his wants and those of his family, and for the entertainment of his friends, and for horse races and boat races, and for a hundred other things. But it is not only to him that you are so generous. Out of your labor, by direct and indirect taxation, are supported the entire government, local, state, and national, the schools and the churches, and all the other institutions whose business it is to protect profits and keep you fooled. You and your fellow workers, labor as a whole, support them all. Do you wonder that they all tell you that everything is all right and that you should be good and keep quiet?

It is good for *them* that you should keep quiet, because they could not keep on duping and robbing you once you open your eyes and see what's happening to you.

That's why they are all strong for this capitalist system, for "law and order."

But is that system good for *you*? Do you think it right and just?

If not, then why do you put up with it? Why do you support it?

"What can I do," you say; "I'm only one."

§ § § §

Are you really only one? Are you not rather one out of many thousands, out of millions, all of them exploited and enslaved the same as you are? Only they don't know it. If they knew it, they wouldn't stand for it. That's sure. So the thing is to make them know it.

Every workingman in your city, every toiler in your country, in every country, in the whole world, is exploited and enslaved the same as you are.

And not only the workingmen. The farmers are duped and robbed in the same manner.

Just like the workingmen, the farmer is dependent on the capitalist class. He toils hard all his life, but most of his labor goes to the trusts and monopolies of the land which by right is no more theirs than the moon is.

The farmer produces the food of the world. He feeds all of us. But before he can get his goods to us, he is made to pay tribute to the class that lives by the work of others, the profit-making, capitalist class. The farmer is mulcted out of the greater part of his product just as the worker is. He is mulcted by the land owner and by the mortgage holder; by the steel trust and the railroad. The banker, the commission merchant, the retailer, and a score of other middlemen squeeze their profits out of the farmer before he is allowed to get his food to you.

Law and government permit and help this robbery by ruling that:

the land, which no man created,
belongs to the landlord;
the railroads, which the workers built,
belong to the railroad magnates;
the warehouses, grain elevators, and storehouses,
erected by the workers, belong to the capitalists;
all those monopolists and capitalists have a right to
get profits from the farmer for using the railroads
and other facilities before he can get his food to you.

You can see then how the farmer is robbed by big capital and business, and how the law helps in that robbery, just as with the workingman.

But it is not only the worker and the farmer who are exploited and forced to give up the greater part of their product to the capitalists, to those who have monopolized the land, the railroads, the factories, the machinery, and all natural resources. The entire country, the whole world is made to pay tribute to the kings of finance and industry.

The small business man depends on the wholesaler; the wholesaler on the manufacturer; the manufacturer on the trust magnates of his industry; and all of them on the money lords and banks for their credit. The big bankers and financiers can put any man out of business by just withdrawing their credit from him. They do so whenever they want to squeeze any one out of business. The business man is entirely at their mercy. If he does not play the game as they want it, to *suit their interests*, then they simply drive him out of the game.

Thus the whole of mankind is dependent upon and enslaved by just a handful of men who have monopolized almost the entire wealth of the world, but who have themselves never created anything.

"But those men work hard," you say.

Well, some of them don't work at all. Some of them are just idlers, whose business is managed by others. Some of them *do* work. But what kind of work do they do? Do they produce anything, as the worker and the farmer do? No, they produce nothing, though they may work. They work to mulct people, to get profits out of them. Does their work benefit *you?* The highwayman also works hard and takes great risks to boot. His "work," like the capitalists, gives employment to lawyers, jailers, and a host of other retainers, all of whom *your* toil supports.

It seems indeed ridiculous that the whole world should slave for the benefit of a handful of monopolists, and that all should have to depend upon them for their right and opportunity to live. But the fact is just that. And it is the more ridiculous when you consider that the workers and farmers, who alone create all wealth, should be the most dependent and the poorest of all the other classes in society.

It is really monstrous, and it is very sad. Surely your common sense must tell you that such a situation is nothing short of madness. If the great masses of the people, the millions throughout the world, could see how they are fooled, exploited and enslaved, as *you* see it now, would they stand for such goings on? Surely they would not!

The capitalists know they wouldn't. That is why they need the government to legalize their methods of robbery, to protect the capitalist system.

And that is why the government needs laws, police and soldiers, courts and prisons to protect capitalism.

But who are the police and the soldiers who protect the capitalists against you, against the people?

If they were capitalists themselves, then it would stand to reason why they want to protect the wealth they have stolen, and why they try to keep up, even by force, the system that gives them the privilege of robbing the people.

But the police and the soldiers, the defenders of "law and order," are not of the capitalist class. They are men from the ranks of the people, poor men who for pay protect the very system that keeps them poor. It is unbelievable, is it not? Yet it is true. It just comes down to this: some of the slaves protect their masters in keeping them and the rest of the people in slavery. In the same way Great Britain, for instance, keeps the Hindus in India in subjection by a police force of natives, of the Hindus themselves. Or as Belgium does with the black men in the Congo. Or as any government does with a subjugated people.

It is the same system. Here is what it amounts to:

Capitalism robs and exploits the whole of the people; the laws legalize and uphold this capitalist robbery; the government uses one part of the people to aid and protect the capitalists in robbing the whole of the people.

The entire thing is kept up by educating the people to believe that capitalism is right, that the law is just, and that the government must be obeyed.

Do you see through this game now?

CHAPTER IV
HOW THE SYSTEM WORKS

But take a closer look at it and see how the system "works." Consider how life and its real meaning have become turned upside down and topsy-turvy. See how your own existence is poisoned and made miserable by the crazy arrangement.

Wherein is the purpose of your life, where the joy of it?

The earth is rich and beautiful, the bright sunshine should gladden your heart. Man's genius and labor have conquered the forces of nature and harnessed the lightning and the air to the service of humanity. Science and invention, human industry and toil have produced untold wealth. We've bridged the shoreless seas, the steam engine has annihilated distance, the electric spark and gasoline motor have unfettered man from the earth and chained even the atmosphere to do his bidding. We have triumphed over space, and the farthest corners of the globe have been brought close together. The human voice now circles the hemispheres, and through the azure there dart fleet messengers, carrying man's greeting to all the peoples of the world.

Yet the people groan under heavy burdens, and there is no joy in their hearts. Their lives are full of misery, their souls cold with want and need. Poverty and crime fill every land; thousands are a prey to disease and insanity, war slaughters millions and brings to the living tyranny and oppression.

Why all this misery and murder in a world so rich and beautiful? Why all the pain and sorrow upon an earth so full of nature's bounty and sunshine?

"It's God's will," says the church.

"People are bad," says the lawmaker.

"It must be so," says the fool.

Is it true? Must it really be so?

You and I and each of us, we all want to live. We have but one life and we want to make the best of it—rightly so. We want some joy and sunshine while we live. What will happen to us when we are dead, we don't know. No one knows. The chances are that once dead we'll stay dead. But whether so or not, while we live our whole being hungers for joy and laughter, for sunshine and happiness. Nature has made us that way. Made you and me, and millions of others like us, to long for life and joy. Is it right and just that we should be deprived of it and forever remain the slaves of a handful of men who lord it over us and over life?

Can that be "God's will," as the church tells you?

But if there be a God, he must be just. Would he permit us to be cheated and despoiled of life and its joys? If there be a God, he must be our father, and all men his children. Would a good father let some of his children go hungry and miserable while others have so much they don't know what to do with it? Would he suffer thousands, even millions, of his children to be killed and slaughtered, just for the glory of some king or the profit of the capitalist? Would he sanction injustice, outrage, and murder? No, my friend, you cannot believe that of a good father, of a just God. If people tell you that God wants such things, they just lie to you.

Maybe you say that God is good, but it is people who are bad, and that is why things are so wrong in the world.

But if people are bad, who made them so? Surely you don't believe that God made people bad, because in that case he himself would be responsible for it. Then it means that if people are bad, something else has made them so. That may well be. Let us look into it.

Let us see how people are, what they are, and how they live. Let us see how *you* live.

From your earliest childhood it has been drilled into you that you must become successful, must "make money." Money means comfort, security, power. It does not matter who you are, you are valued by what you are "worth," by the size of your bank account. So *you* have been taught, and everybody else has been taught the same. Can you wonder that every one's life becomes a chase for money, for the dollar, and your whole existence is turned into a struggle for possession, for wealth?

The money hunger grows on what it feeds. The poor man struggles for a living, for a bit of comfort. The well-to-do man wants greater riches, to give him security and protect him against the fear of tomorrow. And when he becomes a big banker he must not relax his efforts, he must keep a sharp eye on his competitors, for fear of losing the race to some other man.

So every one is compelled to take part in the wild chase, and the hunger for possession gets ever stronger hold of man. It becomes the most important part of life; every thought is on money, all the energies are bent on getting rich, and presently the thirst for wealth becomes a mania, a madness that possesses those who have and those who have not.

Thus life has lost its sole true meaning of joy and beauty; existence has become an unreasoning, wild dance around the golden calf, a mad worship of God Mammon. In that dance and in that worship man has sacrificed all his finer qualities of heart and soul—kindness and justice, honor and manhood, compassion and sympathy with his fellow man.

"Each for himself and the devil take the hindmost"—that must perforce become the principle and urge of most people under such conditions. Is it any wonder that in this mad money chase are developed the worst traits of man—greed, envy, hatred, and the basest passions? Man grows corrupt and evil; he becomes mean and unjust; he resorts to deceit, theft, and murder.

Look closer about you and see how many wrongs and crimes are perpetrated in your city, in your country, in the world at large, for money, for property, for possession. See how full the world is of poverty and misery; see the thousands falling a prey to disease and insanity, to folly and outrage, to suicide and murder—all because of the inhuman and brutalizing *conditions* we live under.

Truly has the wise man said that money is the root of all evil. Wherever you look you will see the corroding and degrading effect of money, of possession, of the mania to have and to hold. Every one is wild to get, to grab by hook or crook, to accumulate as much as he can, so that he may enjoy today and secure himself for tomorrow.

But can you therefore say that man is bad? Is he not *compelled* to take part in this money chase by the conditions of existence, by the crazy system we live in? For you have no choice—you must get into the race or go under.

Is it your fault, then, that life forces you to be and act like that? Is it the fault of your brother or neighbor or of any one? Is it not rather that we are all born into this mad scheme of things and that we have to fall in line?

But is not the scheme itself wrong that makes us act like that? Think it over and you will see that at heart you are not bad at all, but that conditions often compel you to do things that you know are wrong. You would rather not do them. When you can afford it, your urge is to be kind and helpful to others. But if you should follow your inclinations in this direction, you would neglect your own interests and you would soon be in want yourself.

So the conditions of existence suppress and stifle the instincts of kindness and humanity in us, and harden us against the need and misery of our fellow man.

You will see this in *every* phase of existence, in all the relations of men, all through our social life. Of course, if our interests were the same, there would be no need of any one taking advantage of another. Because what would be good for Jack would also be good for Jim. To be sure, as human beings, as children of one humanity, we really do have the same interests. But as members of a foolish and criminal social arrangement, our present day capitalist system, our interests are not at all the same. In fact, the interests of the different classes in society are opposed to each other; they are inimical and antagonistic, as I have pointed out in preceding chapters.

That is why you see men taking advantage of each other when they can profit by it, when their interests dictate it. In business, in commerce, in the relations between employer and employee—everywhere you will find this principle at work. Every one is trying to get ahead of the other fellow. Competition becomes the soul of capitalistic life, beginning with the billionaire banker, the great manufacturer and lord of industry, all through the social and financial scale, down to the last worker in the factory. For even the workers are compelled to compete with each other for jobs and better pay.

In this way our whole life becomes a struggle of man against man, of class against class. In that struggle every method is used to achieve success, to down your competitor, to raise yourself above him by every means possible.

It is clear that such conditions will develop and cultivate the worst qualities of man. It is just as clear that the law will protect those who have power and influence, the rich and the wealthy, however they got their riches. The poor man must inevitably get the worst of it under such circumstances. He will try to do the same as the rich man does. But as he has not the same opportunity to advance his interests under the protection of the law, he will often attempt it outside of the law and he will fall into its meshes. Though he did nothing more than the rich man—took advantage of some one, cheated some one—he did it "illegally," and you call him a criminal.

Look at that poor boy, for instance, on the street corner there. He is ragged, pale, and half-starved. He sees another boy, the son of wealthy parents, and that boy wears nice clothes, he is well fed, and he does not even deign to play with the poor kid. The ragged boy is angry at him, he resents and hates the rich boy. And everywhere the poor boy goes he experiences the same thing: he is ignored and scorned, often kicked about—he feels people don't think him as good as the rich boy, to whom every one is respectful and attentive. The poor boy gets embittered. And when he grows up, he again sees the same thing: the rich are admired and respected, the poor are kicked about and looked down upon. So the poor boy gets to hate his poverty, and he thinks of how he might become rich, get money, and he tries to get it in any way he can, by taking advantage of others, as others have always taken advantage of him, by cheating and lying, and sometimes even by committing a crime.

Then you say that he is "bad." But don't you see what made him bad? Don't you see that the *conditions* of his whole life have made him what he is? And don't you see that the *system* which keeps up such conditions is a greater criminal than the petty thief? The law will step in and punish him, but is it not the same law that permits those bad conditions to exist and upholds the system that makes criminals?

Think it over and see if it is not the law itself, the government, which really creates crime by compelling people to live in conditions that make them bad. See how law and government uphold and protect the biggest crime of all, the mother of all crimes, the capitalistic wage system, and then proceeds to punish the poor criminal.

Consider: does it make any difference whether you do wrong protected by the law, or whether you do it unlawfully? The thing is the same and the effects are the same. Worse even: legal wrongdoing is the greater evil because it causes more misery and injustice than illegal wrong. Lawful crime goes on all the time; it is not punishable and it is made easy, while unlawful crime is not so frequent and is more limited in its scope and effect.

Who causes more misery: the rich manufacturer reducing the wages of thousands of workers to swell his profits, or the jobless man stealing something to keep from starving?

Who commits the greater wrong: the wife of the industrial magnate spending a thousand dollars for a silver collar for her lapdog, or the underpaid girl in the magnate's department store unable to withstand temptation and appropriating some trinket?

Who is the greater criminal: the speculator cornering the wheat market and making a million-dollar profit by raising the price of the poor man's bread, or the homeless tramp committing some theft?

Who is the greater enemy of man: the greedy coal baron responsible for the sacrifice of human lives in his badly ventilated and dangerous mines, or the desperate man guilty of assault and robbery?

It is *not* the wrongs and crimes punishable by law that cause the greatest evil in the world. It is the *lawful* wrongs and unpunishable crimes, justified and protected by law and government, that fill the earth with misery and want, with strife and conflict, with class struggles, slaughter, and destruction.

We hear much about crime and criminals, about burglary and robbery, about offenses against person and property. The columns of the daily press are filled with such reports. It is considered the "news" of the day.

But do you hear much about the crimes of capitalistic industry and business? Do the papers tell you anything about the constant robbery and theft represented by low wages and high prices? Do they write much about the widespread misery caused by market speculation, by adulterating food, by the thousand and one other forms of fraud, extortion, and usury on which business and trade thrive? Do they tell you of the wrong and evils, of the poverty, of the broken hearts and blasted hearths, of disease and premature death, of desperation and suicide that follow in constant and regular procession in the wake of the capitalist system?

Do they tell you of the woe and worry of the thousands thrown out of work, no one caring whether they live or die? Do they tell you about the starvation wages paid to women and girls in our industries, pittances that directly compel many of them to prostitute their bodies to help eke out a living? Do they tell you of the army of unemployed that capitalism holds ready to take the bread from your mouth when you go on strike for better pay? Do they tell you that unemployment, with all its heartache, suffering, and misery is due directly to the system of capitalism? Do they tell you how the wage slave's toil and sweat are coined into profits for the capitalist? How the worker's health, his mind and body are sacrificed to the greed of the lords of industry? How labor and lives are wasted in stupid capitalist competition and unplanned production?

Indeed, they tell you a lot about crimes and criminals, about the "badness" and "evil" of man, especially of the "lower" classes, of the workers. But they don't tell you that capitalist conditions produce most of our evils and crime, and that capitalism itself is the greatest crime of all; that it devours more lives in a single day than all the murderers put together. The destruction of life and property caused by criminals throughout the world since human life began is mere child's play when compared with the ten million killed and twenty million wounded and the incalculable havoc and misery wrought by a single capitalist event, the recent World War. That stupendous holocaust was the legitimate child of capitalism, as all wars of conquest and gain are the result of the conflicting financial and commercial interests of the international bourgeoisie. It was a war for profits, as later admitted even by Woodrow Wilson and his class.

Profits again, as you see. Coining human flesh and blood into profits in the name of patriotism.

"Patriotism!" you protest; "why, that is a noble cause!"

"And unemployment," inquires your friend, "is capitalism responsible for that, too? Is it the fault of my boss that he has no work for me?"

CHAPTER V
UNEMPLOYMENT

I am glad your friend asked the question, for every workingman realizes how important this matter of unemployment is to him. You know what your life is when you are out of work; and when you do have a job, how the fear of losing it hangs over you. You are also aware what a danger the standing army of unemployed is to you when you are out on strike for better conditions. You know that strikebreakers are enlisted from the unemployed whom capitalism always keeps on hand, to help break your strike.

"How does capitalism keep the unemployed on hand?" you ask.

Simply by compelling you to work long hours and as hard as possible, so as to produce the greatest amount. All the modern schemes of "efficiency," the Taylor and other systems of "economy" and "rationalization" serve only to squeeze greater profits out of the worker. It is economy in the interest of the employer *only*. But as concerns you, the worker, this "economy" spells the greatest expenditure of your effort and energy, a fatal waste of your vitality.

It pays the employer to use up and exploit your strength and ability at the highest tension. True, it ruins your health and breaks down your nervous system, makes you a prey to illness and disease (there are even special proletarian diseases), cripples you and brings you to an early grave—but what does your boss care? Are there not thousands of unemployed waiting for your job and ready to take it the moment you are disabled or dead?

That is why it is to the profit of the capitalist to keep an army of unemployed ready at hand. It is part and parcel of the wage system, a necessary and inevitable characteristic of it.

It is in the interest of the people that there should be no unemployed, that all should have an opportunity to work and earn their living; that all should help, each according to his ability and strength, to increase the wealth of the country, so that each should be able to have a greater share of it.

But capitalism is not interested in the welfare of the people. Capitalism, as I have shown before, is interested *only* in profits. By employing less people and working them long hours larger profits can be made than by giving work to more people at shorter hours.

That is why it is to the interest of your employer, for instance, to have 100 people work 10 hours daily rather than to employ 200 at 5 hours. He would need more room for 200 than for 100 persons—a larger factory, more tools and machinery, and so on. That is, he would require a greater investment of capital. The employment of a larger force at less hours would bring less profits, and that is why your boss will not run his factory or shop on such a plan. Which means that a system of profit-making is not compatible with considerations of humanity and the well-being of the workers. On the contrary, the harder and the more "efficiently" you work, and the longer hours you stay at it, the better for your employer and the greater his profits.

You can therefore see that capitalism is not interested in employing all those who want and are able to work. On the contrary: a minimum of "hands" and a maximum of effort is the principle and the profit of the capitalist system. This is the whole secret of all "rationalization" schemes. And that is why you will find thousands of people in every capitalist country willing and anxious to work, yet unable to get employment. This army of unemployed is a constant threat to your standard of living. They are ready to take your place at lower pay, because necessity compels them to it. That is, of course, very advantageous to the boss: it is a whip in his hands constantly held over you, so you will slave hard for him and "behave" yourself.

You can see for yourself how dangerous and degrading such a situation is for the worker, not to speak of the other evils of the system.

"Then why not do away with unemployment?" you demand.

Yes, it would be fine to do away with it. But it could be accomplished only by doing away with the capitalist system and its wage slavery. As long as you have capitalism—or any other system of labor exploitation and profit-making you will have unemployment. Capitalism can't exist without it: it is inherent in the wage system. It is the fundamental condition of successful capitalist production.

"Why?"

Because the capitalist industrial system does not produce for the *needs* of the people; it produces for *profit*. Manufacturers do not produce commodities because the people want them and as much of them as is required. They produce what they expect to sell, and sell at a profit.

If we had a sensible system, we would produce the things which the people want and the quantity they need. Suppose the inhabitants of a certain locality needed 1,000 pairs of shoes; and suppose we'd have 50 shoemakers for the job. Then in 20 hours' work those shoemakers would produce the shoes our community needs.

But the shoe manufacturer of today does not know and does not care how many pairs of shoes are needed. Thousands of people may need new shoes in your city, but they cannot afford to buy them. So what good is it to the manufacturer to know who needs shoes? What he wants to know is who can *buy* the shoes he makes: how many pairs he can *sell* at a profit.

What happens? Well, he will manufacture about as many pairs of shoes as he thinks he will be able to sell. He will try his best to produce them as cheaply and sell them as dearly as he can, so as to make a good profit. He will therefore employ as few workers as possible to manufacture the quantity of shoes he wants, and he will have them work as "efficiently" and hard as he can compel them to.

You see that production *for profit* means longer hours and fewer persons employed than would be the case if production were *for use*.

Capitalism is the system of production for profit, and that is why capitalism always must have unemployed.

But look further into this system of production for profit and you will see how its basic evil works a hundred other evils.

Let us follow the shoe manufacturer of your city. He has no way of knowing, as I have already pointed out, who will or will not be able to buy his shoes. He makes a rough guess, he "estimates," and he decides to manufacture, let us say, 50,000 pairs. Then he puts his product on the market. That is, the wholesaler, the jobber, and the storekeeper put them up for sale.

Suppose only 30,000 pairs were sold; 20,000 pairs remain on hand. Our manufacturer, unable to sell the balance in his own city, will try to dispose of it in some other part of the country. But the shoe manufacturers there have also had the same experience. They also can't sell all they have produced. The supply of shoes is greater than the demand for them, they tell you. They have to cut down production. That means the discharge of some of their employees, thus increasing the army of the unemployed.

"Over-production" this is called. But in truth it is not over-production at all. It is under-consumption, because there are many people who need new shoes, but they can't afford to buy them.

The result? The warehouses are stocked with the shoes the people want but cannot buy; shops and factories close because of the "over-supply." The same things happen in other industries. You are told that there is a "crisis" and your wages must be reduced.

Your wages are cut; you are put on part time or you lose your work altogether. Thousands of men and women are thrown out of employment in that manner. Their wages stop and they cannot buy the food and other things they need.

Are those things not to be had? No, on the contrary; the warehouses and stores are filled with them, there is too much of them, there's "over-production."

So the capitalist system of production for profit results in this crazy situation:

(*1*) people have to starve—not because there is not enough food but because there is too much of it; they have to do without the things they need, because there is too much of those things on hand;

(*2*) because there is too much, manufacturing is cut down, throwing thousands out of work.

(*3*) being out of work and therefore not earning, those thousands lose their buying capacity. The grocer, the butcher, the tailor all suffer as a result. That means increased unemployment all around, and the crisis gets worse.

Under capitalism this happens in *every* industry.

Such crises are inevitable in a system of production for profit. They come from time to time; they return periodically, always getting worse. They deprive thousands and hundreds of thousands of employment, causing poverty, distress, and untold misery. They result in bankruptcy and bank failures, which swallow up whatever little the worker may have saved in time of "prosperity." They cause want and need, drive people to despair and crime, to suicide and insanity.

Such are the results of production for profit; such the fruits of the system of capitalism.

Yet that is not all. There is another result of this system, a result even worse than all the others combined.

That is *War*.

CHAPTER VI
WAR

War! Do you realize what it means? Do you know of any more terrible word in our language? Does it not bring to your mind pictures of slaughter and carnage, of murder, pillage, and destruction? Can't you hear the belching of cannon, the cries of the dying and wounded? Can you not see the battlefield strewn with corpses? Living humans torn to pieces, their blood and brains scattered about, men full of life suddenly turned to carrion. And there, at home, thousands of fathers and mothers, wives and sweethearts living in hourly dread lest some mischance befall their beloved ones, and waiting, waiting for the return of those who will return nevermore.

You know what war means. Even if you yourself have never been at the front, you know that there is no greater curse than war with its millions of dead and maimed, its countless human sacrifices, its broken lives, ruined homes, its indescribable heartache and misery.

"It's terrible," you admit, "but it can't be helped." You think that war must be, that times come when it is inevitable, that you must defend your country when it is in danger.

Let us see, then, whether you really defend your country when you go to war. Let us see what causes war, and whether it is for the benefit of your country that you are called upon to don the uniform and start off on the campaign of slaughter.

Let us consider whom and what you defend in war: who is interested in it and who profits by it.

We must return to our manufacturer. Unable to sell his product at a profit in his own country, he (and manufacturers of other commodities likewise) seeks a market in some foreign land. He goes to England, Germany, France, or to some other country, and tries to dispose there of his "overproduction," of his "surplus."

But there he finds the same conditions as in his own country. There they also have "over-production"; that is, the workers are so exploited and underpaid that they cannot buy the commodities they have produced. The manufacturers of England, Germany, France, etc., are therefore also looking for other markets, just as the American manufacturer.

The American manufacturers of a certain industry organize themselves into a big combine, the industrial magnates of the other countries do the same, and the national combines begin competing with each other. The capitalists of each country try to grab the best markets, especially new markets. They find such new markets in China, Japan, India, and similar countries; that is, in countries that have not yet developed their own industries. When each country will have developed its own industries, there will be no more foreign markets, and then some powerful capitalistic group will become the international trust of the whole world. But in the meantime the capitalistic interests of the various industrial countries fight for the foreign markets and compete with each other there. They compel some weaker nation to give them special privileges, "favored treatment"; they arouse the envy of their competitors, get into trouble about concessions and sources of profit, and call upon their respective governments to defend their interests. The American capitalist appeals to his government to protect "American" interests. The capitalists of France, Germany, and England do the same: they call upon *their* governments to protect *their* profits. Then the various governments call upon their people to *"defend their country."*

Do you see how the game is played? You are not told that you are asked to protect the privileges and dividends of some American capitalist in a foreign country. They know that if they tell you that, you would laugh at them and you would refuse to get yourself shot to swell the profits of plutocrats. But without you and others like you, they can't make war! So they raise the cry of "Defend your country! Your flag is insulted!" Sometimes they actually hire thugs to insult your country's flag in a foreign land, or get some American property destroyed there, so as to make sure the people at home will get wild over it and rush to join the Army and Navy.

Don't think I exaggerate. American capitalists are known to have caused even revolutions in foreign countries (particularly in South America) so as to get a more "friendly" new government there and thus secure the concessions they wanted.

But generally they don't need to go to such lengths. All they have to do is to appeal to your "patriotism," flatter you a bit, tell you that you "can lick the whole world," and they get you ready to don the soldier's uniform and do their bidding.

This is what your patriotism, your love of country is used for. Truly did the great English thinker Carlyle write:

"What, speaking in quite unofficial language, is the net purport and upshot of war? To my own knowledge, for example, there dwell and toil, in the British village of Dumdrudge, usually some five hundred souls. From these, by certain 'natural enemies' of the French there are successively selected, during the French war, say thirty able-bodied men. Dumdrudge, at her own expense, has suckled and nursed them; she has, not without difficulty and sorrow, fed them up to manhood, and even trained them to crafts, so that one can weave, another build, another hammer, and the weakest can stand under thirty stone avoirdupois. Nevertheless, amid much weeping and swearing, they are selected; all dressed in red; and shipped away, at the public charges, some two thousand miles, or say only to the south of Spain; and fed there till wanted.

"And now to that same spot in the south of Spain are thirty similar French artisans, from a French Dumdrudge, in like manner wending; till at length, after infinite effort, the two parties come into actual juxtaposition; and Thirty stands fronting Thirty, each with a gun in his hand.

"Straightway the word 'Fire!' is given, and they blow the souls out of one another, and in place of sixty brisk useful craftsmen, the world has sixty dead carcasses, which it must bury, and anon shed tears for. Had these men any quarrel? Busy as the devil is, not the smallest! They lived far enough apart; were the entirest strangers; nay, in so wide a universe, there was even, unconsciously, by commerce, some mutual helpfulness between them. How then? Simpleton! Their governors had fallen out; and instead of shooting one another, had the cunning to make these poor blockheads shoot."

It is not for your country that you fight when you go to war. It's for your governors, your rulers, your capitalistic masters.

Neither your country or humanity, neither you nor your class—the worker—gain anything by war. It is only the big financiers and capitalists who profit by it.

War is bad for *you*. It is bad for the workers. They have everything to lose and nothing to gain by it. They don't even get any glory from it, for that goes to the big generals and field marshals.

What do *you* get in war? You get lousy, you get shot, gassed, maimed, or killed. That is all that the workers of any country get out of war.

War is bad for your country, bad for humanity: it spells slaughter and destruction. Everything that war destroys—bridges and harbors, cities and ships, fields and factories—all must be built up again. That means that the people are taxed, directly and indirectly, to build it up. For in the last analysis everything comes from the pockets of the people. So war is bad for them materially, not to speak of the brutalizing effect war has upon mankind in general. And don't forget that 999 out of every 1,000 who are killed, blinded, or maimed in war are of the laboring class, sons of workers and farmers.

In modern war there is no victor, for the winning side loses almost as much as the defeated one. Sometimes even more, like France in the late struggle: France is poorer today than Germany. The workers of both countries are taxed to starvation to make good the losses sustained in the war. Labor's wages and standards of living are much lower now in the European countries that participated in the World War than they were before the great catastrophe.

"But the United States got rich through the war," you object.

You mean that a handful of men gained millions, and that the big capitalists made huge profits. Surely they did: the great financiers by lending Europe money at a high rate of interest and by supplying war material and munitions. But where do *you* come in?

Just stop to consider how Europe is paying off its financial debt to America or the interest on it. It does so by squeezing more labor and profits out of the workers. By paying lower wages and producing goods more cheaply the European manufacturers can undersell their American competitors, and for this reason the American manufacturer is compelled also to produce at lower cost. That's where his "economy" and "rationalization" come in, and as a result you must work harder or have your wages reduced, or be thrown out of employment altogether. Do you see how low wages in Europe directly affect your own condition? Do you realize that you, the American worker, are helping to pay the American bankers the interest on their European loans?

There are people who claim that war is good because it cultivates physical courage. The argument is stupid. It is made only by those who have themselves never been to war and whose fighting is done by others. It is a dishonest argument, to induce poor fools to fight for the interests of the rich. People who have actually fought in battles will tell you that modern war has nothing to do with personal courage: it is mass fighting, at a great distance from the enemy. Personal encounters, in which the best man may win, are extremely rare. In modern war you don't see your antagonists: you fight blindly, like a machine. You go into battle scared to death, fearing that the next minute you may be shot to pieces. You go only because you don't have the courage to refuse.

The man who can face vilification and disgrace, who can stand up against the popular current, even against his friends and his country when he knows he is right, who can defy those in authority over him, who can take punishment and prison and remain steadfast—that is a man of courage. The fellow whom you taunt as a "slacker" because he refuses to turn murderer—he needs courage. But do you need much courage just to obey orders, to do as you are told and to fall in line with thousands of others to the tune of general approval and the "Star Spangled Banner"?

War paralyzes your courage and deadens the spirit of true manhood. It degrades and stupefies with the sense that you are not responsible, that "'tis not yours to think and reason why, but to do and die," like the hundred thousand others doomed like yourself. War means blind obedience, unthinking stupidity, brutish callousness, wanton destruction, and irresponsible murder.

I have met persons who say that war is good because it kills many people, so that there is more work for the survivors.

Consider what a terrible indictment this is against the present system. Imagine a condition of things where it is good for the people of a certain community to have some of their number killed off, so the rest could live better! Would it not be the worst man-eating system, the worst cannibalism?

That is just what capitalism is: a system of cannibalism in which one devours his fellow man or is devoured by him. This is true of capitalism in time of peace as in war, except that in war its real character is unmasked and more evident.

In a sensible, humane society that could not be. On the contrary, the greater the population of a certain community the better it would be for all, because the work of each would then be lighter.

A community is no different in this regard than a family. Every family needs a certain amount of work to be done in order to keep its wants supplied. Now the more persons there are in a family to do the necessary work, the easier for each member, the less work for each.

The same holds true of a community or a country, which is only a family on a large scale. The more people there are to do the work necessary to supply the needs of the community, the easier the tasks of each member.*

If the contrary is the case of our present-day society, it merely goes to prove that conditions are wrong, barbaric, and perverse. Nay, more: that they are absolutely criminal if the capitalist system can thrive on the slaughter of its members.

It is evident then that for the workers war means only greater burdens, more taxes, harder toil, and the reduction of their pre-war standard of living.

But there is *one* element of capitalist society for whom war is good. It is the element that coins money out of war, that gets rich on your "patriotism" and self-sacrifice. It is the munitions manufacturers, the speculators of food and other supplies, the warship builders. In short, it is the great lords of finance, industry, and commerce who alone benefit by war.

For these war is blessing. A blessing in more than one way. Because war also serves to distract the attention of the laboring masses from the everyday misery and turns it to "high politics" and human slaughter. Governments and rulers have often sought to avoid popular uprising and revolution by staging a war. History is full of such examples. Of course, war is a double-edged sword. Often it, in turn, leads to revolt. But that is another story to which we shall return when we come to the Russian Revolution.

If you have followed me thus far, you must realize that war is just as much a direct result and inevitable effect of the capitalist system as are the regular financial and industrial crises.

When a crisis comes, in the manner in which I have described it, with its unemployment and hardships, you are told that it is no one's fault, that it is "bad times," the result of "over-production" and similar humbug. And when capitalistic competition for profits brings about a condition of war, the capitalists and their flunkies—the politicians and the press—raise the cry "Save your country!" in order to fill you with false patriotism and make you fight their battles for them.

* There never need be any danger of over-populating the earth. Nature provides her own checks against it. What we need is a more rational distribution of population, intensive agriculture and a more intelligent control of our birth rate.

In the name of patriotism you are ordered to stop being decent and honest, to cease being yourself, to suspend your own judgment, and give up your life; to become a will-less cog in a murderous machine, blindly obeying the order to kill, pillage, and destroy; to give up your father and mother, wife and child, and all that you love, and proceed to slaughter your fellow men who never did you any harm—who are just as unfortunate and deluded victims of their masters as you are of yours.

Only too truly did Carlyle say that "patriotism is the refuge of scoundrels."

Can't you see how you are fooled and duped?

Take the World War, for instance. Consider how the people of America were tricked into participation. They did not want to mix in European affairs. They knew little of them, and they did not care to be dragged into the murderous brawls. They elected Woodrow Wilson on a "he kept us out of the war" slogan.

But the American plutocracy saw that huge fortunes could be gained in the war. They were not satisfied with the millions they were reaping by selling ammunition and other supplies to the European combatants; immeasurably greater profits were to be made by getting a big country like the United States, with its over 100 million of population, into the fray. President Wilson could not withstand their pressure. After all, government is but the maid-servant of the financial powers: it is there to do their bidding.

But how to get America into the war when her people were expressly against it? Didn't they elect Wilson as President on the clear promise to keep the country out of war?

In former days, under absolute monarchs, the subjects were simply compelled to obey the king's command. But that often involved resistance and the danger of rebellion. In modern times there are surer and safer means of making the people serve the interests of their rulers. All that is necessary is to talk them into believing that they themselves want what their masters want them to do; that it is to their own interests, good for their country, good for humanity. In this manner the noble and fine instincts of man are harnessed to do the dirty work of the capitalistic master class, to the shame and injury of mankind.

Modern inventions help in this game and make it comparatively easy. The printed word, the telegraph, the telephone, and radio are all sure aids in this matter. The genius of man, having produced those wonderful things, is exploited and degraded in the interests of Mammon and Mars.

President Wilson invented a new device to snare the American people into the war for the benefit of Big Business. Woodrow Wilson, the former college president, discovered a "war for democracy," a "war to end war." With that hypocritical motto a country-wide campaign was started, rousing the worst tendencies of intolerance, persecution, and murder in American hearts; filling them with venom and hatred against every one who had the courage to voice an honest and independent opinion; beating up, imprisoning, and deporting those who dared to say that it was a capitalistic war for profits. Conscientious objectors to the taking of human life were brutally maltreated as "slackers" and condemned to long penitentiary terms; men and women who reminded their countrymen of the Nazarene's command, "Thou shalt not kill," were branded cowards and shut up in prison; radicals who declared that the war was only in the interest of capitalism and were treated as "vicious foreigners" and "enemy spies." Special laws were rushed through to stifle every free expression of opinion. Dire punishment was meted out to every objector. From the Atlantic to the Pacific hundred-percenters, drunk with murderous patriotism, spread terror. The nation-wide militarist propaganda at last swept the American people into the field of carnage.

Wilson was "too proud to fight," but not too proud to send others to do the fighting for his financial backers. He was "too proud to fight," but not too proud to help the American plutocracy coin gold out of the lives of seventy thousand Americans left dead on European battlefields.

The "war for democracy," the "war to end war" proved the greatest sham in history. As a matter of fact, it started a chain of new wars not yet ended. It has since been admitted, even by Wilson himself, that the war served no purpose except to reap vast profits for Big Business. It created more complications in European affairs than had ever existed before. It pauperized Germany and France, and brought them to the brink of national bankruptcy. It loaded the peoples of Europe with stupendous debts, and put unbearable burdens on their working classes. The resources of every country were strained. The progress of science was registered by new facilities of destruction. Christian precept was proven by the multiplication of murder, and the treaties were signed with human blood.

The World War built huge fortunes for the lords of finance—and tombs for the workers.

And today? Today we stand on the brink of a new war, far greater and more terrible than the last holocaust. Every government is preparing for it and appropriating millions of dollars of the workers' sweat and blood for the coming carnage.

Think it over, my friend, and see what capital and government are doing for you, doing *to* you.

Soon they will again be calling on you to "defend your country!"

In times of peace you slave in field and factory, in war you serve as cannon fodder—all for the greater glory of your masters.

Yet you are told that "everything is all right," that it is "God's will," that it "must be so."

Don't you see that it is not God's will at all, but the doings of capital and government? Can't you see that it is so and "must be so" only because you permit your political and industrial masters to fool and dupe you, so *they* can live in comfort and luxury off your toil and tears, while they treat you as the "common" people, the "lower orders," just good enough to slave for them?

"It has always been so," you remark meekly.

CHAPTER VII
CHURCH AND SCHOOL

Yes, my friend, it has always been so. That is, law and government have always been on the side of the masters. The rich and powerful have always duped you by "God's will," with the help of the church and the school.

But must it always remain so?

In olden days, when the people were the slaves of some tyrant—of a tsar or other autocrat—the church (of every religion and denomination) taught that slavery existed by "the will of God," that it was good and necessary, that it could not be otherwise, and that whoever was against it went against God's will and was a godless man, a heretic, a blasphemer and a sinner.

The school taught that this was right and just, that the tyrant ruled by "the grace of God," that his authority was not to be questioned, and that he was to be served and obeyed.

The people believed it and remained slaves.

But little by little there arose some men who had come to see that slavery was wrong: that it was not right for one man to hold a whole people in subjection and be lord and master over their lives and toil. And they went among the people and told them what they thought.

Then the government of the tyrant pounced upon those men. They were charged with breaking the laws of the land; they were called disturbers of the public peace, criminals, and enemies of the people. They were killed, and the church and the school said that it was right, that they deserved death as rebels against the laws of God and man. And the slaves believed it.

But the truth cannot be suppressed forever. More and more persons gradually came to see that the "agitators" who had been killed were right. They came to understand that slavery was wrong and bad for them, and their numbers grew all the time. The tyrant made severe laws to suppress them: his government did everything to stop them and their "evil designs." Church and school denounced those men. They were persecuted and hounded and executed in the manner of those days.

Sometimes they were put on a big cross and nailed to it, or they had their heads cut off with an ax. At other times they were strangled to death, burned at the stake, quartered, or bound to horses and slowly torn apart.

This was done by the church and the school and the law, often even by the deluded mob, in various countries, and in the museums today you can still see the instruments of torture and death which were used to punish those who tried to tell the truth to the people.

But in spite of torture and death, in spite of law and government, in spite of church and school and press, slavery was at last abolished, though people had insisted that "it was always so and must remain so."

Later, in the days of serfdom, when the nobles lorded it over the common people, church and school were again on the side of the rulers and the rich. Again they threatened the people with the wrath of God if they should dare to become rebellious and refuse to obey their lords and governors. Again they brought down their maledictions upon the heads of the "disturbers" and heretics who dared defy the law and preach the gospel of greater liberty and well-being. Again those "enemies of the people" were persecuted, hounded, and murdered—but the day came when serfdom was abolished.

Serfdom gave place to capitalism with its wage slavery, and again you find church and school on the side of the master and ruler. Again they thunder against the "heretics," the godless ones who wish the people to be free and happy. Again church and school preach to you "the will of God": capitalism is good and necessary, they tell you; you must be obedient to your masters, for "it is God's will" that there be rich and poor, and whoever goes against it is a sinner, a nonconformist, an anarchist.

So you see that church and school are still with the masters against their slaves, just as in the past. Like the leopard, they may change their spots, but never their nature. Still church and school side with the rich against the poor, with the powerful against their victims, with "law and order" against liberty and justice.

Now as formerly they teach the people to respect and obey their masters. When the tyrant was king, church and school taught respect for and obedience to the "law and order" of the king. When the king is abolished and a republic instituted, church and school teach respect for and obedience to republican "law and order." OBEY! that is the eternal cry of church and school, no matter how vile the tyrant, no matter how oppressive and unjust "law and order."

OBEY! For if you will cease obedience to authority you might begin to think for yourself! That would be most dangerous to "law and order," the greatest misfortune for church and school. For then you would find out that everything they taught you was a lie, and was only for the purpose of keeping you enslaved, in mind and body, so that you should continue to toil and suffer and keep quiet.

Such an awakening on your part would indeed be the greatest calamity for church and school, for Master and Ruler.

But if you have gone thus far with me, if you have now begun to think for yourself, if you understand that capitalism robs you and that government with its "law and order" is there to help it do it; if you realize that all the agencies of institutionalized religion and education serve only to delude you and keep you in bondage, then you might rightly feel outraged and cry out, "Is there no justice in the world?"

CHAPTER VIII
JUSTICE

No, my friend, terrible as it is to admit it, there is no justice in the world.

Worse yet: there *can be no justice* as long as we live under conditions which enable one person to take advantage of another's need, to turn it to his profit, and exploit his fellowman.

There can be no justice as long as one man is ruled by another; as long as one has the authority and power to compel another against his will.

There can be no justice between master and servant.

Nor equality.

Justice and equality can exist only among equals. Is the poor street-cleaner the social equal of Morgan? Is the washerwoman the equal of Lady Astor?

Let the washerwoman and Lady Astor enter any place, private or public. Will they receive equal welcome and treatment? Their very apparel will determine their respective reception. Because even their clothes indicate, under present conditions, the difference in their social position, their station in life, their influence, and wealth.

The washerwoman may have toiled hard all her life long, may have been a most industrious and useful member of the community. The Lady may have never done a stroke of work, never been of the least use to society. For all that it is the rich lady who will be welcomed, who will be preferred.

I have chosen this homely example because it is typical of the entire character of our society, of our whole civilization.

It is money and the influence and authority which money commands, that alone count in the world.

Not justice, but possession.

Broaden this example to cover your own life, and you will find that justice and equality are only cheap talk, lies which you are taught, while money and power are the real thing, realities.

Yet there is a deep-seated sense of justice in mankind, and your better nature always resents it when you see injustice done to any one. You feel outraged and you become indignant over it: because we all have an instinctive sympathy with our fellow man, for by nature and habit we are social beings. But when your interests or safety are involved, you act differently; you even feel differently.

Suppose you see your brother do wrong to a stranger. You will call his attention to it, you will chide him for it.

When you see your boss do an injustice to some fellow worker, you also resent it and you feel like protesting. But you will most probably refrain from expressing your sentiments because you might lose your job or get in bad with your boss.

Your *interests* suppress the better urge of your nature. Your dependence upon the boss and his economic power over you influence your behavior.

Suppose you see John beat and kick Bill when the latter is on the ground. Both may be strangers to you, but if you are not afraid of John, you'll tell him to stop kicking a fellow who is down.

But when you see the policeman do the same thing to some citizen you will think twice before interfering, because he might beat you up too and arrest you to boot. He has the authority.

John, who has no authority and who knows that some one might interfere when he is acting unjustly, will—as a rule—be careful what he is about.

The policeman, who is vested with some authority and who knows there is little chance of any one interfering with him, will be more likely to act unjustly.

Even in this simple instance you can observe the effect of authority: its effect on the one who possesses it and on those over whom is it exercised. Authority tends to make its possessor unjust and arbitrary; it also makes those subject to it acquiesce in wrong, subservient, and servile. Authority corrupts its holder and debases its victims.

If this is true of the simplest relations in existence, how much more so in the larger field of our industrial, political, and social life?

We have seen how your economic dependence upon your boss will affect your actions. Similarly it will affect others who are dependent upon him and his good will. Their interests will thus control their actions, even if they are not clearly aware of it.

And the boss? Will he also not be influenced by *his* interests? Will not his sympathies, his attitude and behavior be the result of his particular interests?

The fact is, everyone is controlled, in the main, by his interests. Our feelings, our thoughts, our actions, and our whole life is shaped, consciously and unconsciously, by our interests.

I am speaking of ordinary human nature, of the average man. Here and there you will find cases that seem to be exceptions. A great idea or an ideal, for example, may take such hold of a person that he will entirely devote himself to it and sometimes even sacrifice his life for it. In such an instance it may look as if a man acted against his interests. But that is a mistake—it only seems so. For in reality the idea or ideal for which the man lived or even gave his life, was his chief interest. The only difference is that the idealist finds his main interest in living for some idea, while the strongest interest of the average man is to get on in the world and live comfortably and peacefully. But both are controlled by the dominant interests.

The interests of men differ, but we are all alike in that each of us feels, thinks and acts according to *his* particular interests, his conception of them.

Now, then, can you expect your boss to feel and act against his interests? Can you expect the capitalist to be guided by the interests of his employees? Can you expect the mine owner to run his business in the interests of the miners?

We have seen that the interests of the employer and employee are different; so different that they are opposed to each other.

Can there be justice between them? Justice means that each gets his due. Can the worker get his due or have justice in capitalist society?

If he did, capitalism could not exist: because then your employer could not make any profits out of your work. If the worker would get his due—that is, the things he produces or their equivalent—where would the profits of the capitalist come from? If labor owned the wealth it produces, there would be no capitalism.

It means that the worker cannot get what he produces, cannot get what is due to him, and therefore cannot get justice under wage slavery.

"If that is the case," you remark, "he can appeal to the law, to the courts."

What are the courts? What purpose do they serve? They exist to uphold the law. If some one has stolen your overcoat and you can prove it, the courts would decide in your favor. If the accused is rich or has a clever lawyer, the chances are that the verdict will be to the effect that the whole thing was a misunderstanding, or that it was an act of aberration, and the man will most likely go free.

But if you accuse your employer of robbing you of the greater part of your labor, of exploiting you for his personal benefit and profit, can you get your due in the courts? The judge will dismiss the case, because it is not against the law for your boss to make profits out of your work. There is no law to forbid it. You will get no justice that way.

It is said that "justice is blind." By that is meant that it recognizes no distinction of station, of influence, of race, creed, or color.

This proposition needs only to be stated to be seen as thoroughly false. For justice is administered by human beings, by judges and juries, and every human being has his particular interests, not to speak of his personal sentiments, opinions, likes, dislikes, and prejudices, from which he can't get away by merely putting on a judge's gown and sitting on the bench. The judge's attitude to things—like every one else's—will be determined, consciously and unconsciously, by his education and bringing up, by the environment in which he lives, by his feelings and opinions, and particularly by his interests and the interests of the social group to which he belongs.

Considering the above, you must realize that the alleged impartiality of the courts of justice is in truth a psychological impossibility. There is no such thing, and cannot be. At best the judge can be relatively impartial in cases in which neither his sentiments nor his interests—as an individual or member of a certain social group—are in any way concerned. In such cases you might get justice. But these are usually of small importance, and they play a very insignificant role in the general administration of justice.

Let us take an example. Suppose two business men are disputing over the possession of a certain piece of property, the matter involving no political or social considerations of any kind. In such a case the judge, having no personal feeling or interest in the matter, may decide the case on its merits. Even then his attitude will to a considerable extent depend on his state of health and his digestion, on the mood in which be left home, on a probable quarrel with his spouse, and other seemingly unimportant and irrelevant yet very decisive human factors.

Or suppose that two workingmen are in litigation over the ownership of a chicken coop. The judge may in such a case decide justly, since a verdict in favor of one or the other of the litigants in no way affects the position, feelings, or interests of the judge.

But suppose the case before him is that of a workingman in litigation with his landlord or with his employer. In such circumstances the entire character and personality of the judge will affect his decision, not that the latter will necessarily be unjust. That is not the point I am trying to make. What I want to call your attention to is that, in the given case, the attitude of the judge cannot and will not be impartial. His sentiments toward workingmen, his personal opinion of landlords or employers, and his social views will influence his judgment, sometimes even unconsciously to himself. His verdict may or may not be just; in any case it will not be based exclusively on the evidence. It will be affected by his personal, subjective feelings and by his views regarding labor and capital. His attitude will generally be that of his circle of friends and acquaintances, of his social group, and his opinions in the matter will correspond with the interests of that group. He may even himself be a landlord or have stock in a corporation which employs labor. Consciously or unconsciously his view of the evidence given at the trial will be colored by his own feelings and prejudices, and his verdict will be a result of that.

Besides, the appearance of the two litigants, their manner of speech and behavior, and particularly their respective ability to employ clever counsel, will have a very considerable influence on the impressions of the judge and consequently on his decision.

It is therefore clear that in such cases the verdict will depend more on the mentality and class-consciousness of the particular judge than on the merits of the case.

This experience is so general that the popular voice has expressed it in the sentiment that "the poor man can't get justice against the rich." There may be exceptions now and then, but generally it is true and cannot be otherwise as long as society is divided into different classes with differing interests. So long as that is the case, justice must be one-sided, *class justice*; that is, injustice in favor of one class as against the other.

You can see it still more clearly illustrated in cases involving definite class issues, cases of the class struggle.

Take, for instance, a strike of workers against a corporation or a rich employer. On what side will you find the judges, the courts? Whose interests will the law and government protect? The workers are striking for better conditions of living; they have wives and children at home for whom they are trying to get a little bigger share of the wealth they are creating.

Does the law and government help them in this worthy aim?

What actually happens? Every branch of government comes to the aid of capital as against labor. The courts will issue an injunction against the strikers, they will forbid picketing or make it ineffectual by not permitting the strikers to persuade outsiders not to take the bread out of their mouths, the police will beat up and arrest the pickets, the judges will impose fines on them and railroad them to jail. The whole machinery of the government will be at the service of the capitalists to break the strike, to smash the union, if possible, and reduce the workers to submission. Sometimes the Governor of the state will even call out the militia, the President will order out the regular troops—all in support of capital against labor.

Meanwhile the trust or corporation where the strike is taking place will order their employees to vacate the company houses, will throw them and their families out in the cold, and will fill their places in the mill, mine, or factory with strikebreakers, under the protection and with the aid of the police, the courts, and the government, all of whom are supported by *your* labor and taxes.

Can you speak of justice under such circumstances? Can you be so naive as to believe that justice is possible in the struggle of the poor against the rich, of labor against capital? Can't you see that it is a bitter fight, a struggle of opposed interests, a *war of two classes*? Can you expect justice in war?

Truly the capitalistic class knows that it is war, and it uses every means at its command to defeat labor. But the workers unfortunately do not see the situation as clearly as their masters, and so they still foolishly twaddle about "justice," "equality before the law," and "liberty."

It is useful to the capitalist class that the workers should believe in such fairy tales. It guarantees the continuation of the rule of the masters. Therefore they use every effort to keep up this belief. The capitalistic press, the politician, the public speaker, never miss an opportunity to impress it upon you that law means justice, that all are equal before the law, and that every one enjoys liberty and has the same opportunity in life as the next fellow. The whole machinery of law and order, of capitalism and government, our entire civilization is based on this gigantic lie, and the constant propaganda of it by school, church, and press is for the sole purpose of keeping conditions as they are, of sustaining and protecting the "sacred institutions" of your wage slavery and keeping you obedient to law and authority.

By every method they seek to instill this lie of "justice," "liberty," and "equality" in the masses, for full well they know that their whole power and mastery rest on this faith. On every appropriate and inappropriate occasion they feed you this buncombe; they have even created special days to impress the lesson more emphatically upon you. Their spellbinders fill you full of this stuff on the Fourth of July, and you are permitted to shoot your misery and dissatisfaction off in firecrackers and forget your wage slavery in the big noise and hullabaloo. What an insult to the glorious memory of that great event, the American Revolutionary War, which abolished the tyranny of George III and made the American Colonies an independent republic! Now the anniversary of that event is used to mask your servitude in the country where the workers have neither freedom nor independence. To add insult to injury, they have given you a Thanksgiving Day, that you may offer up pious thanks for what you have not!

So great is the assurance of your masters in your stupidity that they dare do such things. They feel safe in having duped you so thoroughly and reduced your naturally rebellious spirit to such abject worship of "law and order" that you will never dream of opening your eyes and letting your heart cry out in outraged protest and defiance.

At the least sign of your rebellion the entire weight of the government, of law and order, comes down upon your head, beginning with the policeman's club, the jail, the prison, and ending with the gallows or the electric chair. The whole system of capitalism and government is mobilized to crush every symptom of dissatisfaction and rebellion; aye, even any attempt to improve your condition as a workingman. Because your masters well understand the situation and fully know the danger of your waking up to the actual facts of the case, to your real condition of slave. They are aware of their interests, of the interests of their class. They are class conscious, while the workers remain muddled and befuddled.

The industrial lords know that it is good for them to keep you unorganized and disorganized, or to break up your unions when they get strong and militant. By hook and crook they oppose your every advance as a class-conscious worker. Every movement for the improvement of labor's condition they hate and fight tooth and nail. They'll spend millions on the kind of education and propaganda that serves the continuation of their rule rather than on improving your conditions as a worker. They will spare neither expense nor energy to stifle any thought or idea that may reduce their profits or threaten their mastery over you.

It is for this reason that they try to crush every aspiration of labor for better conditions. Consider, for instance, the movement for the eight-hour day. It is comparatively recent history, and probably you remember with what bitterness and determination the employers opposed that effort of labor. In some industries in America and in most European countries the struggle is still going on. In the United States it began in 1886, and it was fought by the bosses with the greatest brutality in order to drive their workers back to the factories under the old conditions. They resorted to lockouts, throwing thousands out of work, to violence by hired thugs and Pinkertons upon labor assemblies and their active members, to the demolition of union headquarters and meeting places.

Where was "law and order"? What side of the struggle was the government on? What did the courts and the judges do? Where was justice?

The local, state, and federal authorities used all the machinery and power at their command to aid the employers. They did not even shrink from murder. The most active and able leaders of the movement had to pay with their lives for the attempt of the workers to reduce their hours of toil.

Many books have been written on that struggle, so that it is unnecessary for me to go into details. But a brief summary of those events will refresh the reader's memory.

The movement for the eight-hour workday started in Chicago, on May 1, 1886, gradually spreading throughout the country. Its beginning was marked by strikes declared in most of the large industrial centers. Twenty-five thousand workers laid down their tools in Chicago on the first day of the strike, and within two days their number was doubled. By the 4th of May almost all unionized labor in the city was on strike.

The armed fist of the law immediately hastened to the aid of the employers. The capitalist press raved against the strikers and called for the use of lead against them. There followed immediately assaults by police upon the strikers' meetings. The most vicious attack took place at the McCormick works, where the conditions of employment were so unbearable that the men were compelled to go on strike already in February. At this place the police and Pinkertons deliberately shot a volley into the assembled workers, killing four and wounding a score of others.

To protest against the outrage a meeting was called at Haymarket Square on the 4th of May, 1886.

It was an orderly gathering, such as were daily taking place in Chicago at the time. The Mayor of the city, Carter Harrison, was present; he listened to several speeches and then—according to his own sworn testimony later on in court—he returned to police headquarters to inform the Chief of Police that the meeting was all right. It was growing late—about ten in the evening; heavy clouds overcast the sky; it looked like rain. The audience began to disperse till only about two hundred were left. Then suddenly a detachment of a hundred policemen rushed upon the scene, commanded by Police Inspector Bonfield. They halted at the speakers' wagon, from which Samuel Fielden was addressing the remnant of the audience. The Inspector ordered the meeting to disperse. Fielden replied: "This is a peaceful assembly." Without further warning the police threw themselves upon the people, mercilessly clubbing and beating men and women. At that moment something whizzed through the air. There was an explosion, as of a bomb. Seven policemen were killed and about sixty wounded.

It was never ascertained who threw the bomb, and even to this day the identity of the man has not been established.

There had been so much brutality by the police and Pinkertons against the strikers that it was not surprising that some one should express his protest by such an act. Who was he? The industrial masters of Chicago were not interested in this detail. They were determined to crush rebellious labor, to down the eight-hour movement, and to stifle the voice of the spokesmen of the workers. They openly declared their determination to "teach the men a lesson."

Among the most active and intelligent leaders of the labor movement at the time was Albert Parsons, a man of old American stock, whose forebears had fought in the American Revolution. Associated with him in the agitation for the shorter workday were August Spies, Adolf Fischer, George Engel, and Louis Lingg. The money interests of Chicago and of the state of Illinois determined to "get" them. Their object was to punish and terrorize labor by murdering their most devoted leaders. The trial of those men was the most hellish conspiracy of capital against labor in the history of America. Perjured evidence, bribed jurymen, and police revenge combined to bring about their doom.

Parsons, Spies, Fischer, Engel, and Lingg were condemned to death, Lingg committing suicide in jail; Samuel Fielden and Michael Schwab were sentenced to prison for life, while Oscar Neebe received 15 years. No greater travesty of justice was ever staged than the trial of these men known as the Chicago Anarchists.

What a legal outrage the verdict was you can judge from the action of John P. Altgeld, later Governor of Illinois, who carefully reviewed the trial proceedings and declared that the executed and imprisoned men had been victims of a plot of the manufacturers, the courts, and the police. He could not undo the judicial murders, but most courageously he liberated the still imprisoned Anarchists, stating that he was merely making good, so far as was in his power, the terrible crime that had been committed against them.

The vengeance of the exploiters went so far that they punished Altgeld for his brave stand by eliminating him from the political life of America.

The Haymarket tragedy, as the case is known, is a striking illustration of the kind of "justice" labor may expect from the masters. It is a demonstration of its class character and of the means to which capital and government will resort to crush the workers.

The history of the American labor movement is replete with such examples. It is not within the scope of this book to review the great number of them. They are dealt with in numerous books and publications, to which I refer the reader for a nearer acquaintance with the Golgotha of the American proletariat. On a smaller scale the Chicago judicial murders are repeated in every struggle of labor. It is sufficient to mention the strikes of the miners in the state of Colorado, with its fiendish Ludlow chapter, where the state militia deliberately shot into the workers' tents, setting the latter afire and causing the death of a number of men, women and children; the murder of strikers in the hop fields of Wheatland, California, in the summer of 1913; in Everett, Washington, in 1916; in Tulsa, Oklahoma; in Virginia and in Kansas; in the copper mines of Montana, and in numerous other places throughout the country.

Nothing so arouses the hatred and vengeance of the masters as the effort to enlighten their victims. This is as true today as it was in the time of slavery and serfdom. We have seen how the church persecuted and martyred her critics and fought every advance of science as a threat to her authority and influence. Similarly has every despot always sought to stifle the voice of protest and rebellion. In the same spirit capital and government today furiously fall upon and tear to pieces everyone who dares shake the foundations of their power and interests.

Take two recent cases as instance of this never-changing attitude of authority and ownership: the Mooney-Billings case and that of Sacco and Vanzetti. One took place in the East, the other in the West, the two separated by a decade and the whole width of the continent. Yet, they were exactly alike, proving that there is neither East nor West, nor any difference of time or place in the masters' treatment of their slaves.

Mooney and Billings are in prison in California for life. Why? If I were to answer in just a few words, I should say, with perfect truth and completeness: because they were intelligent union men who tried to enlighten their fellow employees and improve their condition.

It was just this, and no other reason, that doomed them. The Chamber of Commerce of San Francisco, the money of California, could not tolerate the activities of two such energetic and militant men. Labor in San Francisco was becoming restive, strikes were taking place, and demands were being voiced by the toilers for a greater share of the wealth they were producing.

The industrial magnates of the coast declared war upon organized labor. They proclaimed the "open shop" and their determination to break the unions. That was the preliminary step towards placing the workers in a position of helplessness and then reducing wages. Their hatred and persecution were directed first of all against the most active members of labor.

Tom Mooney had organized the street-car men of San Francisco, a crime for which the traction company could not forgive him. Mooney together with Warren Billings and other workers had also been active in a number of strikes. They were known and admired for their devotion to the union cause. That was enough for the employers and the San Francisco Chamber of Commerce to try to get them out of the way. On several occasions they had been arrested on frame-up charges by agents of the traction and other corporations. But the cases against them were of such flimsy nature that they had to be dismissed. The Chamber of Commerce bided its opportunity to "get" those two labor men, as their agents openly threatened to do.

The opportunity came with the explosion during the Preparedness Parade in San Francisco, July 22, 1916. The labor unions of the city had decided not to participate in the parade, because the latter was merely a show of strength by California capital as against unionized labor which the Chamber of Commerce had set out to crush. The "open shop" was its frankly proclaimed policy, and it made no secret of its determined and bitter hostility to unions.

It has never been ascertained who placed the infernal machine which exploded during the parade, but the San Francisco police never made any serious effort to find the responsible party or parties. Immediately following the tragic occurrence Thomas Mooney and his wife Rena were arrested, as well as Warren Billings, Edward D. Nolan, a member of the machinists' union, and I. Weinberg, of the jitney drivers' union.

The trial of Billings and Mooney proved one of the worst scandals in the history of American courts.

The state witnesses were self-confessed perjurers, bribed and threatened by the police into giving false testimony. Evidence showing the entire innocence of Mooney and Billings was ignored. Mooney was accused of having placed the infernal machine at the very time when he was in the company of friends upon the roof of a house about a mile and a half distant from the scene of the explosion. A photograph taken of the demonstration by a film company during the parade clearly shows Mooney on the roof, and in the background a street clock indicating the time as 2.02 p.m. The explosion having taken place at 2.06 p.m., it would have been a physical impossibility for Mooney to have been at both places at almost the same time.

But it was not a question of evidence, of guilt or innocence. Tom Mooney was bitterly hated by the vested interests of San Francisco. He had to be gotten out of the way. Mooney and Billings were convicted, the former being sentenced to death, the latter receiving a lifetime term.

The outrageous manner in which the trial was conducted, the evident perjury of the state witnesses, and the clear hand of the manufacturers back of the prosecution aroused the country. The matter ultimately was brought up before Congress. The latter passed a resolution ordering the Labor Department to investigate the case. The report of Commissioner John B. Densmore, sent to San Francisco for this purpose, exposed the conspiracy to hang Mooney as one of the methods of the Chamber of

Commerce to destroy organized labor in California.

Since then most of the State witnesses, having failed to receive the reward promised them, confessed to having perjured themselves at the instigation of Charles M. Fickert, then District Attorney of San Francisco and known tool of the Chamber of Commerce. Draper Hand and R. W. Smith, police officials of the city, have both declared in sworn affidavits that the evidence against Mooney and Billings was manufactured from beginning to end by the District Attorney and his bribed witnesses from the lowest social dregs of the coast.

The Mooney-Billings case attracted national and even international attention. President Wilson felt induced to wire to the Governor of California twice, asking for a revision of the case. Mooney's death sentence was commuted to life imprisonment, but no effort has succeeded in securing him a new trial.

The money power of California was bent on keeping Mooney and Billings in the penitentiary. The Supreme Court of the state, obedient to the Chamber of Commerce, steadfastly refused, on technical grounds, to review the trial testimony, the perjured character of which had become a byword in California.

Since then all the surviving jurors have made statements to the effect that if the true facts of the case had been known to them during the trial, they would have never convicted Mooney. Even Judge Fraser, who presided at the trial, has asked for Mooney's pardon, on similar grounds.

Yet both Tom Mooney and Warren Billings still remain in the penitentiary. The Chamber of Commerce of California is determined to keep them there, and their power is supreme with the courts and the government.

Can you still speak of justice? Do you think justice to labor possible under the reign of capitalism?

The judicial murder of the Chicago Anarchists took place many years ago, in 1887. Considerable time has also elapsed since the Mooney-Billings case, in 1916–1917. The latter, moreover, happened far away, on the Pacific Coast, at a time of war hysteria. Such rank injustice could take place only in those days, you might say; it could hardly be repeated today.

Let us then shift the scene to our own day, to the very heart of

America, the proud seat of culture—to Boston, Massachusetts.

It is sufficient to mention Boston to call up the picture of two proletarians, Nicola Sacco and Bartolomeo Vanzetti, one a poor shoemaker, the other a fish peddler, whose names today are known and honored in every civilized country the world over.

Martyrs to humanity, if ever there were any; two men who gave up their lives because of their devotion to mankind, because of their loyalty to the ideal of an emancipated and freed working class. Two innocent men who bravely suffered torture during seven long years, and who died a terrible death with a serenity of spirit rarely equaled by the greatest martyrs of all time.

The story of that judicial murder of two of the noblest of men, the crime of Massachusetts that will neither be forgotten nor forgiven as long as the state exists, is too fresh in the memory of every one to need recapitulation here.

But *why* did Sacco and Vanzetti have to die? This question is of utmost moment; it bears directly upon the matters at issue.

Do you think that if Sacco and Vanzetti had been just a pair of criminals, as the prosecution tried to make you believe, there would have been such ruthless determination to execute them in the face of the appeals, pleadings, and protests of the entire world?

Or if they had been plutocrats actually guilty of murder, with no other issue involved, would they have been executed? Would no appeal to the higher courts of the state have been allowed, would the Federal Supreme Court have refused to consider the case?

You have often heard of some rich fellow killing a man, or of the sons of wealthy parents found guilty of murder in the first degree. But can you name a single one of them ever executed in the United States? Will you even discover many of them in prison? Does not the law always find excuses of "mental excitation," of "brain storm," of "legal irresponsibility" in cases of rich men convicted of crime?

But even if Sacco and Vanzetti had been ordinary criminals sentenced to die, would not appeals from prominent men in all walks of life, from charitable societies, and hundreds of thousands of friends and sympathizers have secured clemency for them? Would not doubt of their guilt, expressed by the highest legal authorities, have resulted in a new trial, a revision of the old testimony, and the consideration of new evidence in their behalf?

Why was all this refused to Sacco and Vanzetti? Why did "law and order," beginning with the local police and Federal detectives, up to the confessedly prejudiced trial judge, all through the Supreme Court of the state, the Governor, and ending with the Federal Supreme Court show such a determination to send them to the electric chair?

Because Sacco and Vanzetti *were dangerous* to the interests of capital. These men voiced the dissatisfaction of the workers with their condition of servitude. They expressed consciously what the workers mostly feel unconsciously. It is because they were *class-conscious* men, Anarchists, that they were a greater menace to the security of capitalism than if they had been a whole army of strikers not conscious of the real objects of the class struggle. The masters know that when you strike you demand only higher pay or shorter hours of work. But the class-conscious struggle of labor against capital is a far more serious matter; it means the entire abolition of the wage system and the freeing of labor from the domination of capital. You can readily understand then why the masters saw a greater danger in such men as Sacco and Vanzetti than in the biggest strike for the mere improvement of conditions within capitalism.

Sacco and Vanzetti threatened the whole structure of capitalism and government. Not those two poor proletarians as individuals. No; rather what those two men represented—the spirit of conscious rebellion against existing conditions of exploitation and oppression.

It is that *spirit* which capital and government meant to kill in the persons of those men. To kill that spirit and the movement for labor's emancipation by striking terror into the hearts of all who might think and feel like Sacco and Vanzetti; to make an example of those two men that would intimidate the workers and keep them away from the proletarian movement.

This is the reason why neither the courts nor the government of Massachusetts could be induced to give Sacco and Vanzetti a new trial. There was danger of their being acquitted in the atmosphere of an aroused public sense of justice; there was the fear that the plot to murder them would be exposed. That is why the justices of the Federal Supreme Court declined to hear the case, just as the judges of the Supreme Court of the state of Massachusetts refused a new trial in spite of important new evidence. For that reason also the President of the United States did not intercede in the matter, though it was no less his moral than his legal duty to do so. His moral duty, in the interests of justice; his legal obligation because as President he had sworn to uphold the Constitution which guarantees every one a fair trial, which Sacco and Vanzetti did not get.

President Coolidge had sufficient precedents for interceding in behalf of justice, notably the example of Woodrow Wilson, in the case of Mooney. But Coolidge had not the courage to do so, being entirely subservient to the Big Interests. No doubt the case of Sacco and Vanzetti was also considered of even greater importance and class significance than that of Mooney. At any rate, both capital and government agreed with their resolve to uphold the courts of Massachusetts at all cost and to sacrifice Nicolo Sacco and Bartolomeo Vanzetti.

The masters were determined to uphold the legend of "justice in the courts," because their whole power rests on the popular belief in such justice. It is not that infallibility is claimed for judges. If that were the attitude, there would be no appeal from the decision of a judge, there would be neither superior nor supreme courts. The fallibility of justice is admitted, but the fact that the courts and all government institutions serve only to support the rule of the masters over their labor slaves—that their justice is but class justice—*that* could not be admitted for even an instant. Because if the people found that out, capitalism and government would be doomed. That is exactly why no impartial review of the evidence in the Sacco and Vanzetti case could be permitted, no new trial given them, for such a proceeding would have exposed the motives and objects back of their prosecution.

Therefore there was no appeal and no new trial—only a star chamber hearing behind closed doors in the Governor's mansion, by men whose loyalty to the dominant class was above suspicion; men who by all their training and education, by their tradition and interests were bound to sustain the courts and clear the Sacco and Vanzetti verdict of any imputation of class justice. Therefore Sacco and Vanzetti had to die.

Governor Fuller of Massachusetts pronounced the final word of their doom. There were, even up to the last moment, thousands who had hoped that the Governor would shrink from committing this cold-blooded murder. But they did not know or had forgotten that years before, in 1919, the same Fuller had stated in Congress that every "radical, socialist, I.W.W., or anarchist should be exterminated"; that is, that those who seek to free labor should be murdered. Could you reasonably expect such a man to do justice to Sacco and Vanzetti, two avowed Anarchists?

Governor Fuller acted according to his sentiments, in keeping with his attitude and interests as a member of the ruling class, in a manner thoroughly class-conscious. Similarly have acted Judge Thayer and all those involved in the prosecution, no less than the "respectable gentlemen" of the Commission appointed by Fuller to "review" the case in secret session. All of them class-conscious, they were interested only in sustaining capitalistic "justice," so as to preserve the "law and order" by which they live and profit.

Is there justice for labor within capitalism and government? Can there be any as long as the present system exists? Decide for yourself.

The cases I have cited are but a few of the numerous struggles of American labor against capital. The same can be duplicated in every country. They clearly demonstrate the fact that

(1) there is only *class* justice in the war of capital against labor; there can be no justice for labor under capitalism;

(2) law and government, as well as all other capitalist institutions (the press, the school, the church, the police, and courts) are always at the service of capital against labor, whatever the merits of any given case. Capital and government are twins with one common interest.

(3) capital and government will use any and all means to keep the proletariat in subjection: they will terrorize the working class and ruthlessly murder its most intelligent and devoted members.

It cannot be otherwise, because there is a life-and-death struggle between capital and labor.

Every time that capital and its servant, the law, hang such men as the Chicago Anarchists or electrocute the Saccos and Vanzettis, they proclaim that they have "freed society from a menace." They want *you* to believe that the executed were your enemies, enemies of society. They also want you to believe that their death has settled the matter, that capitalistic justice has been vindicated, and that "law and order" has triumphed. But the matter is not settled, and the masters' victory is only temporary. The struggle goes on, as it has continued all through the history of man, all through the march of labor and liberty. No matter is ever settled unless it is settled right. You can't suppress the natural yearning of the human heart for freedom and well-being, however much terror and murder governments may resort to. You can't stifle the demand of the toiler for better conditions. The struggle goes on and will continue in spite of everything law, government, and capital may do. But that the workers may not be wasting their energy and efforts in the wrong direction, they must clearly understand that they can no more hope for justice from the courts, from law and government, than they can expect wage slavery to be abolished by their masters.

"What's to be done, then?" you ask. "How shall the workers get justice?"

CHAPTER IX
CAN THE CHURCH HELP YOU?

What's to be done?

How abolish poverty, oppression, and tyranny? How eliminate evil and injustice, weed out corruption, put an end to crime and murder?

How do away with wage slavery?

How secure liberty and well-being, joy and sunshine for every one?

"Turn to God," commands the church; "only a Christian life can save the world."

"Let us pass a new law," says the reformer; "man must be compelled to be good."

"Vote for me!" says the politician; "I'll look after your interests."

"The Trade Union," advises your labor friend; "that's your hope."

"Only Socialism can abolish capitalism and do away with wage slavery," insists the Socialist.

"I'm a Bolshevik," announces another; "only the dictatorship of the proletariat will free the workers."

"We'll remain slaves as long as we have rulers and masters," says the Anarchist; "only liberty can make us free."

The Protectionist and the Free Trader, the Single Taxer and the Fabian, the Tolstoyan and the Mutualist, and a score of other social physicians all prescribe their particular medicine to cure the ills of society, and you wonder who is right and what the true solution might be.

You cannot make any greater mistake than to accept *blindly* this or that advice. You are sure to go wrong.

Only your own reason and experience can decide where the right road lies. Examine the various proposals and determine with your own common sense which is the most reasonable and practical. Only then will you know what is best for yourself, for the worker, and for mankind.

So let us look into the different plans.

§ § § §

Can the church help you?

Maybe you are a Christian, or a member of some other religion—Jew, Mormon, Mohammedan, Buddhist, or what not.

It makes no difference. A man should be free to believe whatever he pleases. The point is not what your religious faith is, but whether religion can abolish the evils we suffer from.

As I said before, we have only one life to live on this earth, and we want to make the best of it. What will happen to us after we are dead we don't know. The chances are we'll never know, and so it's no use bothering about it.

The question here is of life, not of death. It is the living we are concerned with; with you and me and others like ourselves. Can the world be made a better place for us to live in? That's what we want to know. Can religion do it?

Christianity is about 2,000 years old. Has it abolished any evil? Has it done away with crime and murder, has it delivered us from poverty and misery, from despotism and tyranny?

You know that it has *not*. You know that the Christian Church, like all other churches, has always been on the side of the masters, against the people. More: the church has caused worse strife and bloodshed than all the wars of kings and kaisers. Religion has divided mankind into opposing beliefs, and the most bloody wars have been fought on account of religious differences. The church has persecuted people for their opinions, imprisoned and killed them. The Catholic Inquisition terrorized the whole world, tortured so-called heretics, and burned them alive. Other churches did the same when they had the power. They always sought to enslave and exploit the people, to keep them in ignorance and darkness. They condemned every effort of man to develop his mind, to advance, to improve his condition. They damned science, and silenced the men who thirsted for knowledge. Till this very day institutionalized religion is the Judas of its alleged Savior. It approves of murder and war, of wage slavery and capitalistic robbery, and always stands for the "law and order" which crucified the Nazarene.

Consider: Jesus wanted all men to be brothers, to live in peace and good will. The church upholds inequality, national strife, and war.

Jesus condemned the rich as vipers and oppressors of the poor. The church bows before the rich and accumulates vast wealth.

The Nazarene was born in a manger and remained a pauper all his life. His alleged representatives and spokesmen on earth live in palaces.

Jesus preached meekness. The Princes of the Church are haughty and purse-proud.

"As you do unto the least of my children," Christ said, "you do unto me."

The church supports the capitalist system which enslaves little children and brings them to an early grave.

"Thou shalt not kill," commanded the Nazarene. The church approves of executions and war.

Christianity is the greatest hypocrisy on record. Neither Christian nations nor individuals practice the precepts of Jesus. The early Christians did—and they were crucified, burned at the stake, or thrown to the wild animals in the Roman arena. Later the Christian Church compromised with those in power; it gained money and influence by taking the side of the tyrants against the people. It sanctioned everything which Christ condemned, and by that it won the good will and support of kings and masters. Today king, master, and priest are one trinity. They crucify Jesus daily; they glorify him with lip service and betray him for silver pieces; they praise his name and kill his spirit.

It is obvious that Christianity is the greatest sham and shame of humanity, and a complete failure because the Christian appeal is a lie. The churches do not practice what they preach. Moreover, they preach to you a gospel which they know you cannot live up to; they call upon you to become a "better man" without giving you a chance to do so. On the contrary, the churches uphold the conditions that make you "bad," while they command you to be "good." They benefit materially by the existing regime and are financially interested in keeping it up. The Catholic Church, the Protestant, Anglican, Christian Science, Mormon, and other denominations are among the wealthiest organizations in the world today. Their possessions represent the workers' blood and flesh. Their influence is proof of how the people are deluded. The prophets of religion are dead and forgotten; there remain only the profits.

"But if we would lead a truly Christian life," you remark, "the world would be different."

You are right, my friend. But can you live a Christian life under present conditions? Does capitalism allow you to lead such a life? Will the government permit you to do so? Will even the church give you a chance to live a Christian life?

Just try it for one single day and see what happens to you.

As you leave your house in the morning, determine to be a Christian that day and speak only the truth. As you pass the policeman on the corner, remind him of Christ and His commandments. Tell him to "love his enemy as himself," and persuade him to throw away his club and gun.

And when you meet the soldier on the street, impress it upon him that Jesus had said, "Thou shalt not kill."

In your shop or office speak the whole truth to your employer. Tell him of the Nazarene's warning. "What shall it profit you to gain the whole earth and lose your soul and its salvation?" Mention that He commanded us to share our last loaf with the poor; that He said that the rich man has no more chance of getting into heaven than the camel can pass through the eye of a needle.

And when you are brought to court for disturbing the peace of the good Christians, remind the judge: "Judge not that ye be not judged."

You will be declared a fool or a madman, and they will send you to a lunatic asylum or to prison.

You can see, then, what rank hypocrisy it is for the sky pilot to preach the Christian life to you. He knows as well as you that under capitalism and government there is no more chance to lead a Christian life than for a camel to "pass through the needle's eye." All those good folks who pretend to be Christians are just hypocrites who preach what cannot be practiced, for they don't give you any opportunity to lead a Christian life. No, not even to lead an ordinarily decent and honest life, without sham and deceit, without pretense and lying.

It is true that if we could follow the precepts of the Nazarene this would be a different world to live in. There would then be no murder and no war; no cheating and lying and profit-making. There would be neither slave nor master, and we should all live like brothers, in peace and harmony. There would be neither poor nor rich, neither crime nor prison, but that would not be what the church wants. It would be what the Anarchists want, and that we shall discuss further on.

So, my friend, you have nothing to expect from the Christian Church or from *any* church. All progress and improvement in the world has been made *against* the will and wishes of the church. You may believe in whatever religion you please, but don't put any hope of social improvement in the church.

Now let's see whether the reformer or politician can help us.

CHAPTER X
REFORMER AND POLITICIAN

Who is the reformer, and what does he propose?

The reformer wants to "reform and improve." He is not sure what it is that he really wants to change: sometimes he says that "people are bad," and it is them that he wants to "reform"; at other times he means to "improve" conditions. He does not believe in abolishing an evil altogether. Doing away with something that is rotten is "too radical" for him. "For Heaven's sake," he cautions you, "don't be too hasty." He wants to change things gradually, little by little. Take war, for example. War is bad, of course, the reformer admits; it is wholesale murder, a blot upon our civilization. But—abolish it? Oh, no! He wants to "reform" it. He wants to "limit armaments," for instance. With less armaments, he says, we'll kill fewer people. He wants to "humanize" war, to make slaughter more decent, so to speak.

If you should carry out his ideas in your personal life, you would not have a rotten tooth that aches pulled out all at once. You would have it pulled a little today, some more next week, for several months or years, and by then you would be ready to pull it out altogether, so it should not hurt so much. That is the logic of the reformer. Don't be "too hasty," don't pull a bad tooth out all at once.

The reformer thinks he can make people better by law. "Pass a new law," he says whenever anything goes wrong; "compel men to be good."

He forgets that for hundreds, even for thousands, of years laws have been made to force people to "be good," yet human nature remains about what it always was. We have so many laws that even the proverbial Philadelphia lawyer is lost in their maze. The ordinary person can't tell any more what is right or wrong according to statute, what is just, what true or false. A special class of persons—judges—decide what is honest or dishonest, when it is permitted to steal and in what manner, when fraud is legal and when it is not, when murder is right and when it is a crime, which uniform entitles you to kill and which does not. It takes many laws to determine all this, and for centuries legislators have been busy making laws (at a good salary), and yet today we still need more laws, for all the other laws have failed to make you "good."

Still the lawmaker continues to compel people to be good. If the existing laws have not made you better, he says, then we need more laws and stricter ones. Stiffer sentences will diminish and prevent crime, he claims, while he appeals in behalf of his "reform" to the very men who have stolen the earth from the people.

If some one has killed another in a business quarrel, for money or other advantage, the reformer will not admit that money and money-getting rouse the worst passions and drive men to crime and murder. He will argue that the willful taking of human life deserves capital punishment, and he will straightway help the government send armed men to some foreign country to do wholesale killing there.

The reformer cannot think straight. He does not understand that if men act badly it is because they think it is to their advantage to do so. The reformer says that a new law will change all that. He is a born prohibitionist: he wants to prohibit men from being bad. If a man lost his job, for instance, feels blue about it, and gets drunk to forget his troubles, the reformer wouldn't think of helping the man to find work. No, it is drinking that must be prohibited, he insists. He thinks he has reformed you by driving you out of the saloon into the cellar where you stealthily slush on vile moonshine instead of openly taking a drink. In the same way he wants to reform you in what you eat and do, in what you think and feel.

He refuses to see that his "reforms" create worse evils than those they are supposed to suppress; that they cause more deceit, corruption, and vice. He puts one set of men to spy upon another, and he thinks he has "raised the standard of morality"; he pretends to have made you "better" by compelling you to be a hypocrite.

I don't mean to detain you long with the reformer. We are going to meet him again as the politician. Without wishing to be rough on him, I can say frankly that when the reformer is honest he is a fool; when he is a politician he is a knave. In either case, as we shall presently see, he cannot solve our problem of how to make the world a better place to live in.

The politician is first cousin to the reformer. "Pass a new law," says the reformer, "and compel men to be good." "Let *me* pass the law," says the politician, "and things will be better."

You can tell the politician by his talk. In most cases he is a grafter who wants to climb on your shoulders to power. Once there, he forgets his solemn promises and thinks only of his own ambitions and interests.

When the politician is honest he misleads you no less than the grafter. Perhaps worse, because you put confidence in him and are the more disappointed when he fails to do you any good.

The reformer and the politician are both on the wrong track. To try to change men by law is just like trying to change your face by getting a new mirror. For men make laws, not laws men. The law merely *reflects* men as they are, as the mirror reflects your features.

"But the law keeps people from becoming criminals," reformer and politician assert.

If that is true, if the law really prevents crime, then the more laws the better. By the time we have passed enough laws there will be no more crime. Well, why do you smile? Because you know that it is nonsense. You know that the best the law can do is to *punish* crime; it cannot prevent it.

Should the time ever come when the law could read a man's mind and detect there his *intention* to commit a crime, then it might prevent it. But in that case the law would have no policemen to do the preventing, because they'd be in prison themselves. And if the administration of law would be honest and impartial, there would be neither judges nor lawmakers, because they would be keeping the police company.

But seriously speaking, as things stand, how can the law prevent crime? It can do so only when the intention to commit a crime has been announced or has somehow become known. But such cases are very rare. One does not advertise his criminal plans. The claim then that the law prevents crime is entirely baseless.

"But the fear of punishment," you object, "does it not prevent crime?"

If that were the case crime would have stopped long ago, for surely the law has done enough punishing. The whole experience of mankind disproves the idea that punishment prevents crime. On the contrary, it has been found that even the most severe punishments do not frighten people away from crime.

England, as well as other countries, used to punish not only murder but scores of lesser crimes with death. Yet it did not deter others from committing the same crimes. People were then executed publicly, by hanging, by garroting, by the guillotine, in order to inspire greater fear. Yet even the most fearful punishment failed to prevent or diminish crime. It was found that public executions had a brutalizing effect upon the people, and there are cases on record where persons who witnessed an execution immediately committed the very crime the terrible punishment of which they had just witnessed. That is why public execution was abolished: it did more harm than good. Statistics show that there has been no increase of crime in countries that have entirely done away with capital punishment.

Of course, there may be some cases in which the fear of punishment prevents a crime; but on the whole its only effect is to make the criminal more circumspect, so that his detection is more difficult.

There are, generally speaking, two types of crime: some committed in the heat of anger and passion, and in such cases one does not stop to consider the consequences, and so the fear of punishment does not enter as a factor. The other class of crime is committed with cold deliberation, mostly professionally, and in such cases fear of punishment only serves to make the criminal more careful to leave no traces. It is a well-known trait of the professional criminal that he thinks himself sufficiently clever to avoid detection, no matter how often he happens to be caught. He will always blame some particular circumstance, some accidental cause, or just "bad luck" for having been arrested. "Next time I'll be more careful," he says; or, "I won't trust my pal any more." But almost never will you find in him the faintest thought of giving up crime on account of the punishment which may be meted out to him. I have known thousands of criminals, yet hardly any of them ever took possible punishment into consideration.

It is just because fear of punishment has no deterrent effect that crime continues in spite of all laws and courts, prisons and executions.

But let us suppose that punishment does have a deterring effect. Must there not be some powerful reasons that cause people to commit crime, notwithstanding all the dire punishment inflicted?

What are those reasons?

Every prison warden will tell you that whenever there is much unemployment, hard times, the prisons get filled. This fact is also borne out by investigation into the causes of crime. The greatest percentage of it is due directly to conditions, to industrial and economic reasons. That is why the vast majority of the prison population come from the poor classes. It has been established that poverty and unemployment, with their attendant misery and despair, are the chief sources of crime. Is there any law to prevent poverty and unemployment?

Is there any law to abolish these main causes of crime? Are not all the laws designed to keep up the conditions which produce poverty and misery, and thus manufacture crime all the time?

Suppose a pipe bursts in your house. You put a bucket under the break to catch the escaping water. You can keep on putting buckets there, but as long as you do not mend the broken pipe, the leakage will continue, no matter how much you may swear about it.

Our filled prisons are the buckets. Pass as many laws as you want, punish the criminals as you may, the leakage will continue until you repair the broken social pipe.

Does the reformer or politician really want to mend that pipe?

I have said that most crime is of an economic nature. That is, it has to do with money, with possession, with the desire to get something with the least effort, to secure a living or wealth by hook or crook.

But that is just the ambition of our whole life, of our entire civilization. As long as our existence is based on a spirit of this sort, will it be possible to eradicate crime? As long as society is built on the principle of grabbing all you can, we must continue to live that way. Some will try to do it "within the law;" others, more courageous, reckless, or desperate, will do it outside the law. But the one and the other will really be doing the same thing, and it's the thing that is the crime, not the manner in which it is done.

Those who can do it within the law call the others criminals. It's for the "illegal" criminals—and for those who might become such—that most of the laws are made.

The "illegal" criminals are often caught. Their conviction and punishment often depend mainly on how successful they have been in their criminal career. The more successful, the less chance of their conviction, the lighter their punishment. It is not the crime they committed which will ultimately decide their fate, but their ability to employ expensive lawyers, their political and social connections, their money and influence. It will generally be the poor and friendless fellow who will be made to feel the full weight of the law; he'll get speedy "justice" and the heaviest penalty. He is not able to take advantage of the various delays which the law affords to his richer fellow criminal, for appeals to higher courts are expensive luxuries which the moneyless criminal cannot indulge in. That is why you almost never see a rich man behind prison bars; such are occasionally "found guilty," but mighty seldom punished. Nor will you find many professional criminals in prison. These know "the ropes"; they have friends and connections; usually they also have "fall money," for just such occasions, with which to "oil" their

way out of the legal meshes. Those you find in our prisons and peniten-
tiaries are the poorest of society, accidental criminals, mostly workingmen
and farm boys whom poverty and misfortune, striking and picketing,
unemployment and general helplessness have brought behind the bars.

Are these at least reformed by the law and the penalties they
undergo? Hardly. They come out of prison weakened in body and mind,
hardened by the mistreatment and cruelty they suffered from or
witnessed there, embittered by their fate. They have to go back to the
same conditions which had made them law-breakers in the first place,
but now they are labeled "criminals," are looked down upon, scorned
even by former friends, and persecuted and hounded by the police as
men "with a criminal record." It is not long before most of them are
again behind the bars.

So our social merry-go-round revolves. And all the time the
conditions that had made those unfortunates into criminals continue
manufacturing new crops of them, and "law and order" goes on as before,
and the reformer and politician keep busy making more laws.

It is a profitable business, this law-making. Have you ever stopped to
consider whether our courts, police, and the whole machinery of
so-called justice really want to abolish crime? Is it to the interest of the
policeman, the detective, the sheriff, the judge, the lawyer, the prison
contractors, wardens, deputies, keepers, and the thousands of others who
live by the "administration of justice" to do away with crime? Supposing
there were no criminals, could those "administrators" hold their jobs?
Could you be taxed for their support? Would they not have to do some
honest work?

Think it over and see if crime is not a more lucrative source of income
to the "dispensers of justice" than to the criminals themselves. Can you
reasonably believe that they really want to abolish crime?

Their "business" is to apprehend and punish the criminal; but it is not
to their interest to do away with crime, for that's their bread and butter.
That is the reason why they will not look into the *causes* of crime. They
are quite satisfied with things as they are. They are the staunchest
defenders of the existing system, of "justice" and punishment, the
champions of "law and order." They catch and punish "criminals," but
they leave crime and its causes severely alone.

"But what is the law for then?" you demand.

The law is to keep up existing conditions, to preserve "law and order." More laws are constantly made, all for the same purpose of defending and sustaining the present order of things. "To reform men," as the reformer says; "to improve conditions," as the politician assures you.

But the new laws leave men as they are, and conditions remain, on the whole, the same. Since capitalism and wage slavery began, millions of laws have been passed, but capitalism and wage slavery still remain. The truth is, all the laws serve only to make capitalism stronger and perpetuate the workers' subjection. It is the business of the politician, the "science of politics," to make you believe that the law protects you and your interests, while it merely serves to keep up the system which robs, dupes, and enslaves you in body and mind. All the institutions of society have this one object in view: to instill in you respect for law and government, to awe you with its authority and sanctity, and thus support the social framework which rests upon your ignorance and your obedience. The whole secret of the thing is that the masters want to keep their stolen possessions. Law and government are the *means* by which they do it.

There is no great mystery about this matter of government and laws. Nor is there anything sacred or holy about them. Laws are made and unmade; old laws are abolished, and new laws are passed. It is all the work of men, human, and therefore fallible and temporary. There is nothing eternal or unchangeable about them. But whatever laws you make and however you change them, they always serve *one* purpose: to compel people to do certain things, to restrain them from or punish them for doing other things. That is to say, the only purpose of laws and government is to rule the people, to keep them from doing what they want and prescribe to them what certain other people want them to do.

But why must people be kept from doing what they want? And what is it that they want to do?

If you look into this you will find that people want to live, to satisfy their needs, to enjoy life. And in this all people are alike, as I have already pointed out before. But if people are to be prevented from living and enjoying their lives, then there must be some amongst us who have an interest in doing that.

So it is in fact: there are indeed people who don't want us to live and enjoy life, because they have taken the joy out of our lives, and they don't want to give it back to us. Capitalism has done it, and government which serves capitalism. To let the people enjoy life would mean to stop robbing and oppressing them. That is why capitalism needs government, that's why we are taught to respect the "sanctity of the law." We have been made to believe that breaking the law is criminal, though law-breaking and crime are often entirely different things. We have been made to believe that any act against the law is bad for society, though it may be bad only for the masters and exploiters. We have been made to believe that everything which threatens the possessions of the rich is "evil" and "wrong," and that everything which weakens our chains and destroys our slavery is "criminal."

In short, there has been developed in the course of time a kind of "morality" that is useful for the rulers and masters—only a class morality; really a slave morality, because it helps to keep us in slavery. And whoever goes against this slave morality is called "bad," "immoral," a criminal, an anarchist.

If I should rob you of all you have and then persuade you that what I did is good for you and that you should guard my booty against others, it would be a very clever trick on my part, wouldn't it? It would secure me in my stolen possessions. Suppose further that I should also manage to convince you that we must make a rule that no one may touch my stolen wealth and that I may continue to accumulate more in the same manner, and that the arrangement is just and to your own best interests. If such a crazy scheme should be actually carried out, then we'd have the "law and order" of government and capitalism which we have today.

It is clear, of course, that laws would have no force if the people did not believe in them and did not obey them. So the first thing to do is to make them believe that laws are necessary and that they are good for them. And it is still better if you can lead them to think that it is they themselves who make the laws. Then they will be willing and anxious to obey them. That's what is called democracy: to get the people to believe that they are their own rulers and that they themselves pass the laws of their country. That's the great advantage that a democracy or a republic has over a monarchy. In olden times the business of ruling and robbing the people was much harder and more dangerous. The king or feudal lord had to compel people by force to serve him. He would hire armed bands to make his subjects submit and pay tribute to him. But that was expensive and troublesome. A better way was found by "educating" the populace to believe that they "owe" the king loyalty and faithful service. Governing then became much easier, but still the people knew that the king was their lord and commander. A republic, however, is much safer and more comfortable for the rulers, for there the people imagine that they themselves are the masters. And no matter how exploited and oppressed they are, in a "democracy" they think themselves free and independent.

That is why the average workingman in the United States, for instance, considers himself a sovereign citizen, though he has no more to say about the running of his country than the starved peasant in Russia had under the Tsar. He thinks he is free, while in fact he is only a wage slave. He believes he enjoys "liberty for the pursuit of happiness," while his days, weeks and years, and his whole life, are mortgaged to the boss in the mine or factory.

The people under a tyranny know they are enslaved and sometimes they revolt. The people of America are in bondage and don't know it. That is why there are no revolutions in America.

Modern capitalism is wise. It knows that it prospers best under "democratic" institutions, with the people electing their own representatives to the lawmaking bodies, and indirectly casting a vote even for the president. The capitalist masters do not care how or for whom you vote, whether it be the Republican or the Democratic ticket. What difference is it to them? Whoever you elect, he will legislate in favor of "law and order," to protect things as they are. The main concern of the powers that be is that the people should continue to believe in and uphold the existing system. That is why they spend millions for the schools, colleges, and universities which "educate" you to believe in capitalism and government. Politics and politicians, governors and lawmakers are only their puppets. They will see to it that no legislation is passed against their interests. Now and then they will make a show of fighting certain laws and favoring others, else the game would lose its interest for you. But whatever laws there be, the masters will take care that they shouldn't hurt their business, and their well-paid lawyers know how to turn every law to the benefit of the Big Interests, as daily experience proves.

A very striking illustration of it is the famous Sherman Anti-Trust Law, Organized labor spent thousands of dollars and years of energy to pass that legislation. It was directed against growing capitalist monopoly, against the powerful combinations of money which ruled legislatures and courts and lorded it over the workers with an iron hand. After long and expensive effort the Sherman Law was at last passed, and labor leaders and politicians were jubilant over the "new epoch" created by that law, as they enthusiastically assured the toilers.

What has that law accomplished? The trusts have not been hurt by it; they have remained safe and sound; in fact, they have grown and multiplied. They dominate the country and treat the workers as abject slaves. They are more powerful and prosperous than ever before.

But one important thing the Sherman Law did accomplish. Passed especially in the "interests of labor," it has been turned against the workers and their unions. It is now used to break up organizations of labor as being in "prevention of free competition." The labor unions are now constantly menaced by that anti-trust law, while the capitalistic trusts go on their way undisturbed.

My friend, do I need to tell you about the bribery and debauchery of politics, about the corruption of the courts, and the vile administration of "justice?" Do I need to remind you of the big Teapot-Dome and oil lease scandals, and the thousand and one lesser ones of everyday occurrence? It would be to insult your intelligence to dwell upon these universally known things, for they are part and parcel of all politics, in every country.

The great evil is not that politicians are corrupt and the administration of law unjust. If that were the only trouble then we might try, like the reformer, to "purify" politics and to work for a more "just administration." But it is not that which is the real trouble. The trouble is not with impure politics, but that the whole game of politics is rotten. The trouble is not with defects in the administration of the law, but that law itself is an instrument to subject and oppress the people.

The whole system of law and government is a machine to keep the workers enslaved and to rob them of their toil. Every social "reform" whose realization depends on law and government is already *thereby* doomed to failure.

"But the union!" exclaims your friend; "the labor union is the best defense of the worker."

CHAPTER XI
THE TRADE UNION

"Yes, the union is our only hope," you agree; "it makes us strong."

Indeed, there never was a truer word spoken: in union there is strength. It has taken labor a long time to realize this, and even today many proletarians don't understand it thoroughly.

There was a time when the workers did not know anything about organization. Later, when they did begin to get together to improve their condition, laws were passed against it and labor associations were forbidden.

The masters always opposed the organization of their employees, and the governments helped them to prevent and suppress unions. It is not so long ago that England and other countries had very severe laws against workers' getting organized. The attempt to better their situation by joint effort was condemned as "conspiracy" and was prohibited. it took the wage earners a long time to fight out their right of association; and, mind you, they had to *fight* for it. Which shows you that the bosses have never granted anything to the workers except when the latter fought for it and compelled them to yield. Even today many employers oppose the organization of their employees; they prevent it whenever they can: they get labor organizers arrested and driven out of the city, and the law is always on their side and helps them do it. Or they resort to the trick of forming fake labor bosses, yellow company unions, which can be relied on to do the bosses' bidding.

It is easy to understand why the masters don't want you to be organized, why they are afraid of a real labor union. They know very well that a strong, fighting union can compel higher wages and better conditions, which means less profit for the plutocrats. That is why they do everything in their power to stop labor from organizing. When they can't stop it, they try their best to weaken the union or to corrupt its leaders, so that the union should not be dangerous to the bosses' interests.

The masters have found a very effective way to paralyze the strength of organized labor. They have persuaded the workers that they have the same interests as the employers; they have made them believe that capital and labor have "identical interests," and that what is good for the employer is also good for his employees. They have given it the fine sounding name of "Harmony between capital and labor." If your interests are the same as those of your boss, then why should you fight him? That is what they tell you. The capitalist press, the government, the school, and the church all preach the same thing: that you live in peace and amity with your employer. It is good for the industrial magnates to have their workers believe that they are "partners" in a common business: they will then work hard and faithfully because it is "to their own interests"; the workers will not think of fighting their masters for better conditions, but they will be patient and wait till the employer can "share his prosperity" with them. They will also consider the interests and well-being of "their" country and they will not "disturb industry" and the "orderly life of the community" by strikes and stoppage of work. If you listen to your exploiters and their mouthpieces you will be "good" and consider only the interests of your masters, of your city and country—but no one cares about *your* interests and those of your family, the interests of your union and of your fellow workers of the laboring class. "Don't be selfish," they admonish you, while the boss is getting rich by your being good and unselfish. And they laugh in their sleeves and thank the Lord that you are such an idiot.

But if you have followed me till now, then you know that the interests of capital and labor are not the same. No greater lie was ever invented than the so-called "identity of interests." You know that labor produces all the wealth of the world, and capital itself is only the accumulated products of labor. You know that there can be no capital, no wealth of any kind, except as the result of labor. So that by right all the wealth belongs to labor, to the men and women who have created it and keep on creating it by their brain and brawn; that is, to the industrial, agrarian, and mental workers of the world; to the whole working class, in short.

You know also that the capital owned by the masters is stolen property, stolen products of labor. Capitalist industry is the process of continuing to appropriate the products of labor for the benefit of the master class. The masters, in other words, exist and grow rich by keeping for themselves the products of your toil. Yet you are asked to believe that you, the workers, have the same interests as your exploiters and robbers! Can any one but a downright fool be taken in by such a plain fraud?

It is clear that your interests as a worker are *different* from the interests of your capitalistic masters. More than different: they are entirely opposite; in fact, contrary, antagonistic to each other. The better wages the boss pays you, the less profit he makes out of you. It does not require great philosophy to understand that. You can't get away from it, and no twisting and quibbling can change this solid truth.

The very existence of labor unions is itself proof of this, though most of the unions and their members don't understand it. If the interests of labor and capital are the same, why the union? If the boss really believes that what is good for him, as a boss, is also good for you, his employee, then he will certainly treat you right; he will pay you the highest wages possible, so what's the use of having your union? But you know that you do need the union: you need it to help you *fight* for better wages and better conditions of work. To fight whom? Your boss, of course, your employer, the manufacturer, the capitalist. But if you have to fight him, then it does not look as if your interests and his are the same, does it? What becomes of the precious "identity of interests" then? Or maybe you are fighting your boss for better wages because he is so foolish that he does not understand his own interests? Maybe he does not understand that it is good for him to pay you more?

Well, you can see to what nonsense the idea of the "identity of interests" leads. And still, the average labor union is built on this "identity of interests." There are some exceptions, of course, such as the Industrial Workers of the World (I.W.W.), the revolutionary syndicalist unions, and other class-conscious labor organizations. They know better. But the ordinary unions, such as those belonging to the American Federation of Labor in the United States, or the conservative unions of England, France, Germany, and other countries, all proclaim the identity of interests between labor and capital. Yet as we have just seen, their very existence, their strikes and struggles all prove that the "identity" is a fake and a lie. How does it happen then that the unions pretend to believe in the identity of interests, while their very existence and activity deny it?

It is because the average worker does not stop to think for himself. He relies upon his union leaders and the newspapers to do it for him, and they see to it that he should not do any straight thinking. For if the workers should begin to think for themselves, they would soon see through the whole scheme of graft, deceit, and robbery which is called government and capitalism, and they would not stand for it. They would do as the people had done before at various times. As soon as they understood that they were slaves, they destroyed slavery. Later on, when they realized that they were serfs, they did away with serfdom. And as soon as they will understand that they are wage slaves, they will also abolish wage slavery.

You see, then, that it is to the interests of capital to keep the workers from understanding that they are wage slaves. The "identity of interests" swindle is one of the means of doing it.

But it is not only the capitalist who is interested in thus duping the workers. All those who profit by wage slavery are interested in keeping up the system, and all of them naturally try to prevent the workers from understanding the situation.

We have seen before to whose advantage it is to keep things as they are: to rulers and governments, to the churches, to the middle classes—in short, to all who live on the toil of the masses. But even the labor leaders themselves are interested in keeping up wage slavery. Most of them are too ignorant to see through the fraud, and so they really believe that capitalism is all right and that we can't do without it. Yet others, the more intelligent ones, know the truth very well, but as highly paid and influential union officials they benefit by the continuation of the capitalist system. They know that if the workers should see through the whole thing, they would call their leaders to account for having misled and deceived them. They would revolt against their slavery and their misleaders—it might come to a revolution, as has happened often before in history. But labor leaders don't care for revolution; they prefer to let well enough alone, for things are well enough *for them.*

Indeed, the labor misleaders don't favor revolution; they are even opposed to strikes and try to prevent them whenever they can.

When a strike does break out they will see to it that the men "don't go too far," and they will do their best to settle the differences with the employer by "arbitration," in which the workers usually get the worst of it. They will hold conferences with the bosses and beg for some minor concessions, and only too often they will compromise the strike to the advantage of the union—but in any and all cases they will exhort the workers to "preserve law and order,"" to keep quiet, and be patient. They will sit at the same table with the exploiters, be wined and dined by them, and appeal to the government to "intercede" and settle the "trouble," but they will be mighty careful never to mention the source of all the labor troubles, never to touch upon wage slavery itself.

Have you ever seen a single labor leader, of the American Federation of Labor, for instance, stand up and declare that the whole wage system is pure robbery and swindle, and demand for the workers the full product of their toil? Have you ever heard of any "regular" labor leader in any country do that? I never did, nor has any one else. On the contrary, when some decent man dares do so, it is the labor leaders who are the first to declare him a disturber, an "enemy of the workers," a socialist or an anarchist. They are the first to cry "Crucify him!" and the unthinking workers unfortunately echo them.

Such men are crucified, because capital and government feel safe in doing it as long as the people approve of it.

Do you see the point, my friend? Does it look as if your labor leaders want you to get *next* to things, to understand that you are a wage slave? Do they not really serve the interests of the masters?

The union leaders and politicians—the more intelligent ones—know full well what great power labor could wield as the sole producer of the wealth of the world. But they don't want *you* to know it. They don't want you to know that the workers, properly organized and enlightened, could do away with their slavery and subjection. They tell you instead that your union is there only to help you get better wages, though they are aware that you won't improve your condition very much within capitalism, and that you must always remain a wage slave whatever pay the boss may give you. They know very well that even when you do succeed, by means of a strike, in getting a raise, you lose it again in the increased cost of living, not to speak of the wages you lose while you are out on strike.

Statistics show that most of the important strikes are lost. But let us suppose that you won your strike and that you were out only a few weeks. In that time you have lost more in wages than you can gain back working months at the higher pay.

Take a simple example. Suppose you were earning $40 a week when you went on strike. Let us assume the best possible result: we'll say that the strike lasted only 3 weeks and that you gained a five dollar increase. During your 3 weeks' strike you lost $120 in wages. Now you get five dollars a week more, and it will take you 24 weeks to get that lost $120 back again. So, after six months' work at the higher pay you will just stand even. But how about the increased cost of living in the meantime? Because you are not only a producer, you are also a consumer. And when you go to buy things you will find that they are more expensive than before. Higher wages mean increased cost of living. Because what the employer loses by paying you a greater wage he gets back again by raising the price of his product.

You can see, then, that the whole idea of higher wages is in reality very misleading. It makes the worker think that he is actually better off when he gets more pay, but the fact is—so far as the whole working class is concerned—that whatever the worker gains by higher wages he loses as a consumer, and in the long run the situation remains the same. At the end of a year of "higher wages" the worker has no more than after a year of "lower wages." Sometimes he is even worse off, because the cost of living increases much faster than wages.

That is the general rule. Of course there are particular factors that affect wages as well as the cost of living, such as scarcity of materials or of labor. But we need not go into special situations, into cases of industrial or financial crisis, or times of unusual prosperity. What concerns us is the regular situation, the *normal* condition of the workingman. And the normal condition is that he always remains a workingman, a wage slave, earning just enough to enable him to live and to continue to work for his boss. You will find exceptions now and then, as of a worker inheriting or otherwise getting hold of some money, which enables him to go into business, or inventing something that may bring him wealth. But such cases are exceptions and they do not alter *your* condition; that is, the condition of the average toiler, of the millions of workingmen all over the world. So far as those millions are concerned, and so far as you, as one of them, are concerned, you remain a wage slave, whatever your work or your pay, and there is no chance for you to be anything else under the system of capitalism.

Now, then, you might justly ask, "What is the use of the union? What are the union leaders doing about it?"

The truth is that your union leaders do nothing about it. On the contrary, they do everything they can to keep you a wage slave. They do it by making you believe that capitalism is all right and by having you support the existing system with its government and "law and order." They fool you by telling you that it can't be otherwise, just as the boss, the school, the church, and the government do. In fact, your labor leader is doing the same work for capitalism that your political leader is doing for the government: both support and get you to support the present system of injustice and exploitation.

"But the union," you say, "why doesn't the union change things?"

The union *could* change things. But what is the union? The union is just you and the other fellow and more of them—the membership and the officials. You realize now that the officials, the labor leaders, are not interested in changing things. Then it is up to the membership to do it, isn't it?

That's it. But if the membership—the workers in general—don't see what it is all about, then the union can't do anything. It means, therefore, that it is necessary to get the membership to understand the real situation.

This should be the true purpose of the labor union. It should be the union's business to enlighten its members about their condition, to show them why and how they are robbed and exploited, and find ways and means of doing away with it.

That would be fulfilling the union's true purpose of protecting the interests of the worker. The abolition of the capitalistic order of things with its government and law would be the only real defense of labor's interests. And while the union would be preparing for that, it would also be looking after the immediate needs of labor, the improvement of present conditions, so far as that is possible within capitalism.

But the ordinary, conservative union stands, as we have seen, for capitalism and for everything connected with it. It takes it for granted that you are a worker and that you are going to stay one, and that things must remain as they are. It asserts that all the union can do is to help you get a little better wages, cut down your hours of work, and improve the conditions under which you toil. It considers the employer a business partner, as it were, and it makes contracts with him. But it never questions why one of the partners—the boss—gets rich from that kind of contract, while the other partner, the worker, always remains poor, labors hard, and dies a wage slave. It doesn't seem to be an equal partnership, somehow. It looks more like a confidence game, doesn't it?

Well, it is. It is a game in which one side does all the pulling of the chestnuts out of the fire, while the other side takes possession of them. A very unequal partnership, and all the striking of the workers is merely to beg or compel the capitalistic partner to give up a few chestnuts out of his big heap. A skin game, for all that, even when the worker succeeds in getting a few extra nuts.

Yet they speak to you of your dignity, of the "dignity of labor." Can you think of any greater insult? You slave for the masters all your life, you serve them and keep them in comfort and luxury, you let them lord it over you, and in their hearts they laugh at you and despise you for your stupidity—and then they talk to you of your "dignity!"

From pulpit and platform, in the school and lecture room, every labor leader and politician, every exploiter and grafter extols the "dignity of labor," while himself all the time sitting comfortably on your back. Don't you see how they are playing you for a sucker?

What is the union doing about it? What are your labor leaders doing for the fat salary they make you pay them? They are busy "organizing" you, they are busy telling you what a fine fellow you are; how big and strong your union is, and how much your officials are doing for you. But what are they doing? Their time is taken up with petty matters of procedure, with factional fights, with questions of jurisdiction, with elections of officers, with conferences and conventions. You pay for it all, of course, and that is why your officials are always in favor of a big union treasury, but what have *you* got from it? You keep on working in the factory or mill and paying your dues, and your labor leader cares blessed little how hard you toil or how you live, and you have to make a big racket at your union meeting to compel attention to *your* needs and *your* complaints.

When the question of a strike is taken up you will notice, as I have mentioned before, that the leaders generally oppose it—for they also, like the boss and the ruler, want "peace and quiet" instead of the discomforts involved in a fight. Whenever they can, the union leaders will dissuade you from striking, and sometimes even directly prevent and forbid it. They will outlaw your organization if you go on strike without their consent. But if the pressure is too strong for them to resist they will graciously "authorize" the strike. Just imagine—you work hard and from your scanty earnings you support the union officials, who should serve you, yet you have to get *their* permission to improve your condition! It's because you have made them the bosses of your organization, just as you have made the government your master instead of your servant—or as you permit the policeman, whom you pay with your taxes, to order you about instead of you giving him orders.

Did you ever ask yourself how it happens that when you are out on strike (and at all other times as well) the law and the whole machinery of government is always on the side of the boss? Why, the strikers number thousands while the boss is only one, and they and he are supposed to be citizens of equal rights—yet, strange to say, it's the boss who always has the government at his service. He can get the courts to issue an injunction against your "interfering" with "his" business, he can have the police club you off the picket line, he can have you arrested and jailed. Did you ever hear of a mayor, chief of police, or governor order out the police or militia to protect *your* interests in a strike? Queer, isn't it? Again, the boss can get plenty of scabs and blacklegs, under police protection, to help break your strike, because you have been working so many hours that there is always an army of unemployed on hand ready to take your place. Generally you lose your strike because your labor leaders did not permit you to organize in the right way.

I have seen, for instance, bricklayers on a New York skyscraper lay down their tools, while the carpenters and iron workers on the same job remained at work. The strike did not concern them, their unions said, because they belonged to another trade; or they could not join the strikers because that would be breaking the contract their organizations had made with the boss. So they kept at work on the building where their brother union men had struck. That is, they were actually scabbing and helping to break the strike of the bricklayers. Because, forsooth, they belonged to another craft, to a different trade! As if the struggle of labor against capital were a matter of craft and not the common cause of the whole working class!

Another example: the coal miners of Pennsylvania are on strike, and the coal miners of Virginia are taxed to help the strikers with money. The Virginia miners remain at work because they are "bound by contract." They keep on mining coal, so that the coal magnates can supply the market and lose nothing by the strike of the Pennsylvania miners. Sometimes they even gain by making the strike an excuse for raising the price of coal. Can you wonder that the Pennsylvania miners lose the strike, since their own fellow miners scab on them? But if the workers understood their true interests, if they would be organized not by craft or trade but by industries, so that the whole industry—and if necessary the whole working class—could strike as one man, would any strike be lost?

We shall return to this subject. Just now I want to point out to you that your union, as at present organized, and your union officials are not built for effectively fighting capitalism. Not built even for successfully conducting strikes. They cannot materially improve your condition.

They serve only to keep the workers divided into different and often opposing organizations; they train them to believe that capitalism is all right; they paralyze their initiative and ability to think and act in a class-conscious manner. That is why the labor leaders and the conservative unions are the strongest bulwark of existing institutions. They are the backbone of capitalism and of government, the best support of "law and order," and the reason why you remain in wage slavery.

"But we ourselves choose our union officials," you object; "if the present ones are no good, we can elect others."

Of course, you can elect new leaders, but does it make any difference whether this or that man is your leader, whether it is Gompers or Green, Jouhaux in France, or Thomas in England, as long as your union sticks to the same foolish ideas and false methods, believes in capitalism and supports the "harmony of interests," divides the workers and reduces their strength by craft organization, makes contracts with the boss which bind the membership and keep them scabbing on their fellows, and in many other ways upholds the regime of your bondage?

"Then the union is no good?" you demand.

In union there is strength, but it has to be a real union, a true organization of labor, because the workers everywhere have the *same* interests, no matter what work they do or to what particular craft they belong. Such a union would be based on the mutual interests and solidarity of labor throughout the world. It would be conscious of its tremendous power as the creator of all wealth.

"Power!" you object. "You said we're slaves! What power can slaves have?"

Let us see about it, then.

CHAPTER XII
WHOSE IS THE POWER?

People talk about the greatness of their country, about the strength of the government and the power of the capitalist class. Let us see what that power really consists of, wherein it lies, and who actually has it.

What is the government of a country? It is the King with his ministers, or the President with his cabinet, the Parliament or the Congress, and the officials of the various state and federal departments. Altogether a small number of persons as compared with the entire population.

Now, when is that handful of men, called government, strong and in what does its strength consist?

It is strong when the people are with it. Then they supply the government with money, with an army and navy, obey it, and enable it to function. In other words, the strength of a government depends entirely on the support it receives.

But can any government exist if the people are actively opposed to it? Could even the strongest government carry out any undertaking without the aid of the populace, without the help of the masses, the workers of the country?

It is clear, of course, that no government can accomplish anything alone. It can do only what the people approve of or at least permit to be done.

Take the great World War, for instance. The American financiers wanted the United States to get into it, because they knew that they would rake in tremendous profits, as they actually did. But labor had nothing to gain from the war, for how can the toilers benefit by the slaughter of their fellows in some other land? The masses of America were not in favor of mixing in the European inbroglio. As previously mentioned, they had elected Woodrow Wilson President; on a "keep us out of war" platform. Had the American people persisted in this determination, could the government have gotten us into the carnage?

How was it managed, then, that the people of the United States were induced to go to war when they had voted against it by electing Wilson? I have already explained it in a previous chapter. Those interested in entering the war started a great propaganda in favor of it. It was carried on in the press, in the schools and pulpit; by preparedness parades, patriotic spellbinders, and shouting for "democracy" and "war to end war." It was a heinous way of fooling the people into believing that the war was for some "ideal" instead of being just a capitalist war for profits, as all modern wars are. Millions of dollars were spent on that propaganda, the money of the people, of course, for in the end the people pay for everything. An artificial enthusiasm was worked up, with all kinds of promises to the workers of the wonderful things that would result for them from the war. It was the greatest fraud and humbug, but the people of the United States fell for it, and they went to war, though not voluntarily, but by conscription.

And the spokesmen of the workers, the labor leaders? As usual, they proved the best "patriots," calling upon their union members to go and get themselves killed, for the greater glory of Mammon. What did the late Samuel Gompers, then President of the American Federation of Labor, do? He became the right-hand man of President Wilson, his chief recruiting lieutenant. He and his union officials turned sergeants of capital in rounding up labor for the slaughter. The labor leaders of the other countries did the same.

Every one knows that the "war to end war" really ended nothing. On the contrary, it has caused more political complications than there have ever been before in Europe, and has prepared the field for a new and more terrible war than the last one. But that question does not belong here. I have referred to the matter merely to show you that without Gompers and the other labor leaders, without the consent and support of the toiling masses, the government of the United States would have been entirely unable to carry out the wishes of the lords of finance, industry, and commerce.

Or consider the case of Sacco and Vanzetti. Could Massachusetts have executed them if the organized workers of America had been against it, if they had taken action to prevent it? Suppose that Massachusetts labor had refused to support the state government in its murderous intention: suppose the workers had boycotted the Governor and his agents, stopped supplying them with food, cut off their means of communication, and shut off the electric current in Boston and Charleston prison. The government would have been powerless to function.

If you look at this matter with clear, unprejudiced eyes, you will realize that it is not the people who are dependent upon the government, as is generally believed, but just the other way about.

When the people withhold their aid from the government, when they refuse obedience and pay no taxes, what happens? The government cannot support its officials, cannot pay its police, cannot feed its army and navy. It remains without funds, without means to carry out its orders. It is paralyzed. The handful of persons calling themselves the government become helpless—they lose their power and authority. If they can gather enough men to aid them, they may try to fight the people. If they cannot, or lose the fight, they have to give it up. Their "governing" is at an end.

That is to say, the power of even the strongest government rests entirely in the people, in their willing support and obedience. It follows that government *in itself* has no power at all. The moment the people refuse to bow to its authority, the government ceases to exist.

Now, what strength has capitalism? Does the power of the capitalists rest in themselves, or where does it come from?

It is evident that their strength lies in their capital, in their wealth. They own the industries, the shops, factories, and land. But those possessions would do them no good but for the willingness of the people to work for them and pay tribute to them. Suppose the workers should say to the capitalists: "We are tired of making profits for you. We won't slave for you any more. You didn't create the land, you didn't build the factories, nor the mills or shops. We built them and from now on we will use them to work in, and what we produce will not be yours but will belong to the people. You will get nothing, and we won't even give you any food for your money. You'll be just like ourselves, and you will work like the rest of us."

What would happen? Why, the capitalists would appeal to the government for aid. They would demand protection for their interests and possessions. But if the people refuse to recognize the authority of the government, the latter itself would be helpless.

You might say that is revolution. Maybe it is. But whatever you call it, it would amount to this: the government and the capitalists—the political and financial rulers—would find out that all their boasted power and strength disappear when the people refuse to acknowledge them as masters, refuse to let them lord it over them.

Can this happen, you wonder. Well, it has happened many times before, and not so very long ago again in Russia, in Germany, in Austria. In Germany that mighty war lord, the Kaiser, had to flee for his life, because the masses had decided they did not want him any more. In Austria the monarchy was driven out because the people got tired of its tyranny and corruption. In Russia the most powerful Tsar was glad to give up his throne to save his head, and failed even in that. In his own capital he could not find a single regiment to protect him, and all his great authority went up in smoke when the populace refused to bow to it. Just so the capitalists of Russia were made helpless when the people stopped working for them and took the land, the factories, the mines, and mills for themselves. All the money and "power" of the bourgeoisie in Russia could not get them a pound of bread when the masses declined to supply it unless they did honest work.

What does it all prove?

It proves that so-called political, industrial, and financial power, all the authority of government and capitalism is *really* in the hands of the people. It proves that only the people, the masses, have power.

This power, the people's power, is *actual*: it cannot be taken away, as the power of the ruler, of the politician, or of the capitalist can be. It cannot be taken away because it does not consist in possessions but in ability. It is the ability to create, to produce; the power that feeds and clothes the world, that gives us life, health and comfort, joy and pleasure.

How great this power is you will realize when you ask yourself:

Would life be possible at all if the workers did not toil? Would the cities not starve if the farmers failed to supply them food?

Could the railroads run if the railroad men suspended work? Could any factory, shop, or mill continue operations but for the coal miners?

Could trade or commerce go on if the transport workers went on strike?

Would the theaters and movies, your office and house have light if the electricians would not supply the current?

Truly has the poet spoken:

"All the wheels stand still
When your strong arms so will."

That is the productive, industrial power of labor.

It does not depend on any politics, or on king, president, parliament, or congress. It depends neither on the police, nor on the army and navy— for these only consume and destroy, they create nothing. Nor does it depend on laws and rules, on legislators or courts, on politician or plutocrat. It rides entirely and exclusively in the ability of the workers in factory and field, in the brain and brawn of the industrial and agricultural proletariat to labor, to create, to produce.

It is the *productive* power of the workers—of the man with the plow and with the hammer, of the man of mind and muscle, of the masses, of the entire *working class.*

It follows, therefore, that the working class, in every country, is the most important part of the population. In fact, it is the only vital part. The rest of the people help in the social life, but if need be we could do without them, while we could not live even a single day without the man of labor. His is the all-important *economic power.*

The strength of government and capital is external, *outside* of themselves.

The strength of labor is *not* external. It lies *in* itself, in its ability to work and create. It is the only *real* power.

Yet labor is held lowest in the social scale.

Is it not a topsy-turvy world, this world of capitalism and government? The workers, who as a class are the most essential part of society, who alone have real power, are powerless under present conditions. They are the poorest class, the least influential and least respected. They are looked down upon, the victims of every kind of oppression and exploitation, the least appreciated and least honored. They live wretchedly in ugly and unhealthy tenements, the death rate is greatest among them, the prisons are filled with them, the gallows and electric chair are for them.

This is the reward of labor in our society of government and capitalism; that is what you get from the "law and order" system.

Does such law and order deserve to live? Should such a social system be permitted to continue? Should it not be changed for something else, something better, and is not the worker interested more than any one else in seeing to it? Should not his own organization, built especially for his interests—the union—help him do it?

How?

CHAPTER XIII
SOCIALISM

When you ask this question, the Socialist tells you:

"Vote the Socialist ticket. Elect our party. We'll abolish capitalism and establish Socialism."

What does the Socialist want, and how does he propose to get it?

There are many varieties of Socialists. There are Social Democrats, Fabian Socialists, National Socialists, Christian Socialists, and other labels. Generally speaking, they all believe in the abolition of poverty and unjust social conditions. But they disagree very much as to what would be "just" conditions and, still more, how to bring them about.

These days even mere attempts to improve capitalism are often called "Socialism," while in reality they are only reforms. But such reforms cannot be considered socialistic because true Socialism does not mean to "improve" capitalism but to abolish it altogether. Socialism teaches that the conditions of labor cannot be essentially bettered under capitalism; on the contrary, it shows that the lot of the worker must steadily get worse with the advancing development of industrialism, so that efforts to "reform" and "improve" capitalism are directly opposed to Socialism and only delay its realization.

We have seen in preceding chapters that the enslavement of the workers, inequality, injustice, and other social evils are the result of monopoly and exploitation, and that the system is upheld by the political machine called government. It would therefore serve no purpose to discuss those schools of Socialism (improperly so called) that do not stand for the abolition of capitalism and wage slavery. Just as useless it would be for us to go into allegedly socialistic proposals such as "more just distribution of wealth" "equalization of income," "single tax," or other similar plans. These are not Socialism; they are only reforms. Mere parlor Socialism, such as Fabianism, for example, is also of no vital interest to the masses.

Let us therefore examine that school of Socialism which deals with capitalism and the wage system fundamentally, which deals with the worker, with the disinherited, and which is known as the Social Democratic movement.* It considers all other forms of Socialism

* Organized under the various names of "Social Democratic Party," "Social Democratic Labor Party," or "Socialist Labor Party."

impractical and utopian; it calls itself the only sound and scientific theory of true Socialism as formulated by Karl Marx, the author of *Capital*, which is the gospel and guide of all Social Democrats.

Now, then, what do the Socialist followers of Karl Marx—known as Marxian Socialists, and whom, for the sake of brevity, we'll call simply Socialists—propose?

They say that the workers can never become free and secure well-being unless they abolish capitalism. The sources of production and the means of distribution must be taken out of private hands, they teach. That is to say, the land, machinery, mills, factories, mines, railroads, and other public utilities should not be owned privately, because such ownership enslaves the workers as well as mankind in general. Private possession of the things without which humanity cannot exist must therefore cease. The means of production and distribution should become public property. Opportunity for free use would do away with monopoly, with interest and profit, with exploitation and wage slavery. Social inequality and injustice would be eliminated, the classes would be abolished, and all men would become free and equal.

These views of Socialism are also in full accord with the ideas of most Anarchists.

The present owners—Socialism further teaches—will not give up their possessions without a struggle. All history and past experience prove that. The privileged classes have always held on to their advantages, always opposed every attempt to weaken their power over the masses. Even today they fight ruthlessly against every attempt of labor for betterment. It is therefore certain that in the future, as in the past, the plutocracy will resist if you try to deprive them of their monopolies, special rights, and privileges. That resistance will bring about a bitter struggle, a revolution.

True Socialism is therefore *radical* and *revolutionary*. Radical, because it goes to the very root of the social trouble (radix meaning root, in Latin); it does not believe in reforms and makeshifts; it wants to change things from the very bottom. Revolutionary, not because it wants blood shed, but because it clearly foresees that revolution is inevitable; it knows that capitalism cannot be changed to Socialism without a violent struggle between the possessing class and the dispossessed masses.

"But if a revolution," you ask, "why do the Socialists want me to vote them into office? Is the revolution to be fought there?"

Your question is to the point. If capitalism is to be abolished by revolution, what do the Socialists seek office for, why do they try to get into the government?

Here is just where the great contradiction of Marxian Socialism comes in, a fundamental contradiction that has been fatal to the Socialist movement in every country, and that has made it ineffectual and powerless to be of any use to the working class.

It is very necessary to realize that contradiction clearly in order to understand why Socialism has failed, why the Socialists have gotten into a blind alley and can't lead the workers to emancipation.

What is that contradiction? Marx taught that "revolution is the midwife of capitalism pregnant with a new society;" that is, that capitalism will not be changed to Socialism except by revolution. But in his "Communist Manifesto," on the other hand, Marx insists that the proletariat must get hold of the political machinery, of the government, in order to conquer the bourgeoisie. The working class—he teaches—must grasp the reins of the State, by means of the Socialist parties, and use the political power to usher in Socialism.

This contradiction has created the greatest confusion among Socialists and has split the movement into many factions. The majority of them, the regular Socialist parties in every country, now stand for the conquest of political power, for the establishment of a Socialist government whose business it will be to abolish capitalism and bring about Socialism.

Judge for yourself if such a thing is possible. In the first place, Socialists themselves admit that the possessing classes will not give up their wealth and privileges without a bitter fight and that it will result in revolution.

Again, is the thing at all practical? Take the United States, for instance. For over fifty years the Socialists have been trying to elect party members to Congress with the result that after half a century of political work they have now just one member in the House of Representatives in Washington. How many centuries will it take at that rate (and the rate is declining rather than growing) to get a Socialist majority in Congress?

But even suppose that the Socialists could some day secure that majority. Will they then be able to change capitalism to Socialism? It would require amending and altering the Constitution of the United States, as well as in the individual states, for which a two-thirds vote would be necessary. Just stop and consider: the American plutocrats, the trusts, the bourgeoisie, and all the other forces that benefit by capitalism would they just sit quietly and permit the changing of the Constitution in such a manner as to deprive them of their wealth and privileges? Can you believe that? Do you remember what Jay Gould said when he was accused of getting his millions illegally and in defiance of the Constitution?

"To Hell with the Constitution!" he replied. And so every plutocrat feels, even if he is not as frank as Gould. Constitution or no constitution, the capitalists would fight to the death for their wealth and privileges. And that is just what is meant by revolution. You can judge for yourself then whether capitalism can be abolished by electing Socialists to office or whether Socialism can be voted in by the ballot. It is not hard to guess who'll win a fight between ballots and bullets.

In former days the Socialists realized this very well. Then they claimed that they meant to use politics only for the purpose of propaganda. It was in the days when Socialist agitation was forbidden, particularly in Germany. "If you elect us to the Reichstag" (the German Parliament), the Socialists told the workers then, "we'll be able to preach Socialism there and educate the people to it." There was some reason in that, because the laws which prohibited Socialist speeches did not apply to the Reichstag. So the Socialists favored political activity and took part in elections in order to have an opportunity to advocate Socialism.

It may seem a harmless thing, but it proved the undoing of Socialism. Because nothing is truer than that the means you use to attain your object soon themselves become your object. So money, for example, which is only a means to existence, has itself become the aim of our lives. Similarly with government. The "elder" chosen by the primitive community to attend to some village business becomes the master, the ruler. Just so, it happened with the Socialists.

Little by little they changed their attitude. Instead of electioneering being merely an educational method, it gradually became their only aim to secure political office, to get elected to legislative bodies and other government positions. The change naturally led the Socialists to tone down their revolutionary ardor; it compelled them to soften their criticism of capitalism and government in order to avoid persecution and secure more votes. Today the main stress of Socialist propaganda is not laid any more on the educational value of politics but on the actual election of Socialists to office.

The Socialist parties do not speak of revolution any more. They claim now that when they get a majority in Congress or Parliament they will legislate Socialism into being: they will legally and peacefully abolish capitalism. In other words, they have ceased to be revolutionists; they have become reformers who want to change things by law.

Let us see, then, how they have been doing it during the past several decades.

In almost every European Country the Socialists have secured great political power. Some countries now have Socialist governments; in others the Socialist parties have a majority; in others again Socialists occupy the highest positions in the State, such as cabinet offices, even those of Prime Ministers. Let us examine what they have accomplished for Socialism and what they are doing for the workers.

In Germany, the mother of the Socialist movement, the Social Democratic Party holds numerous government offices; its members are in the municipal and national legislative bodies, in the judiciary, and in the Cabinet. Two German Presidents, Haase and Ebert, were Socialists. The present Reichskanzler (Chancellor), Dr. Herman Muller, is a Socialist. Herr Loebe, President of the Reichstag, is also a member of the Socialist Party. Scheidemann, Noske, and scores of others in the highest positions in the government, in the army and navy, are all leaders of the powerful German Social Democratic Party. What have they done for the proletariat whose cause the Party is supposed to champion? Have they brought about Socialism? Have they abolished wage slavery? Have they made the least attempt toward those objects?

The uprising of the workers in Germany, in 1918, forced the Kaiser to flee the country, and the reign of the Hohenzollern was at an end. The people put their trust in the Social Democrats and voted them into power. But once secure in the government, the Socialists turned against the masses. They combined with the German bourgeoisie and the military clique, and themselves became the bulwark of capitalism and militarism. They not only disarmed the people and suppressed the toilers, but they even shot and imprisoned every Socialist who dared protest against their treachery. Noske, as Socialist chief of the army during the Revolution, ordered his soldiers out against the workers and massacred them wholesale—the very proletarians who had voted him into power, his own brother Socialists. At his hands perished Karl Liebknecht and Rosa Luxemburg, two of the most devoted and loyal revolutionists, cold-bloodedly murdered in Berlin on January 16, 1919, by army officers, with the secret connivance of the Socialist government. The Anarchist poet and thinker, Gustav Landauer, and scores of the best friends of labor shared the same fate all over Germany.

Haase, Ebert, Scheidemann, Noske, and their Socialist lieutenants did not permit the Revolution to accomplish anything vital. The moment they got into power they used it to crush rebellious labor. The open and stealthy murder of the truly revolutionary elements was but one of the means used by the Socialist government to subdue the Revolution. Far from introducing any changes for the benefit of the workers, the Socialist Party became the most zealous defender of capitalism, preserving all the prerogatives and benefits of the aristocracy and master class. That is why the German Revolution accomplished nothing except to drive out the Kaiser. The nobility remained in possession of all its titles, holdings, special rights, and privileges; the military caste retained the power it had under the monarchy; the bourgeoisie has been strengthened, and the financial kings and industrial magnates lord it over the German toiler today with even greater arbitrariness than before. The Socialist Party of Germany, with many million votes behind it, has *succeeded*—in getting into office. The workers slave and suffer as before.

The same picture you find in the other countries. In France the Socialist Party is strongly represented in the government. The Minister of Foreign Affairs, Aristide Briand, who has also held the post of Prime Minister, was formerly one of the greatest lights of the Party in France. Today he is the strongest champion of capitalism and militarism. Many of his former fellow-Socialists are his colleagues in the government, and many more present-day Socialists are in the French Parliament and other important offices. What are they doing for Socialism? What are they doing for the workers?

They are helping to defend and "stabilize" the capitalistic regime of France; they are busy passing laws increasing the taxes so that the high government officials may get better salaries; they are engaged in collecting the war indemnity from Germany, whose workers, just as their French brothers, have to bleed for it. They are working hard to help "educate"

France, and particularly her school children, to hate the German people; they are aiding to build more warships and military airplanes for the next war which they are themselves preparing by cultivating the spirit of jingoism and vengeance against their neighbor countries. The new laws mobilizing every adult man and woman of France in case of war was introduced by the prominent Socialist, Paul Boncour, and passed with the aid of the Socialist members of the Chamber of Deputies.

In Austria and Belgium, in Sweden and Norway, in Holland and Denmark, in Czecho-Slovakia, and in most other European lands the Socialists have risen to power. In some countries entirely so, in others partly. And everywhere, without a single exception, they have followed the same course, everywhere they have forsworn their ideals, have duped the masses, and turned their political elevation to their own profit and glory.

"These men who rose to power on the backs of labor and then betrayed the workers are scoundrels," I hear you say in just indignation. True, but that is not all. There is a deeper reason for this constant and regular betrayal, a greater and more significant cause for this almost universal phenomenon. Socialists are not essentially different from other men. They are human, just as you and I. And no man turns scoundrel or traitor over night.

It is *power* which corrupts. The consciousness that you possess power is itself the worst poison that corrodes the finest metal of man. The filth and contamination of politics everywhere sufficiently prove that. Moreover, even with the best intentions Socialists in legislative bodies or in government positions find themselves entirely powerless to accomplish anything of a socialistic nature, anything of benefit to the workers. For politics is not a means to better the conditions of labor. It never was and never can be.

The demoralization and vitiation take place little by little, so gradually that one hardly notices it himself. Just visualize for a moment the condition of a Socialist elected to Congress, for instance. He is all alone, as against several hundred men of other political parties. He senses their opposition to his radical ideas, and he finds himself in a strange and unfriendly atmosphere. But he is there and he must participate in the business that is being transacted. Most of that business—the bills brought in, the laws proposed—is entirely foreign to him. It has no bearing whatever on the things the Socialist believes in, no connection with the interests of the working class voters who elected him. It is just the routine of legislation. It is only when a bill of some bearing upon labor or on the industrial and economic situation comes up, that our Socialist can take part in the proceedings. He does, and he is ignored or laughed at for his impractical ideas on the matter. For they are indeed impractical. Even at best, when the proposed law is not specially designed to grant new privileges to monopoly, it deals with matters involved in capitalist business, with some commercial treaty or agreement between one government and another. But he, the Socialist, was elected on a Socialist ticket, and it is his business to abolish the capitalistic government, to do away with the system of commerce and profit altogether, so how can he speak "practically" on the submitted bills? Of course he becomes a butt of ridicule to his colleagues, and soon he begins to see how stupid and useless his presence is in the halls of legislation. That is why some of the best men of the Socialist Party in Germany turned against political action, as did John Most, for instance. But there are few persons of such honesty and courage. As a rule the Socialist remains in his position, and every day he is compelled to realize more and more what a senseless role he is playing. He comes to feel that he must find some way to take a serious part in the work, express sound opinions in the discussions and become a real factor in the proceedings. This is imperative in order to preserve his own dignity, to compel the respect of his colleagues, and also to show to his constituents that they did not elect a mere dummy.

So he begins to acquaint himself with the routine. He studies river dredging and coast improvement, reads up on appropriations, examines the hundred and one bills which come up for consideration, and when he occasionally gets the floor—which is not very often—he tries to explain the proposed legislation from the Socialist standpoint, as he is in duty bound to do. He "makes a Socialist speech." He dwells on the suffering of the workers and the crimes of wage slavery; he informs his colleagues that capitalism is an evil, that the rich must be abolished and the whole system done away with. He finishes his peroration and sits down. The politicians exchange glances, smile and joke, and the assembly goes over to the business in hand.

Our Socialist perceives that he is regarded as a laughing stock. His colleagues are getting tired of his "hot air," and he finds more and more difficulty in securing the floor. He is often called to order and told he must speak to the point, but he knows that neither by his talk nor by his vote can he influence the proceedings in the slightest degree. His speeches don't even reach the public; they are buried in the *Congressional Record* which no one reads, and he is painfully aware of being a solitary and unheeded voice in the wilderness of political machinations.

He appeals to the voters to elect more comrades to the legislative bodies. A lone Socialist cannot accomplish anything, he tells them. Years pass, and at last the Socialist Party succeeds in having a number of its members elected. Each of them goes through the same experience as their first colleague, but now they quickly come to the conclusion that preaching Socialist doctrines to the politicians is worse than useless. They decide to participate in the legislation. They must show that they are not just "spouting revolution" but that they are practical men, statesmen, that they are doing something for their constituency, looking after its interests.

In this manner the situation compels them to take a "practical" part in the proceedings, to "talk business," to fall in line with the matters actually dealt with in the legislative body. Full well they know that these things have no relation to Socialism or to the abolition of capitalism. On the contrary, all this law-making and political mummery only strengthens the hold of the masters upon the people; worse, it misleads the workers into believing that the legislatures may do something for them and deludes them with the false hope that they may get results by politics. In this way it keeps them looking to the law and government to "change things," to "improve" their condition.

So the machinery of government carries on its work, the masters remain secure in their position, and the workers are held off with promises of "action" by their representatives in the legislative bodies, by new laws that are to give them "relief."

For years this process has been going on in all the countries of Europe. The Socialist parties have succeeded in electing many of their members to various legislative and government positions. Spending years in that atmosphere, enjoying good jobs and pay, the elected Socialists have themselves become part and parcel of the political machinery. They have come to feel that it is no use waiting for the Socialist revolution to abolish capitalism. It is more practical to work for some "betterment," to try to get a Socialist majority in the government. For when they have a majority they will need no revolution, they now say.

Slowly, by degrees, the Socialist change has taken place. With growing

success in elections and securing political power they turn more conservative and content with existing conditions. Removed from the life and
suffering of the working class, living in the atmosphere of the bourgeoisie,
of affluence and influence, they have become what they call "practical."
Seeing at first hand the political machinery at work, knowing its debauchery and corruption, they have realized that there is no hope for Socialism in
that swamp of deceit, bribery, and corruption. But few, very few Socialists
find the courage to enlighten the workers about the hopelessness of politics
to aid the cause of labor. Such a confession would mean the end of their
political career, with its emoluments and advantages. So the great majority
of them are content to keep their own counsel and let well enough alone.
Power and position have gradually stifled their conscience, and they have
not the strength and honesty to swim against the current.

That is what has become of Socialism, which had once been the hope
of the oppressed of the world. The Socialist parties have joined hands with
the bourgeoisie and the enemies of labor. They have become the strongest
bulwark of capitalism, pretending to the masses that they are fighting for
their interests, while in reality they have made common cause with the
exploiters. They have so far forgotten and gone back on their original
Socialism that in the great World War the Socialist parties in every country
in Europe helped their governments to lead the workers to slaughter.

The war has clearly demonstrated the bankruptcy of Socialism. The
Socialist parties, whose motto was "Workers of the world, unite!" sent the
toilers to murder each other. From having been bitter enemies of militarism
and war they became defenders of "their" land, urging the workers to don
the soldiers' uniform and kill their fellow workers in other countries.

Strange indeed! For years they had been telling the proletarians that
they have no country, that their interests are opposed to those of their masters, that labor has "nothing to lose but its chains," but at the first sign of
war they called upon the toilers to join the army and voted support and
money for the government to do the work of carnage. This happened in
every country in Europe. True, there were Socialist minorities that
protested against the war, but the dominant majority in the Socialist parties
condemned and ignored them, and lined up for the slaughter.

It was a most terrible betrayal not only of Socialism but of the whole
working class, of humanity itself. Socialism, whose purpose it was to
educate the world to the evils of capitalism, to the murderous character of

patriotism, to the brutality and uselessness of war; Socialism, which was the champion of man's rights, of liberty and justice, the hope and promise of a better day, miserably turned into a defender of the government and the masters, became the handmaiden of the militarists and jingo nationalists. The former Social Democrats became "social patriots."

This did not happen because of mere treachery, however. To take that view would be to miss the main point and misunderstand its warning lesson. Treachery it was indeed, both in its nature and effect, and the results of that treachery have bankrupted Socialism, disillusioned the millions that earnestly believed in it, and filled the world with black reaction. But it was not only treachery, not treachery of the ordinary kind. The real cause lies much deeper.

We are what we eat, a great thinker said. That is, the life we lead, the environment we live in, the thoughts we think, and the deeds we do—all subtly fashion our character and make us what we are.

The Socialists' long political activity and cooperation with bourgeois parties gradually turned their thoughts and mental habits from Socialist ways of thinking. Little by little they forgot that the purpose of Socialism was to educate the masses, to make them see through the game of capitalism, to teach them that government is their enemy, that the church keeps them in ignorance, that they are duped by ideas designed to perpetuate the superstitions and wrongs on which present day society is built. In short, they forgot that Socialism was to be the Messiah who would drive darkness out of the minds and lives of men, lift them from the slough of ignorance and materialism, and rouse their natural idealism, the striving for justice and brotherhood, toward liberty and light.

They forgot it. They had to forget it in order to be "practical," to "accomplish" something, to become successful politicians. You cannot dive into a swamp and remain clean. They had to forget it, because their object had become to "get results," to win elections, to secure power. They knew that they could not have success in politics by telling the people the whole truth about conditions—for the truth not only antagonizes the government, the church, and the school; it also offends the prejudices of the masses. These it is necessary to educate, and that is a slow and difficult process. But the political game demands success, quick results. The Socialists had to be careful not to come in too great conflict with the powers that be; they could not afford to lose time in educating the people.

It therefore became their main object to win votes. To achieve that they had to trim their sails. They had to lop off, little by little, those parts of Socialism which might result in persecution by the authorities, in disfavor from the church, or which would keep bigoted elements from joining their ranks. They had to compromise.

They did. First of all they stopped talking revolution. They knew that capitalism cannot be abolished without bitter struggle, but they decided to tell the people that they could bring about Socialism by legislation, by law, and that all that is necessary is to put enough Socialists in the government.

They ceased denouncing government as an evil; they quit enlightening the workers about its real character as an agency for enslavement. Instead they began asserting that *they*, the Socialists, are the staunchest upholders of "the State" and its best defenders; that far from being opposed to "law and order," they are its truest friends; that they are, indeed, the only ones who sincerely believe in government, except that the government must be socialistic; that is, that they, the Socialists, are to make the laws and run the government.

Thus, instead of weakening the false and enslaving belief in law and government, to weaken it so that those institutions could be abolished as a means of oppression, the Socialists actually worked to *strengthen* the people's faith in forcible authority and government, so that today the members of the Socialist parties the world over are the strongest believers in the State and are therefore called Statists. Yet their great teachers, Marx and Engels, clearly taught that the State serves only to suppress, and that when the people will achieve real liberty the State will be abolished, will "disappear."

Socialist compromise for political success did not stop there. It went further. To gain votes, the Socialist parties decided not to educate the people about the falsity, hypocrisy, and menace of organized religion. We know what a bulwark of capitalism and slavery the church, as an institution, is and always has been. It is obvious that people who believe in the church, swear by the priest and bow to his authority, will naturally be obedient to him and his commands. Such people, steeped in ignorance and superstition, are the easiest victims of the masters. But in order to achieve greater success in their election campaigns, the Socialists decided to eliminate educational anti-religious propaganda so as not to offend popular prejudices. They declared religion a "private matter," and excluded all criticism of the church from their agitation.

What you personally believe in is indeed your private affair; but when you get together with other people and organize them into a body to impose your belief on others, to force them to think as you do, and to punish them (to the extent of your power) if they entertain other beliefs, then it is no more your "private matter." You might as well say that the Inquisition, which tortured and burned people alive as heretics, was a "private affair."

It was one of the worst betrayals of the cause of liberty by the Socialists, this declaration that religion is a "private matter." Mankind has slowly grown out of the fearful ignorance, superstition, bigotry, and intolerance which made religious persecution and inquisitions possible. The advance of science and invention, the printed word and means of communication have brought enlightenment, and it is that *enlightenment* which has to some extent freed the human mind from the clutches of the church. Not that it has entirely ceased to damn those who do not accept her dogmas. There is still enough of that persecution, but the advance of knowledge has robbed the church of her former absolute sway over the mind, the life, and liberty of man; just as progress has in the same way deprived government of the power to treat the people as absolute slaves and serfs.

You can easily see then how important it is to continue the work of enlightenment which has proven such a liberating blessing for the people in the past; to continue it, so that it may some day help us do away entirely with all the forces of superstition and tyranny.

But the Socialists determined to give up this most necessary work, declaring religion to be a "private matter."

Those compromises and the repudiation of the real aims of Socialism paid rather well. The Socialists gained political strength at the sacrifice of ideals. But that "strength" has in the long run spelled weakness and ruin.

There is nothing more corrupting than compromise. One step in that direction calls for another, makes it necessary and compelling, and soon it swamps you with the force of a rolling snowball become a landslide.

One by one those features of Socialism which were really significant, educational, and liberating were sacrificed on behalf of politics, to secure more favorable public opinion, lessen persecution, and accomplish "something practical"; that is, to get more Socialists elected to office. In this process, which has been going on for years in every country, the Socialist parties in Europe acquired a membership that numbered millions. But those millions were not socialistic at all; they were party followers who had no conception of the real spirit and meaning of Socialism; men and women steeped in old prejudices and capitalistic views; bourgeois-minded people, narrow nationalists, church members, believers in divine authority and consequently also in human government, in the domination of man by man, in the State and its institutions of oppression and exploitation, in the necessity of defending "their" government and country, in patriotism and militarism.

Is it any wonder, then, that when the Great War broke out Socialists in every country, with few exceptions, took up arms to "defend the fatherland," the fatherland of their rulers and masters? The German Socialist fought for his autocratic Kaiser, the Austrian for the Hapsburg monarchy, the Russian for the Tsar, the Italian for his King, the Frenchman for the "republic," and so the "Socialists" of every country and their followers went on slaughtering each other until ten million of them lay dead, and twenty million were blinded, maimed, and crippled.

It was inevitable that the policy of political, parliamentary activity should lead to such results. For in truth so-called political "action" is, so far as the cause of the workers and of true progress is concerned, worse than inaction. The very essence of politics is corruption, sail-trimming, the sacrifice of your ideals and integrity for success. Bitter are the fruits of that "success" for the masses and for every decent man and woman the world over.

As a direct consequence of it millions of workers in every country are discouraged and disheartened. Socialism—they justly feel—has deluded and betrayed them. Fifty, nay, almost a hundred, years of Socialist "work" have resulted in the entire bankruptcy of the Socialist parties, in the disillusionment of the masses, and have brought about a reaction which now dominates the entire world and holds labor by the throat with an iron grip.

Do you still think that the Socialist parties with their elections and politics can help the proletariat out of wage slavery?

By their fruits you shall know them.

"But the Bolsheviki," you protest "they did not betray the workers. They have Socialism in Russia today!"

Let us take a look at Russia, then.

CHAPTER XIV
THE FEBRUARY REVOLUTION

In Russia the Bolsheviki, known as the Communist Party, are in control of the government. The Revolution of October, 1917, put them in power.*

That Revolution was the most important event in the world since the French Revolution in 1789–1793. It was even greater than the latter, because it went much deeper to the rock bottom of society. The French Revolution sought to establish political freedom and equality, believing that it would thereby also secure brotherhood and welfare for all. It was a mighty step in advance on the road of progress and it ultimately changed the entire political face of Europe. It abolished the monarchy in France, established a republic, and gave the death blow to feudalism, to the absolute rule of the church and the nobility. It influenced every country on the Continent along progressive lines, and helped to further democratic sentiment throughout Europe.

But fundamentally it altered nothing. It was a *political* revolution, to secure political rights and liberties. It did secure them. France is a "democracy" today and the motto, "Liberty, Brotherhood, Equality," is written even on every prison building. But it did not free man from exploitation and oppression; and that is, after all, the thing which is needed most.

The French Revolution put the middle classes, the bourgeoisie, into the government, in place of the aristocracy and nobility. It gave certain constitutional rights to the farmer and worker, who until then were mere serfs. But the power of the bourgeoisie, its industrial mastery, made the farmer its abject dependent and turned the city worker into a wage slave.

It could not be otherwise, because liberty is an empty sound as long as you are kept in bondage economically. As I have pointed out before, freedom means that you have the *right* to do a certain thing; but if you have no *opportunity to* do it, that right is sheer mockery. The opportunity lies in your economic condition, whatever the political situation may be. No political rights can be of the least use to the man who is compelled to slave all his life to keep himself and family from starvation.

* According to the old Russian calendar, in November.

Great as the French Revolution was as a step toward emancipation from the despotism of king and noble, it could accomplish nothing for the *real* freedom of man because it did not secure for him economic opportunity and independence.

It is for that reason that the Russian Revolution was a far more significant event than all the previous upheavals. It not only abolished the Tsar and his absolute sway; it did something more important: it destroyed the *economic* power of the possessing classes, of the land barons and industrial kings. For that reason it is the greatest happening in all history, the first and only time that such a thing has been tried.

This could not have been done by the French Revolution, because the people then still believed that political emancipation would be enough to make men free and equal. They did not realize that the basis of all liberty is economic. But that is by no means to the discredit of the French Revolution; the times were not ripe for a fundamental economic change.

Coming a hundred and twenty-eight years later, the Russian Revolution was more enlightened. It went to the root of the trouble. It knew that no political freedom would do any good unless the peasants got the soil and the workers the factories in their possession, so that they should not remain at the mercy of the land monopolists and the capitalistic owners of the industries.

Of course, the Russian Revolution did not accomplish this great work over night. Revolutions, like everything else, grow: they begin small, accumulate strength, develop, and broaden.

It was during the war that the Russian Revolution started, because of the dissatisfaction of the people at home and the army at the front. The country was tired of fighting; it was worn out by hunger and misery. The soldiers had had enough of slaughter; they began to ask why they must kill or be killed—and when soldiers begin asking questions, no war can continue much longer.

The despotism and corruption of the Tsarist government added oil to the fire. The court had become a public scandal, with the priest Rasputin debauching the Empress and through his influence over her and the Tsar controlling the affairs of State. Intrigues, bribery, and every form of venality were rampant. The army funds were stolen by high officials, and the soldiers were often forced to go into battle without enough ammunition and supplies. Their boots were paper-soled, and many had no footgear at all. Some regiments revolted; others refused to fight. More and more frequently the soldiers fraternized with the "enemy"—young men like themselves, who had the misfortune of being born in a different country; and who, like the Russians, had been ordered to war without knowing why they must shoot or be shot. Great numbers dropped their guns and returned home. There they told the folks about the fearful conditions at the front, the useless carnage, the wretchedness, and disaster. That helped to increase the discontent of the masses, and presently voices began to be heard against the Tsar and his regime.

Day by day this sentiment grew; it was fanned into flame by increased taxes and great want, by the shortage of food and provisions.

In February, 1917, the Revolution broke out. As usual in such cases, the powers that be were stricken with blindness. The autocrat and his ministers, the aristocrats and their advisers all believed that it was just a matter of some street disorders, of strikes, and bread riots. They imagined themselves safe in the saddle. But the "disorder" continued, spreading over the entire country, and presently the Tsar saw himself forced to quit the throne. Before long the once mighty monarch was arrested and exiled to Siberia, where he himself had formerly sent thousands to their death, and where be and his whole family later met their doom.* The Russian autocracy was abolished. The February Revolution against the most powerful government in Europe was accomplished almost without firing a gun.

"How could it be done so easily?" you wonder.

The Romanov regime was an absolutism; Russia under the Tsars was the most enslaved country in Europe. The people practically had no rights. The whim of the autocrat was supreme, the order of the police the highest law. The masses lived in poverty and suffered the greatest oppression. They longed for freedom.

For over a hundred years libertarians and revolutionists in Russia worked to undermine the regime of tyranny, to enlighten the people and rouse them to rebellion against their subjection. The history of that movement is replete with the consecration and devotion of the finest men and women. Thousands, even hundreds of thousands of them, lined the road of Golgotha, filling the prisons, tortured and done to death in the frozen wilds of Siberia. Beginning with the Decembrist attempt to secure a

---

* Executed by the Bolsheviki in Ekaterinburg, Siberia, in 1918.

constitution, over a hundred years ago, all through the century, the fires of liberty were kept burning by the heroic self-sacrifice of the nihilists and revolutionists. The story of that great martyrdom has no equal in the annals of man.

Apparently it was a losing struggle, for the complete denial of freedom made it practically impossible for the pioneers of liberty to reach the people, to enlighten the masses. Tsardom was well protected by its numerous police and secret service, as well as by the official church, press, and school which trained the people in abject servility to the Tsar and unquestioning obedience to "law and order." Dire punishment was visited upon anyone daring to voice a liberal sentiment; the most severe laws punished even the attempt to teach the peasants to read and write. The government, the nobility, the clergy, and the bourgeoisie all combined, as usual, to stamp out and crush the least effort to enlighten the masses. Deprived of every means of spreading their ideas, the liberal elements in Russia were driven to the necessity of employing violence against the barbarous tyranny, of resorting to acts of terror in order by such means to mitigate, even to a small extent, the rule of despotism, and at the same time to compel the attention of their country and of the world at large to the unbearable conditions. It was this tragic necessity that gave rise in Russia to terroristic activities, turning idealists, to whom human life was sacred, into executioners of tyrants. Nature's noblemen they were, those men and women who willingly, even eagerly, gave their lives to lift the fearful yoke from the people. Like bright stars on the firmament of the age-long warfare between oppression and liberty stand out the names of Sophie Perovskaya, Kibaltchitch, Grinevitsky, Sasonov, and countless other martyrs, known and unknown, of darkest Russia.

It was a most uneven struggle, apparently a hopeless fight. For the revolutionists were but a handful as against the almost limitless power of Tsardom with its large armies, numerous police, special bureaus of political spies, its notorious Third Department, the secret Okhrana, its universal system of house janitors as police aids, and with all the other great resources of a vast country of over a hundred million population.

A losing fight. And yet, the splendid idealism of the Russian youth—particularly of the student element—their unquenchable enthusiasm and devotion to liberty were not in vain. The people came out the victor, as they ultimately always do in the struggle of light against darkness. What a lesson to the world, what encouragement to the weak in spirit, what hope it holds for the further never-ceasing advance of mankind in spite of all tyranny and persecution!

In 1905 broke out the first revolution in Russia. Still strong was the autocracy, and the uprising of the masses was crushed, though not without its having compelled the Tsar to grant certain constitutional rights. But fearfully did the government avenge even those small concessions. Hundreds of revolutionists paid for them with their lives, thousands were imprisoned, and many other thousands doomed to Siberia.

Again despotism drew a fresh breath and felt itself secure against the people. But not for long. The hunger for liberty may be suppressed for a time; yet never exterminated. Man's natural instinct is for freedom, and no power on earth can succeed in crushing it for very long.

Twelve years later—a very short time in the life of a people—came another revolution, that of February, 1917. It proved that the spirit of 1905 was not dead, that the price paid for it in human lives had not been in vain. Truly has it been said that the blood of the martyrs nourishes the tree of liberty. The work and self-sacrifice of the revolutionists had borne fruit. Russia had learned much from past experience, as succeeding events proved.

The people had learned. In 1905 they had demanded only some mitigation of the despotism, some small political liberties; now they demanded the complete abolition of the tyrannical rule.

The February Revolution sounded the death-knell of Tsardom. It was the least bloody revolution in all history. As I have explained before, the power of even the strongest government evaporates like smoke the moment the people refuse to acknowledge its authority, to bow to it, and withhold their support. The Romanov regime was conquered almost without a fight, naturally enough, since the entire people had become tired of its rule and had decided that it was harmful and unnecessary, and that the country would be better off without it. The ceaseless agitation and educational work carried on by the revolutionary elements (the Socialists of various groups, including the Anarchists) had taught the masses to understand that Tsardom must be done away with. So widespread had this sentiment become that even the army—the most unenlightened group in Russia, as in every land—had lost faith in the existing conditions. The people had *outgrown* the despotism, had freed themselves in mind and spirit from it, and thereby gained the strength and possibility of freeing themselves actually, physically.

That is why the all-powerful autocrat could find no more support in Russia; no, not even a single regiment to protect him. The mightiest government in Europe broke down like a house of cards.

A temporary, provisional government, took the place of the Tsar, Russia was free.

CHAPTER XV
BETWEEN FEBRUARY
AND OCTOBER

I remember attending a very large mass-meeting in Madison Square Garden, New York, called to celebrate the dethronement of the Tsar. The huge hall was crowded with twenty thousand people wrought up to the highest pitch of enthusiasm. "Russia is free!" the leading speaker began. A veritable hurricane of applause, shouts, and hurrahs greeted the declaration. It continued for many minutes, breaking out again and again. But when the audience became quiet and the orator was about to proceed, there came a voice from the crowd:

"Free for what?"

There was no reply. The speaker continued his harangue.

The Russians are a simple and naive people. Never having had any constitutional rights, they had no interest in politics and were not corrupted by it. They knew little of congresses and parliaments, and cared less about them.

"Free for what?" they wondered.

"You are free from the Tsar and his tyranny," they were told.

That was very fine, they thought. "But how about the war?" the soldier asked. "How about the land?" the peasant demanded. "How about a decent existence?" the proletarian urged. You see, my friend, those Russians were so "uneducated" they were not satisfied just to be free *from* something; they wanted to be free *for* something, free *to do* what they wanted. And what they wanted was a chance to live, to work and enjoy the fruits of their labor. That is, they wanted access to the land, so they could raise food for themselves; access to the mines, shops, and factories, so as to produce what they needed. But under the Provisional Government, just as under the Romanovs, those things belonged to the wealthy; they remained "private property."

As I say, the simple Russian knew nothing about politics, but he knew exactly what he wanted. He lost no time in making his wants known, and he was determined to get them. The soldiers and sailors chose spokesmen from their own midst to present to the Provisional Government their demand to terminate the war. Their representatives organized themselves as soldiers' councils, called *Soviets* in Russia. The peasants and the city workers did the same. In this manner every branch of the army and navy, every agricultural and industrial district, every factory even, established its own Soviets. In the course of time the various Soviets formed the All-Russian Soviet of Workers', Soldiers', and Peasants' Deputies, which held its sessions in Petrograd.

Through the Soviets the people presently began to voice their demands.

The Provisional Government, the new "liberal" regime under the leadership of Miliukov, paid no attention. It is characteristic of all political parties alike that, once in power, they turn a deaf ear to the needs and wants of the masses. The Provisional Government was no different in this than the Tsarist autocracy. It failed to understand the spirit of the time, and it stupidly believed that a few minor reforms would satisfy the country. It kept busy talking and discussing, proposing new bills and enacting more legislation. But it was not laws the people wanted. They wanted peace, while the government insisted on continuing the war. They cried for land and bread, but what they got was more laws.

If history teaches anything at all its clearest lesson is that you can't defy or resist the will of a whole people. You can suppress it for a while, stem the tide of popular protest, but the more violently will the storm rage when it comes. Then it will break down every obstacle, sweep away all opposition, and its momentum will carry it even further than its original intention.

That has been the story of every great conflict, of every revolution.

Recall the American War for Independence, for instance. The rebellion of the colonies against Great Britain began with the refusal to pay the tea tax exacted by the government of George III. The comparatively unimportant objection to "taxation without representation," meeting with the King's opposition, resulted in war and ended in completely freeing the American colonies from English rule. Thus was born the Republic of the United States.

The French Revolution similarly began with the demand for small improvements and reforms. The refusal of Louis XVI to lend ear to the popular voice cost him not only his throne but also his head, and brought about the destruction of the entire feudal system in France.

Just so did Tsar Nicholas II believe that a few insignificant concessions would stop the revolution. He also paid for his stupidity with his crown and life. The same fate overtook the Provisional Government. That is why a wise man said that "history repeats itself." It always does with government.

The Provisional Government consisted mostly of conservative men who did not understand the people and who were far removed from their needs. The masses demanded peace first of all. The provisional government, under the leadership of Miliukov and later under Kerensky, was determined to continue the war even in the face of the general dissatisfaction and the serious breakdown of the industrial and economic life of the country. The rising waves of the Revolution were soon to sweep it away: the Soviet of Workers' and Soldiers' Deputies was preparing to take matters into its own hands.

Meanwhile the people did not wait. The soldiers at the front had already themselves decided to quit the war as unnecessary and useless slaughter. By the hundred thousands they were leaving the fields of battle and returning home to their farms and factories. There they began carrying into effect the real objects of the Revolution. For to them the Revolution did not mean printed constitutions and paper rights, but the land and the workshop. Between June and October, 1917, while the provisional government kept on endlessly discussing "reforms," the peasants started confiscating the estates of the large landholders and the workers took possession of the industries.

This was called *expropriating* the capitalist class: that is, depriving the masters of the things they had no right to monopolize, the things they had appropriated from the laboring classes, from the people.

In this manner the soil was expropriated from the landlords, the mines and mills from their "owners," the warehouses from the speculators. The workers and farmers took everything in charge through their labor unions and agrarian organizations.

The "liberal" government of Miliukov had insisted on keeping up the war because the Allies wanted it. The "revolutionary" government of Kerensky also remained deaf to the popular demands. It passed drastic laws against the "unauthorized" taking of land by the peasantry. Kerensky did everything in his power to keep the army at the front and even reintroduced the death penalty for "desertion." But the people now ignored the government.

The situation again proved that the real power of a country lies in the hands of the masses, of those who fight, toil, and produce, and not in any parliament or government. Kerensky at one time was the adored idol of Russia, more powerful than any Tsar. Yet his authority was lost, his government fell, and he himself had to flee for his life when the people realized that he was not serving their cause. While he was still the head of the Provisional Government, the actual power began to go over to the Petrograd Soviet, most of whose members were revolutionary workers, peasants, and soldiers.

Various and even opposing views were represented in the Soviet, as is inevitable in bodies composed of different classes of the population with their particular interests. But the greatest influence under such circumstances is always exerted by those who voice the deepest feelings and needs of the people. Therefore, the more revolutionary elements in the Soviet gradually gained the mastery, for they expressed the true wants and aspirations of the masses.

There were those in the Soviet who held that a constitution, something like that of the United States, was all that Russia needed to attain freedom and well-being. They asserted that capitalism was all right: there must be masters and servants, rich and poor; the people should be satisfied with the rights and liberties which a democratic government would grant them. These were the Constitutional Democrats, called for short *Cadets* in Russia. They quickly lost their influence, because the "naive" Russian workers and peasants knew that it was not rights and liberties on paper they wanted, but a chance to work and enjoy the fruits of their labor. They pointed to America with its Constitution and Declaration of Independence, and said that they did not care for the injustice, corruption, and wage slavery which constitutionally existed in that country.

The next more liberal element were the Social Democrats, known as Mensheviki. As Socialists they believed in the abolition of capitalism, but they declared that the Revolution was not the time to do it. Why not? Because it was not a proletarian revolution, they claimed, even if it looked like one. They maintained that it could not be a social revolution and therefore it should not alter the fundamental economic conditions of the country. According to them it was only a bourgeois revolution, a political one, and as such it should make only political changes. It could not be anything more than a bourgeois revolution, the Mensheviki argued, because had not the great Karl Marx taught that a proletarian revolution could take place only in a country where capitalism had reached its highest stage of development? Russia was very backward industrially, and therefore it would be against the teachings of Marx to consider the Revolution proletarian. For that reason capitalism must remain in Russia and be given a chance to ripen before the people could think of abolishing wage slavery.

The Social Democrats had a large following among the workers of Russia, many labor unions being Menshevik. But the argument that the Revolution was not proletarian only because Marx had fifty years before said that it couldn't be, did not appeal to the toilers. They had made the Revolution, they had fought and bled for it. They had driven out the Tsar and his clique, and they were now driving out their industrial masters, thus abolishing wage slavery and capitalism. They could not see why they could not do what they were actually doing only because some one who was dead long ago had believed that it couldn't be done. The reasoning of the Socialist leaders was too "scientific" for them. Their common sense told them that it was pure nonsense, and the Mensheviki lost most of their following among the workers.

Another political party was called Socialists Revolutionists. To this party belonged many of the terrorists who had been active against Tsardom in the past. The Socialists Revolutionists had numerous adherents, mainly among the farming population. But they alienated them by taking a stand for the continuation of the war when the country was against it. This attitude also caused a split in the party, the conservative element becoming known as the Right Socialists Revolutionists, while the more revolutionary faction called itself Left Socialists Revolutionists. The latter, led by Maria Spiridonova, who had suffered many years of Siberian imprisonment under the Tsar, advocated the termination of the war and secured a very considerable following, particularly among the poorer agricultural classes.

The most radical element in Russia were the Anarchists, who demanded immediate peace, free land for the peasant, and the socialization of the means of production and distribution. They wanted the abolition of capitalism and wage slavery, equal rights for all and special privileges to none. The land, the factories and mills, the machinery of production and the means of distribution were to become the possession of the whole people. Each able person was to work according to his ability and receive according to his needs. There was to be full liberty for every one and joint use on the basis of mutual interests. The Anarchists warned the proletariat against delegating power to any government or placing a political party in authority. Government of any kind, they said, would stifle the Revolution and rob the workers of the results already achieved. The life and welfare of a country depended on economics, not on politics, they argued. That is, what people want is to live, to work and satisfy their needs. For this, sensible management of industry is necessary, not politics. Politics, they insisted, is a game to rule and govern men, not to help them live. In short, the Anarchists advised the toilers to permit no one to become their master again, to abolish political government, and to manage their agrarian, industrial, and social affairs for the good of all instead of for the benefit of rulers and exploiters. They called upon the masses to stand by their Soviets and look after their interests by means of their own organizations.

The Anarchists were, however, comparatively small in numbers. As the most advanced and revolutionary element they had been persecuted by the Tsarist regime even worse than the Socialists. Many of them had been executed, others imprisoned and their organizations suppressed as illegal. It was most dangerous to belong to the Anarchists, and their work of education was exceedingly difficult. Therefore, the Anarchists were not strong and could not exert much influence upon the people at large in a vast country of 120 million in population.

But they had a great advantage in that their idea appealed to the healthy instincts and sound sense of the masses. To the extent of their ability and limited power the Anarchists encouraged the demand for peace, land, and bread, and actively helped carry out those demands by direct expropriation and the formation of a free communal life.

There was another political party in Russia which was far more numerous and better organized than the Anarchists. That party realized the value of the Anarchist ideas and set to work to carry them out.

It was the Bolsheviki.

CHAPTER XVI
THE BOLSHEVIKI

Who were the Bolsheviki, and what did they want?

Up to the year 1903, the Bolsheviki were members of the Russian Socialist Party; that is, Social Democrats, followers of Karl Marx and his teachings. In that year the Social Democratic Labor Party of Russia split on the question of organization and other minor matters. Under the leadership of Lenin the opposition formed a new party, which called itself Bolshevik. The old party became known as Menshevik.*

The Bolsheviki were more revolutionary than the other party from which they seceded. When the world war broke out they did not betray the cause of the workers and join the patriotic jingoes, as did the majority of the other Socialist parties. To their credit be it said that, like most of the Anarchists and Left Socialists Revolutionists, the Bolsheviki opposed the war on the ground that the proletariat had no interest in the quarrels of conflicting capitalist groups. When the February Revolution began the Bolsheviki realized that political changes alone would do no good, would not solve the labor and social problems. They knew that putting one government in place of another would not help matters. What was needed was a radical, fundamental change.

Though Marxists like their Menshevik step-brothers (believers in the theories of Karl Marx), the Bolsheviki did not agree with the Mensheviki in their attitude to the great upheaval. They scorned the idea that Russia could not have a proletarian revolution because capitalist industry had not developed there to its fullest possibilities. They realized that it was not merely a bourgeois political change that was taking place. They knew that the people were not satisfied with the abolition of the Tsar and not content with a constitution. They saw that things were developing further. They understood that the taking of the land by the peasantry and the growing expropriation of the possessing classes did not signify "reform." Closer to the masses than the Mensheviki, the Bolsheviki felt the popular pulse and more correctly judged the spirit and purpose of the tremendous events. It was foremost of all Lenin, the Bolshevik leader, who believed that the time was approaching when he and his Party might grasp the reins of government and establish Socialism on the Bolshevik plan.

* From the Russian word *bolshe*, meaning "more" or majority; *menshe* signifying "less."

Bolshevik Socialism meant the seizing of political power by the Bolsheviki in the name of the proletariat. They agreed with the Anarchists that Communism would be the best economic system; that is, the land, the machinery of production and distribution, and all public utilities should be owned in common, excluding private possession in those things. But while the Anarchists wanted the people as a whole to be the owners, the Bolsheviki held that everything must be in the hands of the State, which meant that the government would not only be the political ruler of the country but also its industrial and economic master. The Bolsheviki as Marxists believed in a strong government to run the country, with absolute power over the lives and fortunes of the people. In other words, the Bolshevik idea was a dictatorship, that dictatorship to be in the hands of themselves, of *their* political Party.

They called such an arrangement the "dictatorship of the proletariat," because their Party, they said, represented the best and foremost element, the advance guard of the working class, and their Party should therefore be dictator in the name of the proletariat.

The great difference between the Anarchists and the Bolsheviki was that the Anarchists wanted the masses to decide and manage their affairs for themselves, through their own organizations, without orders from any political party. They wanted real liberty and voluntary cooperation in joint ownership. The Anarchists therefore called themselves *free* Communists, or Communist Anarchists, while the Bolsheviki were *compulsory*, governmental or State Communists. The Anarchists didn't want any State to dictate to the people, because such dictation, they argued, always means tyranny and oppression. The Bolsheviki, on the other hand, while repudiating the capitalist State and bourgeois dictatorship, wanted the State and the dictatorship to be *theirs*, of their Party.

You can therefore see that there is all the difference in the world between the Anarchists and the Bolsheviki. The Anarchists are opposed to all government; the Bolsheviki are strong for government on condition that it is in their hands. "They are not against the big stick," as a clever friend of mine is wont to say; "they only want to be at the right end of it."

But the Bolsheviki realized that the views and methods advocated by the Anarchists were sound and practical, and that only such methods could assure the success of the Revolution. They decided to make use of Anarchist ideas for their own purposes. So it happened that although the

Anarchists were themselves too weak in numbers to reach the masses, they succeeded in influencing the Bolsheviki, who presently began to advocate Anarchist methods and tactics, pretending of course that they were their own.

But they were not their own. You might say that it does not matter who advocates or helps to carry out an idea that will benefit the people. But if you think it over a bit you will realize that it matters very much, as all history and particularly the Russian Revolution proves.

It matters because everything depends on the *motives*, on the purpose and spirit in which a thing is carried out. Even the best idea can be applied in such a manner as to bring much harm. Because the masses, fired by the great idea, may fail to notice *how*, in what manner, and by what means it a being carried out. But if carried out in the wrong spirit or by false means, even the noblest and finest idea can be turned to the ruin of the country and its people.

That is just what happened in Russia. The Bolsheviki advocated and partly carried out Anarchist ideas, but the Bolsheviki were not Anarchists and they did not at heart believe in those ideas. They used them for their own purposes—purposes that were not Anarchistic, that were really anti-Anarchistic, against the Anarchist idea. What were those Bolshevik purposes?

The Anarchist idea was to do away with oppression of every kind, to abolish the rule of one class over another, to substitute the management of things for the mastery of man over man, to secure liberty and well-being for all. Anarchist methods were calculated to bring about such a result.

The Bolsheviki used the Anarchist methods for an entirely different purpose. They did not want to abolish political domination and government: they only meant to get it into their own hands. Their object was, as already explained, to gain control of political power by their Party and establish a Bolshevik dictatorship. It is necessary to get this very clearly in order to understand what happened in the Russian Revolution and why "proletarian dictatorship" quickly became a Bolshevik dictator-ship *over* the proletariat.

It was soon after the February Revolution that the Bolsheviki began to proclaim Anarchist principles and tactics. Among these were "direct action," "the general strike," "expropriation," and similar modes of action by the masses. As I have said, the Bolsheviki as Marxists did not believe in such methods. At least they had not believed in them until the Revolution. For years previously Socialists everywhere, including the Bolsheviki, had ridiculed the Anarchist advocacy of the general strike as the strongest weapon of the workers in their struggle against capitalist exploitation and government oppression. "The general strike is general nonsense," was the war cry of Socialists against the Anarchists. Socialists did not want the workers to resort to direct mass action and the general strike, because it might lead to revolution and the taking of things into their own hands. The Socialists wanted no independent revolutionary action by the masses. They advocated political activity. They wanted the workers to put them, the Socialists, in power, so *they* could do the revolutionizing.

If you glance over the Socialist writings for the past forty years, you will be convinced that Socialists were always against the general strike and direct action, as they were also opposed to expropriation and revolutionary syndicalism, which is another name for workers' Soviets. Socialist congresses passed drastic resolutions against, and Socialist agitators fiercely denounced, all such revolutionary tactics.

But the Bolsheviki accepted these Anarchist methods and began advocating them with new-born conviction. Not, of course, at the outbreak of the Revolution, in February, 1917. They did it much later, when they saw that the masses were not content with mere political changes and were demanding bread instead of a constitution. The swiftly moving events of the Revolution *compelled* the Bolsheviki to fall in line with the most radical popular aspirations in order not to be left behind by the Revolution, as happened to the Mensheviki, to the Right Socialists Revolutionists, the Constitutional Democrats, and to other reformers.

Very sudden was this Bolshevik acceptance of Anarchist methods, because only a short time before they had been insistently calling for the Constituent Assembly. For months following the February Revolution they were demanding the convocation of a representative body to determine the form of government that Russia was to have. It was right for the Bolsheviki to favor the Constituent Assembly, since they were Marxists and pretended to believe in majority rule. The Constituent Assembly was to be elected by the entire people, and the majority in the Assembly was to decide matters. But the real reason why the Bolsheviki agitated for the Assembly was that they believed the masses were with them and that they, the Bolshevik Party, would be sure of a majority in the Assembly. Presently, however, it became clear that they would prove an insignificant minority in that body. Their hope to dominate it vanished. As good governmentalists and believers in majority rule they should have bowed to the will of the people. But that did not suit the plans of Lenin and his friends. They looked about for other ways of getting control of the government, and their first step was to begin a vehement agitation *against* the Constituent Assembly.

To be sure, the Assembly could give nothing of value to the country. It was a mere talking machine, lacking all vitality, and unable to accomplish any constructive work. The Revolution was a fact outside and independent of the Constituent Assembly, independent of any legislative or governmental body. It began and was developing in spite of government and constitution, in spite of all opposition, in defiance of law. In its entire character it was unlawful, non-governmental, even anti-governmental. The Revolution followed the healthy natural impulses of the people, their needs and aspirations. In the truest sense it was Anarchistic in spirit and deed. Only the Anarchists, those governmental heretics who believe in liberty and popular initiative as the cure for social ills, welcomed the Revolution as it was and worked for its further growth and deepening, so as to bring the entire life of the country within the sphere of its influence.

All the other parties, including the Bolsheviki, had the sole object of lassoing the revolutionary movement and tying it to their particular band-wagon. The Bolsheviki needed the support of the masses to wrest political power for their Party and to proclaim the Communist dictatorship. Seeing that there was no hope of accomplishing this through the Constituent Assembly, they turned against it, joined the Anarchists in condemning it, and later forcibly dispersed it. But you can see that while the Anarchists could do this honestly, in keeping with their no-government ideas, similar action on the part of the Bolsheviki was rank hypocrisy and political trickery.

Together with their opposition to the Constituent Assembly the Bolsheviki borrowed from the Anarchist arsenal a number of other militant tactics. Thus they proclaimed the great war cry, "All power to the Soviets," advised the workers to ignore and even defy the Provisional Government, and to resort to direct mass action to carry out their demands. At the same time they also adopted the Anarchist methods of the general strike and energetically agitated for the "expropriation of the expropriators."

It is important to keep in mind that these tactics of the Bolsheviki were not, as I have already pointed out, the logical outcome of their ideas, but only a means of gaining the confidence of the masses with the object of achieving political domination. Indeed, those methods were really *opposed* to Marxist theories and were not believed in by the Bolsheviki. It was therefore not surprising that, once in power, they repudiated all those anti-Marxist ideas and tactics.

The Anarchist mottoes proclaimed by the Bolsheviki did not fail to bring results. The masses rallied to their flag. From a Party with almost no influence, with its main leaders, Lenin and Zinoviev, discredited* and hiding, with Trotsky and others in prison, they quickly became the most important factor in the movement of the revolutionary proletariat.

Attentive to the demands of the masses, particularly of the soldiers and workers, voicing their needs with energy and persistence, the Bolsheviki constantly gained greater influence among the people and in the Soviets, especially in those of Petrograd and Moscow. The inactivity of the Provisional Government and its failure to undertake any important changes aggravated the general dissatisfaction and resentment, which were soon to break into fury. The pusillanimous character of the Kerensky regime served to strengthen the hands of the Bolsheviki in the Soviets. Daily the rupture between the latter and the government grew, presently developing into open antagonism and struggle.

The evident helplessness of the government, the decision of Kerensky to renew an aggressive movement at the front, together with the reintroduction of the death penalty for military desertion, the persecution of the revolutionary elements and the arrest of their leaders, all hastened the crisis. On July 3, 1917,** thousands of armed workers, soldiers, and sailors demonstrated in the streets of Petrograd in spite of government prohibition, demanding "All power to the Soviets." Kerensky sought to suppress the popular movement. He even recalled "trusted" regiments from the front to teach the proletariat of Petrograd a "salutary lesson." But in vain were all the efforts of the bourgeoisie, represented by Kerensky, by the Social Democratic leaders and Right Socialists Revolutionists, to stem the rising tide. The July demonstrations were suppressed, but within a short

---

* Because of the widely believed but false charge against Lenin of being in the pay of Germany.

** July 16, new style.

time the revolutionary movement swept the provisional government away. The Petrograd Soviet of soldiers and workers declared the government abolished, and Kerensky saved his life only by fleeing in disguise.

The masses backed the Petrograd Soviet. The example of the capital was soon followed by Moscow, thence spreading throughout the country.

It was on October 25th* that the Provisional Government was declared abolished, its members arrested, and the Winter Palace taken by the military-revolutionary committee of the Petrograd Soviet. On the same day the Second All-Russian Congress of Soviets opened its sessions. Political government was practically abolished in Russia. All power was now in the hands of the workers, soldiers, and peasants represented in the Congress. The latter immediately began to consider steps to carry out the will of the masses: to terminate the war, secure land for the peasants, the industries for the workers, and establish liberty and welfare for all.

This was the status of the Russian Revolution in October, 1917. Beginning with the abolition of the Tsar, it gradually widened and developed into a thorough industrial and economic reorganization of the country. The spirit of the people and their needs marked out the further progress of the Revolution toward the rebuilding of life on the foundation of political freedom, economic equality, and social justice.

This could be accomplished only as the previous great changes, from February to October, had been; by the joint effort and free cooperation of the workers and peasants, the latter now joined by the bulk of the army.

But such a development did not come within the scheme of the Bolsheviki. As already explained, their aim was to establish a dictatorship wielded by their Party. But a dictatorship means dictation, the imposing of the ruler's will upon the country. The Bolsheviki now felt themselves strong enough to carry out their real object. They dropped the revolutionary and Anarchist mottoes. There must be a vigorous political power, they declared, to carry on the work of the Revolution. Under the guise of protecting the people against the monarchists and the bourgeoisie they began to use repressive measures. As a matter of fact, there were no Tsarist supporters or monarchists in Russia worth mentioning. The people had grown out of Tsarism, and there was no more chance whatever, for a monarchy in Russia. As to the bourgeoisie, there had never been any organized capitalist class in

* November 7, new style.

Russia, such as we have in highly developed industrial countries—in the United States, England, France, and Germany. The Russian bourgeoisie was small in numbers and weak. It continued to exist after the February Revolution only by the protection of the Kerensky government. The moment the latter was abolished, the bourgeoisie went to pieces. It had neither strength nor means to stop the confiscation of its lands and factories by the peasants and workers. Strange as it may seem, it is a fact that throughout this whole period of the Revolution the Russian bourgeoisie did not make any organized and effectual attempt to regain its possessions.*

Consider how different it would have been in America. There the capitalists, who are strong and well organized, would have offered the greatest resistance. They would have formed defense bodies to protect themselves and their interests by force of arms. I have no doubt they will do so when things begin to happen there as they did in Russia in 1917. Not that they will succeed, however. But as I say, the Revolution in Russia did not produce any organized and effective bourgeois resistance, for the simple reason that there was no real bourgeoisie or capitalist class in that country. Military attempts there were indeed, such as that of the Tsarist General Kornilov to attack Petrograd with Cossacks brought from the front, but so harmless was that adventure that Kornilov's army melted away even before he could reach the capital. His men went over to the revolutionary garrison of Petrograd almost without firing a gun.**

The point is that when the masses are with the Revolution, there can be no thought of successful resistance by any enemy, no chance of suppressing the Revolution. That was the situation in Russia in October, 1917, when the Soviets took the power into their hands.

The Bolshevik plan was to gain entire and exclusive control of the government for their Party. It did not fit into their scheme to permit the people themselves to manage things, through their Soviet organizations. As long as the Soviets had the whole say the Bolsheviki could not achieve their purpose. It was therefore necessary either to abolish the Soviets or to gain control of them.

* In the South of Russia (the Ukraine) the bourgeoisie did offer some resistance, but only during the rule of the Hetmen Skoropadsky and Petlura, aided by the Allied armies. As soon as foreign aid was withdrawn, the Ukrainian bourgeoisie also became helpless.
** Real counter-revolution began much later, when Bolshevik terror and dictatorship were in full sway, which alienated the masses and resulted in insurrections.

To abolish the Soviets was impossible. They represented the toiling masses; the Soviet idea had been a cherished dream of the Russian people for centuries. Even in the far past Russia had soviets of various kinds, and the entire village life was built on the Soviet principle; that is, on the equal right and representation of all members alike. The ancient Russian *mir*, the public assembly to transact the business of the village or town, was one of the forms of the Soviet idea.

The Bolsheviki knew that the revolutionary workers and peasants, as well as the soldiers (who were workers and peasants in uniform), would not stand for the abolition of their Soviets. There remained the only alternative of getting control of them. Holding to the Lenin principle that the "end justifies the means," the Bolsheviki did not shrink from any methods whatever to discredit and eliminate the other revolutionary elements from the Soviets. They carried on a persistent campaign of venom and detraction for the purpose of deluding the masses and turning them against the other parties, particularly against the Left Socialists Revolutionists and the Anarchists. Systematically and by the most jesuitic means they sought to become the sole power, so as to be able to carry out Lenin's scheme of "proletarian dictatorship."

By such tactics the Bolsheviki finally succeeded in organizing a Soviet of People's Commissars, which in reality became the new government. All its members were Bolsheviki, with two minor exceptions: the Commissariats of justice and of Agriculture were headed by Left Socialist Revolutionists. Before long these were also eliminated and replaced by Bolsheviki. The Soviet of People's Commissars was the political machine of the Bolshevik Party, which was now re-christened into the Communist Party of Russia.

What this Communist Party stood for, what its objects and purposes were, we already know. It openly avowed determination to secure exclusive Bolshevik domination the label of the "dictatorship of the proletariat."

This was fatal to the Revolution and its great aim of a deep social and economic reconstruction, as the subsequent history of Russia has proven.

Why?

CHAPTER XVII
REVOLUTION AND DICTATORSHIP

Because the Revolution and the Bolshevik dictatorship were things of an entirely different and even opposite nature. And here is where most people make the greatest mistake in confusing the Russian Revolution with the Communist Party and speaking of them as if they were one and the same, which emphatically they are not.

This will become clear to us if we compare the aims of the Revolution with the ends sought by the Bolsheviki.

The Revolution was a mighty uprising against oppression and misery. It voiced the longing of the masses for liberty and justice. It attempted to do away with everything that kept man in subjection, made him a slave and a beast of burden. The Revolution tried to establish new forms of life, conditions of real equality and brotherhood.

We have already seen that the Revolution was not a superficial change, that it did not stop with the February events. The Tsar had been abolished and the power of his autocracy broken, but the result was only another *form* of government. The economic and social conditions remained the same. Yet it was just those that the people meant to change. That is why the October Revolution took place. Its purpose was to rebuild life altogether, on new social foundations.

How was it to be rebuilt? It is evident that taking Romanov out of the Kremlin palace and putting Lenin in his place would not do it. Something more was necessary. It was necessary to give the soil to the peasant, to put the factories in the hands of the workers and their labor organizations. In short, it was the aim of October to afford the people an opportunity to make use of the political freedom won in February.

That is the way the masses sized up the situation. And they acted upon it. They began to apply liberty to their needs. They wanted peace, so they stopped the war, first of all. It was months later that the Bolshevik government signed the Brest-Litovsk treaty and concluded an official peace with Germany. But so far as the Russian armies were concerned, war was at an end long before, without diplomatic negotiations. Trotsky frankly admits this in his work on the Revolution.*

* *1917,* by Leon Trotsky. Moscow, 1925.

The Russian workers and peasants, temporarily in soldiers' uniforms, had taken matters into their own hands and terminated the war by leaving the fronts.

Similarly did the peasantry and the proletariat act in solving the industrial and agrarian problems. While the Provisional Government was still discussing land reforms, the masses themselves acted, through their local councils and Soviets. The peasants *took* the land they needed and began cultivating it. With simple common sense and inherent popular justice they settled the agrarian problem over which politicians and lawgivers had been breaking their heads for many decades without result. The Bolsheviki, when they came to power, "legalized" what the peasants had already accomplished without asking anybody's permission.

In like manner did the workers' Soviets start to solve the industrial problem by taking over the factories and mines and managing them for the general benefit instead of for the profit of the "owners." That was actual abolition of capitalism and wage slavery, long before the Bolshevik government declared capitalist ownership "legally" at an end.

All the other problems of everyday life the Revolution was similarly solving by the practical and direct activity of the masses themselves. Cooperative organizations brought city and village together for the exchange of products; house committees looked after the housing question; street and district committees were organized for the safety of the city, and other voluntary bodies were formed for the defense of the people's interests and of the Revolution.

The requirements of the situation directed the efforts of the masses; liberty of action brought initiative into play and the wants of the people shaped their creative capacities to the needs of the hour.

These collective activities constituted the Revolution. They were the Revolution. For "revolution" is not some vague thing without definite meaning and purpose; nor does it signify political scene shifting or new legislation. The *actual* Revolution took place neither in February nor in October, but between those months. It consisted in the free play and interplay of the revolutionary energies and efforts of the people, in independent popular initiative and creative work, inspired by common need and mutual interests.

That was the spirit and tendency of the great economic and social upheaval in Russia. It solved problems as they arose, on the basis of liberty and free cooperation.

This process of the Revolution was stopped in its development by the Communist Party seizing political power and constituting itself a new government.

We have just seen what the aim of the Revolution was; we know what the masses of Russia wanted and what means they used to achieve it.

The objects of the Bolsheviki as a political party, on the other hand, were of an entirely different nature. As frankly admitted by themselves, their immediate goal was a dictatorship; that is, the formation of a powerful Bolshevik State which should direct the life and activities of the country according to the views and theories of the Communist Party

To give due credit to the Bolsheviki let me say right here that there never was any political party more devoted to its cause, more whole-hearted in its efforts to advance it, more determined and energetic in the achievement of its purpose. But *those purposes* were entirely foreign to the Revolution and opposed to its real needs. They were, in fact, so contrary to the spirit and aims of the Revolution that their achievement meant the destruction of the Revolution itself. No doubt the Bolsheviki really thought that only by means of their dictatorship could Russia be converted into a Socialist paradise for the worker and farmer. Indeed, as Marxists they could not see things in any other way. Believers in an all-powerful State, they had no confidence in the people; they had no faith in the initiative and creative ability of the toilers. They distrusted them as a "multi-colored mob which has to be forced into liberty." They agreed with the cynical maxim of Rousseau that the masses "can be made free only by compulsion."

"Proletarian compulsion in all its forms," wrote Bukharin, the foremost Communist theoretician, "beginning with summary execution and ending with compulsory labor is, however paradoxical it may sound, a method of reworking the human material of the capitalistic epoch into Communist humanity."

That was the Bolshevik gospel; it was the attitude of a party that believed a revolution could be run by the orders of a Central Committee.

What followed was the logical outcome of the Bolshevik idea.

Claiming that only the dictatorship of their Party could properly conduct the Revolution, they bent all energies to secure that dictatorship. It meant that they had to take things exclusively into their own hands, to have the designs of the Party accomplished at any cost.

We need not go into the details of the schemes and political manipulations of those days which finally resulted in the Communist Party gaining the upper hand. The important point is that the Bolsheviki did contrive to carry out their plans. Within a few months after the October Revolution, by April, 1918, they were in entire control of the government.

By taking advantage of the excitement of the revolutionary days and the inevitable confusion, they exploited the situation for their own objects. They used the political differences to rouse fierce party passions, resorted to every means to denounce their opponents as enemies of the people, branded them counter-revolutionists, and finally succeeded in damning them in the eyes of the workers and soldiers. Declaring that the Revolution must be protected against those alleged enemies, they were enabled to proclaim their own dictatorship. In the name of "saving the Revolution" they began eliminating all other revolutionary elements, non-Bolshevik, from positions of influence, finishing by suppressing them entirely.

It must be left to future historians to determine whether Bolshevik repression of the bourgeoisie, with which they started their rule, was not merely a means toward the ulterior purpose of suppressing all other non-Bolshevik elements. For the Russian bourgeoisie was not dangerous to the Revolution. As already explained, it was an insignificant minority, unorganized and powerless. The revolutionary elements, on the contrary, were a real obstacle to the dictatorship of any political party.

Because dictatorship would meet with the strongest opposition not from the bourgeoisie but from the truly revolutionary classes which considered dictatorship inimical to the best interests of the Revolution, the elimination of these would therefore be of prime necessity to any political party seeking dictatorship. Such a policy, however, could not successfully *begin* with the suppression of the revolutionists: it would provoke the disapproval and resistance of the workers and soldiers. It would have to be begun at the bourgeois end and means found gradually to spread the net over the other elements. Distrust and antagonism would have to be wakened, intolerance and persecution stimulated, popular fear created for the safety of the Revolution in order to secure the people's support for an ever-widening campaign of elimination and suppression, for the introduction of the bloody hand of red terror into the life of the Revolution.

But as I have said, it is the place of the future historian to determine to what extent such motives fashioned the events of those days. Here we are more concerned with what actually happened.

What happened was that before long the Bolsheviki established the exclusive dictatorship of their Party.

"What was that dictatorship," you ask, "and what did it achieve?"

CHAPTER XVIII
THE DICTATORSHIP AT WORK

It achieved the complete mastery of the Bolsheviki over a country of 140 million of population. In the name of the "proletarian dictatorship" *one* political organization, the Communist Party, became the absolute ruler of Russia. The proletarian dictatorship was not dictatorship by the proletariat. Millions of people cannot all be dictators. Nor can thousands of party members be dictators. By its very nature a dictatorship is limited to a small number of persons. The less of them, the stronger and more unified the dictatorship. In actual practice dictatorship is always in the hands of *one* person, the strong man whose will compels the consent of his nominal co-dictators. It cannot be otherwise, and so it was with the Bolsheviki.

The real dictator was neither the proletariat nor even the Communist Party. Theoretically the power was held by the Central Committee of the Party, but actually it was wielded by the inner circle of that Committee, called the political bureau or "politbureau." But even the politbureau was not the real dictator, though its membership was less than a score. For in the politbureau there were differing views on every important question, as there must be when there are many heads. The real dictator was the man whose influence secured the support of the majority of the politbureau. That man was Lenin, and it was he who was the real "proletarian dictatorship," just as Mussolini, for instance, and not the Fascist Party, is dictator in Italy. It was always the views and ideas of Lenin that were carried out, from the very inception of the Bolshevik Party to the last day of Lenin's life; carried out when the entire Party was opposed to his opinion and even when the Central Committee bitterly fought his proposals on their first presentation. It was Lenin who always won, his will that prevailed. It was so in every critical period of Bolshevik history. It could not help being so, because dictatorship always means domination by the strongest personality, the supremacy of a single will.

The whole history of the Communist Party, as that of every dictatorship, indisputably demonstrates this. Bolshevik writings themselves prove it. Here it is sufficient to mention but a few of the most vital events to substantiate my contention.

In March, 1917, when Lenin returned home from exile in Switzerland, the Central Committee of his Party in Russia had decided to enter the Coalition Government formed after the abolition of the Tsarist regime. Lenin was opposed to cooperation with the bourgeois and Mensheviki who were in the government. Yet notwithstanding that the Party had already decided the question and that Lenin was almost alone in his opposition, his influence carried. The Central Committee reversed itself and took up Lenin's position.

Later, in July, 1917, Lenin advocated an immediate revolution against the Kerensky government. His proposal was roundly condemned even by his nearest comrades and friends as foolhardy and criminal. But again Lenin won, even at the cost of Zinoviev, Kamenev, and other influential Bolsheviki refusing to be parties to the scheme and resigning from the Central Committee. Incidentally, the *Putsch* (the attempt to upset Kerensky) proved a failure and cost many workers' lives.

The red terror instituted by Lenin as soon as he came to power after the October Revolution was bitterly denounced by his co-workers as entirely uncalled for and as a direct betrayal of the Revolution. But in spite of the official protests of the most active and influential members of the Party, Lenin had his way.*

During the Brest-Litovsk negotiations it was again Lenin who insisted that "peace on any terms" be made with Germany, while Trotsky, Radek, and other important Bolshevik leaders opposed the Kaiser's conditions as humiliating and destructive. Once more Lenin scored.

The "new economic policy" (the "NEP") submitted by Lenin to his Party during the Kronstadt events** was fought by the Central Committee as nullifying all the revolutionary achievements and as a death blow to Communism. It was indeed a complete reversal of everything the Revolution stood for and a return to the very conditions that the great October change had abolished. But Lenin's will again prevailed and his resolution was carried at the IX Communist Congress held in Moscow, in March, 1921.

As you see, the alleged dictatorship of the proletariat was only the dictatorship of Lenin. He dictated to the politbureau, the politbureau to the Central Committee, the Central Committee to the Party, the Party to

---

* See the official protests by Bolsheviki of long standing, such as Lodovsky and others, quoted by Trotsky in his work *1917*.
** The revolt of the Kronstadt sailors in March, 1921. See *The Kronstadt Rebellion*, by the author.

the proletariat and the rest of the people. Russia counted a population of over a hundred million; the Communist Party had less than fifty thousand members; the Central Committee consisted of several score; the politbureau numbered about a dozen; and Lenin was one. But that one was *the* proletarian dictatorship.

Russia is a country of vast extent, spread over half of Europe and a goodly part of Asia. It is peopled by numerous races and nationalities speaking different languages, with diversified psychology, varied interests and outlook upon life. We know what the dictatorship of the Tsars did to the country. Let us now see what the "proletarian" dictatorship accomplished.

Today, after over a decade of Bolshevik rule in Russia. we can form a fair estimate of its effects and examine the results it achieved. Let us sum them up.

Politically the aim of the Revolution was to abolish governmental tyranny and oppression and make the people free. The Bolshevik government is admittedly the worst despotism in Europe, with the sole exception of Fascist rule in Italy. The citizen has no rights which the government feels bound to respect. The Communist Party is a political monopoly, with all the other parties and movements outlawed. Security of person and domicile is unknown. Freedom of speech and press does not exist. Even within the Party the least difference of opinion is suppressed and punished by imprisonment and exile, as witness the fate of Trotsky and his followers of the Opposition. Independent opinion is not tolerated. The G.P.U., the secret service formerly called Tcheka, is a super-government with unlimited arbitrary powers over the liberty and lives of the people. Only those who are entirely on the side of the dominant Party clique enjoy freedom and privileges. But such "liberty" is to be had under the worst despotism: if you have nothing to say you are perfectly free to say it even in the land of Mussolini. As a prominent member of a recent Communist Congress put it, "There is room for all political parties in Russia: the Communist Party is in the government, the others are in prison."

Economically it was the fundamental aim of the Revolution to abolish capitalism and establish Communism and equality.

The Bolshevik dictatorship began by instituting a system of unequal compensation and discriminating rewards, and ended by reintroducing capitalistic ownership after it had been abolished by the direct action of the industrial and agrarian proletariat. Today Russia is a country partly State capitalistic and partly privately capitalistic.

The dictatorship and the red terror by which it was maintained proved the main factors in paralyzing the economic life of the country. High-handed Bolshevik rule antagonized the people, its despotism embittered the masses. The repression of every independent effort alienated the best elements from the Revolution and made them feel that it had become the private concern of the political Party in power. Facing a new tyranny instead of the longed-for liberty, the workers became discouraged. They felt their revolutionary achievements taken from them and used as a weapon against themselves and their aspirations. The proletarian saw his factory committee subjected to the dictates of the Communist Party and made helpless to protect his interests as a toiler. His labor union became the mouthpiece and transmitter of Bolshevik orders, and he found himself deprived of all voice, not only in the management of industry but even in his own factory where he was kept at work long hours at the poorest pay. The toilers soon realized that the Revolution had been taken out of their hands, that their Soviets had been emasculated of all power, and that the country was being ruled by some people far away in the Kremlin, just as it was in the days of the Tsars. Eliminated from revolutionary and creative activity, living only to obey the new masters, constantly harassed by Bolsheviki and Tchekists, and ever in fear of prison or execution for the least expression of protest, the worker became embittered against the Revolution. He deserted the factory and sought the village where he might be furthest removed from the dreaded rulers and at least secure of his daily bread. Thus broke down the industries of the country.

The peasant saw leather-clad and armed Communists descend upon his quiet village, despoil it of the fruit of his hard labor, and treat him with the brutality and insolence of the old Tsarist officials. He saw his Soviet dominated by some lazy, good-for-nothing village loafer calling himself Bolshevik and holding power from Moscow. He had willingly, even generously, given his wheat and corn to the workers and the soldiers, but he saw his provisions lie rotting at the railroad stations and in the warehouses, because the Bolsheviki could not themselves manage things and would let no one else do it. He knew that his brothers in the factory and in the army suffered for lack of food because of Communist inefficiency, bureaucracy, and corruption. He understood why more was always demanded of him saw his few possessions, his own family provisions, confiscated by Tchekists who often took even his last horse without which the peasant could neither work nor live. He saw his neighbor villages, that rebelled against these outrages, leveled to the ground and the peasants whipped and shot, just as in the old days. He turned against the Revolution and in his desperation he determined to plant and sow no more than he needed for himself and family and to hide even that in the forest.

Such were the results of the dictatorship, of Lenin's military communism and Bolshevik methods. Industry stood still, and famine overwhelmed the country. The general suffering, the bitterness of the workers, and the peasant uprisings began to threaten the existence of the Bolshevik regime. To save the dictatorship Lenin decided to introduce a new economic policy, known as the "NEP."

The purpose of the "NEP" was to revive the economic life of the country. It was to encourage greater production by the peasantry by allowing them to sell their surplus instead of having it forcibly confiscated by the government. It was also to enable exchange of products by legalizing trade and reviving the cooperatives formerly suppressed as counter-revolutionary. But the determination of the Communist Party to hold on to its dictatorship made all these economic reforms ineffectual, because industry cannot develop under a despotic regime. Economic growth, as well as trade and commerce, requires security of person and property, a certain amount of freedom and non-interference in order to function. But dictatorship does not permit that freedom; its "guarantees" cannot inspire confidence. Hence the new economic policy has not produced the results desired, and Russia remains in the throes of poverty, constantly on the brink of economic disaster.

Industrially the dictatorship has emasculated the Revolution of its basic purpose of placing production in the hands of the proletariat and making the worker independent of economic masters. The dictatorship merely changed masters: the government has become the boss instead of the individual capitalist, though the latter is now also developing as a new class in Russia. The toiler has remained dependent as before. In fact, more so. His labor organizations have been deprived of all power, and he has lost even the right to strike against his governmental employer. "Since the workers, as a class, wield the dictatorship," the Communists argue, "they cannot strike against themselves." Accordingly the proletarians in Russia pay themselves wages that are not sufficient for bare existence, live crowded in unhygienic quarters, work under most unsanitary conditions, endanger their health and lives because of lack of industrial precaution and safety, and arrest and imprison themselves for an expression of discontent.

Culturally the Bolshevik regime is a training school in Communism and party fanaticism, with no access to ideas differing from the views of the dominant clique. It is the rearing of an entire people in the dogmas of a political church, with no opportunity to broaden and cultivate the mind outside the circle of opinions permitted by the ruling class. No press exists in Russia except the official Communist publications and such others as are approved of by the Bolshevik censor. No public sentiment can find expression there, since the government has a monopoly of speech, press, and assembly.

It is no exaggeration to say that there is less freedom of opinion and opportunity to voice it under the Bolshevik dictatorship than there had been under the Tsars. When Russia was ruled by the Romanovs you could at least secretly issue pamphlets and books, since the government then had no monopoly of the paper supply and printing presses. These were in private hands, and the revolutionists could always find ways to use them for their propaganda.

Today in Russia all the means of publication and distribution are in the exclusive possession of the government, and no person can express his views to the public unless he first secures Bolshevik permission. Thousands of illegal publications had been issued by the revolutionary parties during the autocratic Romanov regime. Under Communist rule such a happening is most exceptional, as witness the indignant amazement of the Bolsheviki when it was discovered that Trotsky had succeeded in publishing the platform of the Opposition element in the Party.

Socially Bolshevik Russia, ten years after the Revolution, is a country where no man can enjoy political security or economic independence, where the hidden hand of the G.P.U. is always at work, terrorizing the people by sudden night searches, arrests for no known cause, secret denunciation for alleged counter-revolution out of personal revenge, imprisonment without hearing or trial, and year-long exile to the frozen North of Siberia or the arid wastes of Western Asia. A huge prison, where equality means the fear of all alike, and "freedom" signifies unquestioning submission to the powers that be.

Morally Russia represents the struggle of the finer qualities of man against the degrading and corrupting effects of a system built on coercion and intimidation. The Revolution brought the best instincts of man to the fore: his manhood, his consciousness of human value, his love of liberty and justice. The revolutionary atmosphere inspired and cultivated these tendencies lying dormant in the people, particularly the feeling against oppression, the hunger for freedom, the spirit of mutual helpfulness and cooperation. But the dictatorship has had the effect of counteracting these traits and arousing instead fear and hatred, the spirit of intolerance and persecution. Bolshevik methods have systematically weakened the people's morale, have encouraged servility and hypocrisy, created disillusionment and distrust, and have developed an atmosphere of time-serving now dominant in Russia.

Such is the situation today in that unhappy land, such the effects of the Bolshevik idea that you can make a people free by compulsion, the dogma that dictatorship can lead to liberty.

"So you think that the Revolution failed because of dictatorship?" you ask. "Was not Russia too backward to make a success of it?"

It failed because of Bolshevik ideas and methods. The Russian masses were not too "backward" to abolish the Tsar, to defeat the provisional government, to destroy capitalism and the wage system, to turn the land over to the peasantry and the industries to the workers. So far the Revolution was the greatest success, and the people were beginning to build their new life upon the foundation of equal liberty, opportunity, and justice. But the moment a political party usurped the reins of government and proclaimed its dictatorship, disastrous results were inevitable.

Revolution, when it comes, must deal with conditions as it finds them. It is the means and methods used, and the purpose for which they are used, that are vital. Upon them depends the course and fate of the revolution.

Whatever the social, political, or economic situation of a given country—be it "backward" Russia or "advanced" America—the most important problem is what you want to accomplish and what means will best secure your objects.

If the purpose of the Russian Revolution was to establish a dictatorship, then the Bolshevik methods were right and their success complete.

But if the aim of the Revolution was to abolish oppression and servitude, then the Bolsheviki and their policies are proving the greatest failure.

It all depends, as you see, on what your purpose is, what you want to accomplish. Your aims must determine the means. Means and aims are in reality the same: you cannot separate them. It is the means that shape your ends. The means are the seeds which bud into flower and come to fruition. The fruit will always be of the nature of the seed you planted. You can't grow a rose from a cactus seed. No more can you harvest liberty from compulsion or justice and manhood from dictatorship.

Let us learn this lesson well because the fate of revolution depends on it. "You shall reap what you sow" is the acme of all human wisdom and experience.

You cannot make a sick man well by drawing out his blood. The free activity of the masses is the life-blood of revolution. Eliminate or repress it, and revolution becomes anemic and dies.

It means that the aims of the revolution must fashion its methods. Not coercion and dictatorship, but only liberty and the free expression of the masses can serve the objects of revolution. In revolution, as in ordinary life, there is no middle road: it is either compulsion or liberty.

Dictatorship and terror have been tried in Russia. The lesson of that experiment is clear and convincing: those methods imply the destruction of revolution. A new way must be found.

"Is there any other way?" you ask.

There is only the way of liberty, and that has never been tried, yet.

I don't know whether you are willing to try it: most people are afraid of freedom. But I do know that unless that way is tried, the way of liberty, justice, and reason, revolution must lead to dictatorship, to failure and death.

Dictatorship, whether white or red, always means the same thing: it means compulsion, oppression, and misery. That is its character and essence. It cannot be anything else. Dictatorship is a government that governs most. But as Thomas Jefferson wisely said, "That government is best which governs least."

That is what the Anarchists claim, and so let us turn from Socialism and Bolshevism, from Marx and Lenin, to consider what Anarchism has to offer us.

PART TWO —

ANARCHISM

CHAPTER XIX
IS ANARCHISM VIOLENT?

You have heard that Anarchists throw bombs, that they believe in violence, and that Anarchy means disorder and chaos.

It is not surprising that you should think so. The press, the pulpit, and everyone in authority constantly din it in to your ears. But most of them know better, even if they have a reason for not telling you the truth. It is time you should hear it.

I mean to speak to you honestly and frankly, and you can take my word for it, because it happens that I am just one of those Anarchists who are pointed out as men of violence and destruction. I ought to know, and I have nothing to hide.

"Now, does Anarchism really mean disorder and violence?" you wonder.

No, my friend, it is capitalism and government which stand for disorder and violence. Anarchism is the very reverse of it; it means order without government and peace without violence.

"But is that possible?" you ask.

That is just what we are going to talk over now. But first your friend demands to know whether Anarchists have never thrown bombs or used any violence.

Yes, Anarchists have thrown bombs and have sometimes resorted to violence.

"There you are!" your friend exclaims. "I thought so."

But do not let us be hasty. If Anarchists have sometimes used violence, does it mean necessarily that Anarchism means violence?

Ask yourself this question and try to answer it honestly. When a citizen puts on a soldier's uniform, he may have to throw bombs and use violence. Will you say, then, that citizenship stands for bombs and violence?

You will indignantly resent the imputation. It simply means, you will reply, that *under certain conditions* a man may have to resort to violence. The man may happen to be a Democrat, a Monarchist, a Socialist, Bolshevik, or Anarchist.

You will find that this applies to all men and to all times.

Brutus killed Cesar because he feared his friend meant to betray the republic and become king. Not that Brutus "loved Cesar less but that he loved Rome more." Brutus was not an Anarchist. He was a loyal republican.

William Tell, as folklore tells us, shot to death the tyrant in order to rid his country of oppression. Tell had never heard of Anarchism.

I mention these instances to illustrate the fact that from time immemorial despots met their fate at the hands of outraged lovers of liberty. Such men were rebels against tyranny. They were generally patriots, Democrats or Republicans, occasionally Socialists or Anarchists. Their acts were cases of individual rebellion against wrong and injustice. Anarchism had nothing to do with it.

There was a time in ancient Greece when killing a despot was considered the highest virtue. Modern law condemns such acts, but human feeling seems to have remained the same in this matter as in the old days. The conscience of the world does not feel outraged by tyrannicide. Even if publicly not approved, the heart of mankind condones and often even secretly rejoices at such acts. Were there not thousands of patriotic youths in America willing to assassinate the German Kaiser whom they held responsible for starting the World War? Did not a French court recently acquit the man who killed Petlura to avenge the thousands of men, women and children murdered in the Petlura pogroms against the Jews of South Russia?

In every land, in all ages, there have been tyrannicides; that is, men and women who loved their country well enough to sacrifice even their own lives for it. Usually they were persons of no political party or idea, but simply haters of tyranny. Occasionally they were religious fanatics, like the devout Catholic Kullmann, who tried to assassinate Bismarck.* or the misguided enthusiast Charlotte Corday who killed Marat during the French Revolution.

In the United States three Presidents were killed by individual acts. Lincoln was shot in 1865, by John Wilkes Booth, who was a Southern Democrat; Garfield, in 1881, by Charles Jules Guiteau, a Republican; and McKinley, in 1901, by Leon Czolgosz. Out of the three only one was an Anarchist.

The country that has the worst oppressors produces also the greatest number of tyrannicides, which is natural. Take Russia, for instance. With complete suppression of speech and press under the Tsars, there was no way of mitigating the despotic regime than by "putting the fear of God" into the tyrant's heart.

* July 13, 1874.

Those avengers were mostly sons and daughters of the highest nobility, idealistic youths who loved liberty and the people. With all other avenues closed, they felt themselves compelled to resort to the pistol and dynamite in the hope of alleviating the miserable conditions of their country. They were known as nihilists and terrorists. They were not Anarchists.

In modern times individual acts of political violence have been even more frequent than in the past. The women suffragettes in England, for example, frequently resorted to it to propagate and carry out their demands for equal rights. In Germany, since the war, men of the most conservative political views have used such methods in the hope of re-establishing the kingdom. It was a monarchist who killed Karl Erzberger, the Prussian Minister of Finance; and Walter Rathenau, Minister of Foreign Affairs, was also laid low by a man of the same political party.

Why, the original cause of, or at least excuse for, the Great War itself was the killing of the Austrian heir to the throne by a Serbian patriot who had never heard of Anarchism. In Germany, Hungary, France, Italy, Spain, Portugal, and in every other European country men of the most varied political views have resorted to acts of violence, not to speak of the wholesale political terror, practiced by organized bodies such as the Fascists in Italy, the Ku Klux Klan in America, or the Catholic Church in Mexico.

You see, then, that Anarchists have no monopoly of political violence. The number of such acts by Anarchists is infinitesimal as compared with those committed by persons of other political persuasions.

The truth is that in every country, in every social movement, violence has been a part of the struggle from time immemorial. Even the Nazarene, who came to preach the gospel of peace, resorted to violence to drive the money changers out of the temple.

As I have said, Anarchists have no monopoly on violence. On the contrary, the teachings of Anarchism are those of peace and harmony, of non-invasion, of the sacredness of life and liberty. But Anarchists are human, like the rest of mankind, and perhaps more so. They are more sensitive to wrong and injustice, quicker to resent oppression, and therefore not exempt from occasionally voicing their protest by an act of violence. But such acts are an expression of individual temperament, not of any particular theory.

You might ask whether the holding of revolutionary ideas would not naturally influence a person toward deeds of violence. I do not think so, because we have seen that violent methods are also employed by people of the most conservative opinions. If persons of directly opposite political views commit similar acts, it is hardly reasonable to say that their ideas are responsible for such acts.

Like results have a like cause, but that cause is not to be found in political convictions; rather in individual temperament and the general feeling about violence.

"You may be right about temperament," you say. "I can see that revolutionary ideas are not the cause of political acts of violence, else every revolutionist would be committing such acts. But do not such views to some extent justify those who commit such acts?"

It may seem so at first sight. But if you think it over you will find that it is an entirely wrong idea. The best proof of it is that Anarchists who hold exactly the same views about government and the necessity of abolishing it, often disagree entirely on the question of violence. Thus Tolstoyan Anarchists and most Individualist Anarchists condemn political violence, while other Anarchists approve of or at least justify it.

Is it reasonable, then, to say that Anarchist views are responsible for violence or in any way influence such acts?

Moreover, many Anarchists who at one time believed in violence as a means of propaganda have changed their opinion about it and do not favor such methods any more. There was a time, for instance, when Anarchists advocated individual acts of violence, known as "propaganda by deed." They did not expect to change government and capitalism into Anarchism by such acts, nor did they think that the taking off of a despot would abolish despotism. No, terrorism was considered a means of avenging a popular wrong, inspiring fear in the enemy, and also calling attention to the evil against which the act of terror was directed. But most Anarchists today do not believe any more in "propaganda by deed" and do not favor acts of that nature.

Experience has taught them that though such methods may have been justified and useful in the past, modern conditions of life make them unnecessary and even harmful to the spread of their ideas. But their ideas remain the same, which means that it was not Anarchism which shaped their attitude to violence. It proves that it is not certain ideas or "isms" that lead to violence, but that some other causes bring it about.

We must therefore look somewhere else to find the right explanation.

As we have seen, acts of political violence have been committed not only by Anarchists, Socialists, and revolutionists of all kinds, but also by patriots and nationalists, by Democrats and Republicans, by suffragettes, by conservatives and reactionaries, by monarchists and royalists, and even by religionists and devout Christians.

We know now that it could not have been any particular idea or "ism" that influenced their acts, because the most varied ideas and "isms" produced similar deeds. I have given as the reason individual temperament and the general feeling about violence.

Here is the crux of the matter. What is this general feeling about violence? If we can answer this question correctly, the whole matter will be clear to us.

If we speak honestly, we must admit that every one believes in violence and practices it, however he may condemn it in others. In fact, all of the institutions we support and the entire life of present society are based on violence.

What is the thing we call government? Is it anything else but organized violence? The law orders you to do this or not to do that, and if you fail to obey, it will compel you by force. We are not discussing just now whether it is right or wrong, whether it should or should not be so. Just now we are interested in the fact that *it is* so—that all government, all law and authority finally rest on force and violence, on punishment or the fear of punishment.

Why, even spiritual authority, the authority of the church and of God rests on force and violence, because it is the fear of divine wrath and vengeance that wields power over you, compels you to obey, and even to believe against your own reason.

Wherever you turn you will find that our entire life is built on violence or the fear of it. From earliest childhood you are subjected to the violence of parents or elders. At home, in school, in the office, factory, field, or shop, it is always some one's *authority* which keeps you obedient and compels you to do his will.

The right to compel you is called authority. Fear of punishment has been made into duty and is called obedience.

In this atmosphere of force and violence, of authority and obedience, of duty, fear and punishment we all grow up; we breathe it throughout our lives. We are so steeped in the spirit of violence that we never stop to ask whether violence is right or wrong. We only ask if it is legal, whether the law permits it.

You don't question the right of the government to kill, to confiscate and imprison. If a private person should be guilty of the things the government is doing all the time, you'd brand him a murderer, thief, and scoundrel. But as long as the violence committed is "lawful," you approve of it and submit to it. So it is not really violence that you object to, but to people using violence "unlawfully."

This lawful violence and the fear of it dominate our whole existence, individual and collective. Authority controls our lives from the cradle to the grave—authority parental, priestly and divine, political, economic, social, and moral. But whatever the character of that authority, it is always the same executioner wielding power over you through your fear of punishment in one form or another. You are afraid of God and the devil, of the priest and the neighbor, of your employer and boss, of the politician and policeman, of the judge and the jailer, of the law and the government. All your life is a long chain of fears—fears which bruise your body and lacerate your soul. On those fears is based the authority of God, of the church, of parents, of capitalist and ruler.

Look into your heart and see if what I say is not true. Why, even among children the ten-year-old Johnny bosses his younger brother or sister by the authority of his greater physical strength, just as Johnny's father bosses him by his superior strength, and by Johnny's dependence on his support. You stand for the authority of priest and preacher because you think they can "call down the wrath of God upon your head." You submit to the domination of boss, judge, and government because of their power to deprive you of work, to ruin your business, to put you in prison—a power, by the way, that you yourself have given into their hands.

So authority rules your whole life, the authority of the past and the present, of the dead and the living, and your existence is a continuous invasion and violation of yourself, a constant subjection to the thoughts and the will of some one else.

And as you are invaded and violated, so you subconsciously revenge yourself by invading and violating others over whom *you* have authority or can exercise compulsion, physical or moral. In this way all life has become a crazy quilt of authority, of domination and submission, of command and obedience, of coercion and subjection, of rulers and ruled, of violence and force in a thousand and one forms.

Can you wonder that even idealists are still held in the meshes of this spirit of authority and violence, and are often impelled by their feelings and environment to invasive acts entirely at variance with their ideas?

We are all still barbarians who resort to force and violence to settle our doubts, difficulties, and troubles. Violence is the method of ignorance, the weapon of the weak. The strong of heart and brain need no violence, for they are irresistible in their consciousness of being right. The further we get away from primitive man and the hatchet age, the less recourse we shall have to force and violence. The more enlightened man will become, the less he will employ compulsion and coercion. The really civilized man will divest himself of all fear and authority. He will rise from the dust and stand erect: he will bow to no tsar either in heaven or on earth. He will become fully human when he will scorn to rule and refuse to be ruled. He will be truly free only when there shall be no more masters.

Anarchism is the ideal of such a condition; of a society without force and compulsion, where all men shall be equals and live in freedom, peace, and harmony.

The word Anarchy comes from the Greek, meaning without force, without violence or government, because government is the very fountainhead of violence, constraint, and coercion.

Anarchy* therefore does not mean disorder and chaos, as you thought before. On the contrary, it is the very reverse of it; it means no government, which is freedom and liberty. Disorder is the child of authority and compulsion. Liberty is the mother of order.

"A beautiful ideal," you say; "but only angels are fit for it."

Let us see, then, if we can grow the wings we need for that ideal state of society.

---

* Anarchy refers to the condition. Anarchism is the theory or teaching about it.

CHAPTER XX
WHAT IS ANARCHISM?

"Can you tell us briefly," your friend asks, "what Anarchism really is?"

I shall try. In the fewest words, Anarchism teaches that we can live in a society where there is no compulsion of any kind.

A life without compulsion naturally means liberty; it means freedom from being forced or coerced, a chance to lead the life that suits you best.

You cannot lead such a life unless you do away with the institutions that curtail your liberty and interfere with your life, the conditions that compel you to act differently than you really would like to.

What are those institutions and conditions? Let us see what we have to do away with in order to secure a free and harmonious life. Once we know what has to be abolished and what must take its place, we shall also find the way to do it.

What must be abolished, then, to secure liberty?

First of all, of course, the thing that invades you most, that handicaps or prevents your free activity; the thing interferes with your liberty and compels you to life differently from what would be your own choice.

That thing is government.

Take a good look at it and you will see that government is the greatest invader; more than that, the worst criminal man has ever known of. It fills the world with violence, with fraud and deceit, with oppression and misery. As a great thinker once said, "its breath is poison." It corrupts everything it touches.

"Yes, government means violence and it is evil," you admit; "but can we do without it?"

That is just what we want to talk over. Now, if I should ask you whether *you* need government, I'm sure you would answer that you don't, but that it is for the others that it is needed.

But if you should ask any one of those "others," he would reply as you do: he would say that he does not need it, but that it is necessary "for the others."

Why does every one think that he can be decent enough without the policeman, but that the club is needed for "the others?"

"People would rob and murder each other if there were no government and no law," you say.

If they really would, *why* would they? Would they do it just for the pleasure of it or because of certain reasons? Maybe if we examine their reasons, we'd discover the cure for them.

Suppose you and I and a score of others had suffered shipwreck and found ourselves on an island rich with fruit of every kind. Of course, we'd get to work to gather the food. But suppose one of our number should declare that it all belongs to him, and that no one shall have a single morsel unless he first pays him tribute for it. We would be indignant, wouldn't we? We'd laugh at his pretensions. If he'd try to make trouble about it, we might throw him into the sea, and it would serve him right, would it not?

Suppose further that we ourselves and our forefathers had cultivated the island and stocked it with everything needed for life and comfort, and that someone should arrive and claim it all as his. What would we say? We'd ignore him, wouldn't we? We might tell him that he could share with us and join us in our work. But suppose that he insists on his ownership and that he produces a slip of paper and says that it proves that everything belongs to him? We'd tell him that he's crazy and we'd go about our business. But if he should have a government in back of him, he would appeal to it for the protection of "his rights," and the government would send police and soldiers who would evict us and put the "lawful owner in possession."

That is the function of government; that is what government exists for and what it is doing all the time.

Now, do you still think that without this thing called government we should rob and murder each other?

Is it not rather true that *with* government we rob and murder? Because government does not secure us in our rightful possessions, but on the contrary takes them away for the benefit of those who have no right to them, as we have seen in previous chapters.

If you should wake up tomorrow morning and learn that here is no government any more, would your first thought be to rush out into the street and kill someone? No, you know that is nonsense. We speak of sane, normal men. The insane man who wants to kill does not first ask whether there is or isn't a government. Such men belong to the care of physicians and alienists; they should be placed in hospitals to be treated for their malady.

The chances are that if you or Johnson should awaken to find that there is no government, you would get busy arranging your life under the new conditions.

It is very likely, of course, that if you should then see people gorge themselves while you go hungry, you would demand a chance to eat, and you would be perfectly right in that. And so would every one else, which means that people would not stand for any one hogging all the good things of life: they would want to share in them. It means further that the poor would refuse to stay poor while others wallow in luxury. It means that the worker will decline to give up his product to the boss who claims to "own" the factory and everything that is made there. It means that the farmer will not permit thousands of acres to lie idle while he has not enough soil to support himself and family. It means that no one will be permitted to monopolize the land or the machinery of production. It means that private ownership of the *sources of life* will not be tolerated any more. It will be considered the greatest crime for some to own more than they can use in a dozen lifetimes, while their neighbors have not enough bread for their children. It means that all men will share in the social wealth, and that all will help to produce that wealth.

It means, in short, that for the first time in history right, justice, and equality would triumph instead of law.

You see therefore that doing away with government also signifies the abolition of monopoly and of personal ownership of the means of production and distribution.

It follows that when government is abolished, wage slavery and capitalism must also go with it, because they cannot exist without the support and protection of government. Just as the man who would claim a monopoly of the island, of which I spoke before, could not put through his crazy claim without the help of government.

Such a condition of things where there would be liberty instead of government would be Anarchy. And where equality of use would take the place of private ownership, there would be Communism.

It would be Communist Anarchism.

"Oh, Communism," your friend exclaims, "but you said you were not a Bolshevik!"

No, I am not a Bolshevik, because the Bolsheviki want a powerful government or State, while Anarchism means doing away with the State or government altogether.

"But are not the Bolsheviki Communists?" you demand.

Yes, the Bolsheviki are Communists, but they want their dictatorship, their government, to *compel* people to live in Communism. Anarchist Communism, on the contrary, means voluntary Communism, Communism from free choice.

"I see the difference. It would be fine, of course," your friend admits. "But do you really think it possible?"

CHAPTER XXI
IS ANARCHY POSSIBLE?

"It might be possible," you say, "if we could do without government. But can we?"

Perhaps we can best answer your question by examining your own life. What role does the government play in your existence? Does it help you live? Does it feed, clothe, and shelter you? Do you need it to help you work or play? If you are ill, do you call the physician or the policeman? Can the government give you greater ability than nature endowed you with? Can it save you from sickness, old age and death?

Consider your daily life and you will find that in reality, the government is no factor in it at all except when it begins to interfere in your affairs, when it compels you to do certain things and prohibits you from doing others. It forces you, for instance, to pay taxes and support it, whether you want to or not. It makes you don a uniform and join the army. It invades your personal life, orders you about, coerces you, prescribes your behavior, and generally treats you as it pleases. It tells you even what you must believe and punishes you for thinking and acting otherwise. It directs you what to eat and drink, and imprisons or shoots you for disobeying. It commands you and dominates every step of your life. It treats you as a bad boy or as an *irresponsible* child who needs the strong hand of a guardian, but if you disobey it holds you *responsible* nevertheless.

We shall consider later the details of life under Anarchy and see what conditions and institutions will exist in that form of society, how they will function, and what effect they are likely to have upon man.

For the present we want to make sure first that such a condition is possible, that Anarchy is practical.

What is the existence of the average man today? Almost all your time is given to earning your livelihood. You are so busy making a living that you hardly have time to live, to enjoy life. Neither the time nor the money. You are lucky if you have some source of support, some job. Now and then comes slack-time: there is unemployment and thousands are thrown out of work, every year, in every country.

That time means no income, no wages. It results in worry and privation, in disease, desperation, and suicide. It spells poverty and crime. To alleviate that poverty we build homes of charity, poorhouses, free hospitals, all of which you support with your taxes. To prevent crime and to punish the criminals it is again you who have to support police, detectives, State forces, judges, lawyers, prisons, keepers. Can you imagine anything more senseless and impractical? The legislatures pass laws, the judges interpret them, the various officials execute them, the police track and arrest the criminal, and finally the prison warden gets him into custody. Numerous persons and institutions are busy keeping the jobless man from stealing and punish him if he tries to. Then he is provided with the means of existence, the lack of which had made him break the law in the first place. After a shorter or longer term he is turned loose. If he fails to get work he begins the same round of theft, arrest, trial, and imprisonment all over again.

This is a rough but typical illustration of the stupid character of our system; stupid and inefficient. Law and government support that system.

Is it not peculiar that most people imagine we could not do without government, when in fact our real life has no connection with it whatever, no need of it, and is only interfered with where law and government step in?

"But security and public order," you object, "could we have that without law and government? Who will protect as against the criminal?"

The truth is that what is called "law and order" is really the worst disorder, as we have seen in previous chapters. What little order and peace we do have is due to the good common sense and joint efforts of the people, mostly in spite of the government. Do you need government to tell you not to step in front of a moving automobile? Do you need it to order you not to jump off the Brooklyn Bridge or from the Eiffel Tower?

Man is a social being: he cannot exist alone; he lives in communities or societies. Mutual need and common interests result in certain arrangements to afford us security and comfort. Such co-working is free, voluntary; it needs no compulsion by any government. You join a sporting club or a singing society because your inclinations lie that way, and you cooperate with the other members without any one coercing you. The man of science, the writer, the artist, and the inventor seek their own kind for inspiration and mutual work. Their impulses and needs are their best urge: the interference of any government or authority can only hinder their efforts.

All through life you will find that the needs and inclinations of people make for association, for mutual protection and help. That is the difference between managing things and governing men; between doing something from free choice and being compelled. It is the difference between liberty and constraint, between Anarchism and government, because Anarchism means voluntary cooperation instead of forced participation. It means harmony and order in place of interference and disorder.

"But who will protect us against crime and criminals?" you demand.

Rather ask yourself whether government really protects us against them. Does not government itself create and uphold conditions which make for crime? Does not the invasion and violence upon which all governments rest cultivate the spirit of intolerance and persecution, of hatred and more violence? Does not crime increase with the growth of poverty and injustice fostered by government? Is not government itself the greatest injustice and crime?

Crime is the result of economic conditions, of social inequality, of wrongs and evils of which government and monopoly are the parents. Government and law can only punish the criminal. They neither cure nor prevent crime. The only real cure for crime is to abolish its causes, and this the government can never do because it is there to preserve those very causes. Crime can be eliminated only by doing away with the conditions that create it. Government cannot do it.

Anarchism means to do away with those conditions. Crimes resulting from government, from its oppression and injustice, from inequality and poverty, will disappear under Anarchy. These constitute by far the greatest percentage of crime.

Certain other crimes will persist for some time, such as those resulting from jealousy, passion, and from the spirit of coercion and violence which dominates the world today. But these, the offspring of authority and possession, will gradually disappear under wholesome conditions with the passing away of the atmosphere that cultivated them.

Anarchy will therefore neither breed crime nor offer any soil for its thriving. Occasional anti-social acts will be looked upon as survivals of former diseased conditions and attitudes, and will be treated as an unhealthy state of mind rather than as crime.

Anarchy would begin by feeding the "criminal" and securing him work instead of first watching him, arresting, trying, and imprisoning him, and finally ending by feeding him and the many others who have to watch and feed him. Surely even this example shows how much more sensible and simpler life would be under Anarchism than now.

The truth is, present life is impractical, complex and confused, and not satisfactory from any point of view. That is why there is so much misery and discontent. The worker is not satisfied; nor is the master happy in his constant anxiety over "bad times" involving loss of property and power. The specter of fear for tomorrow dogs the steps of poor and rich alike.

Certainly the worker has nothing to lose by a change from government and capitalism to a condition of no government, of Anarchy.

The middle classes are almost as uncertain of their existence as the workers. They are dependent upon the good will of the manufacturer and wholesaler, of the large combines of industry and capital, and they are always in danger of bankruptcy and ruin.

Even the big capitalist has little to lose by the changing of the present day system to one of Anarchy, for under the latter everyone would be assured of his living and comfort; the fear of competition would be eliminated with the abolition of private ownership. Every one would have full and unhindered opportunity to live and enjoy his life to the utmost of his capacity.

Add to this the consciousness of peace and harmony; the feeling that comes with freedom from financial or material worries; the realization that you are in a friendly world with no envy or business rivalry to disturb your mind; in a world of brothers, in an atmosphere of liberty and general welfare.

It is almost impossible to conceive of the wonderful opportunities which would open up to man in a society of Communist Anarchism. The scientist could fully devote himself to his beloved pursuits, without being harassed about his daily bread. The inventor would find every facility at his disposal to benefit humanity by his discoveries and inventions. The writer, the poet, the artist—all would rise on the wings of liberty and social harmony to greater heights of attainment.

Only then would justice and right come into their own. Do not underestimate the role of these sentiments in the life of man or nation. We do not live by bread alone. True existence is not possible without opportunity to satisfy our physical needs. But the gratification of these by no means constitutes all of life. Our present system of civilization has, by disinheriting millions, made the belly the center of the universe, so to speak. But in a sensible society, with plenty for all, the matter of mere existence, the security of a livelihood would be considered self-evident and free as the air is for all. The feelings of human sympathy, of justice and right would have a chance to develop, to be satisfied, to broaden and grow. Even today the sense of justice and fair play is still alive in the heart of man, in spite of centuries of repression and perversion. It has not been exterminated, it cannot be exterminated because it is inborn, innate in man, an instinct as strong as that of self-preservation, and just as vital to our happiness. For not all the misery we have in the world today comes from the lack of material welfare. Man can better stand starvation than the consciousness of injustice. The consciousness that you are treated unjustly will rouse you to protest and rebellion just as quickly as hunger, perhaps even quicker. Hunger may be the immediate cause of every rebellion or uprising, but beneath it is the slumbering antagonism and hatred of the masses against those at whose hands they are suffering injustice and wrong. The truth is that right and justice play a far more important role in our lives than most people are aware of. Those who would deny this know as little of human nature as of history. In everyday life you constantly see people grow indignant at what they consider to be an injustice. "That isn't right," is the instinctive protest of man when he feels wrong done. Of course, every one's conception of wrong and right depends on his traditions, environment and bringing up. But whatever his conception, his natural impulse is to resent what he thinks wrong and unjust.

Historically the same holds true. More rebellions and wars have been fought for ideas of right and wrong than because of material reasons. Marxists may object that our views of right and wrong are themselves formed by economic conditions, but that in no way alters the fact that the sense of justice and right has at all times inspired people to heroism and self-sacrifice in behalf of ideals.

The Christs and the Buddhas of all ages were not prompted by material considerations but by their devotion to justice and right. The pioneers in every human endeavor have suffered calumny, persecution, even death, not for motives of personal aggrandizement but because of their faith in the justice of their cause. The John Husses, the Luthers, Brunos, Savonarolas, Gallileos and numerous other religious and social idealists fought and died championing the cause of right as they saw it. Similarly in paths of science, philosophy, art, poetry, and education men from the time of Socrates to modern days have devoted their lives to the service of truth and justice. In the field of political and social advancement, beginning with Moses and Spartacus, the noblest of humanity have consecrated themselves to ideals of liberty and equality. Nor is this compelling power of idealism limited only to exceptional individuals. The masses have always been inspired by it. The American War of Independence, for instance, began with popular resentment in the Colonies against the injustice of taxation without representation. The Crusades continued for two hundred years in an effort to secure the Holy Land for the Christians. This religious ideal inspired six million of men, even armies of children, to face untold hardships, pestilence, and death in the name of right and justice. Even the late World War, capitalistic as it was in cause and result, was fought by millions of men in the fond belief that it was being waged for a just cause, for democracy and the termination of all wars.

So all through history, past and modern, the sense of right and justice has inspired man, individually and collectively, to deeds of self-sacrifice and devotion, and raised him far above the mean drabness of his everyday existence. It is tragic, of course, that this idealism expressed itself in acts of persecution, violence, and slaughter. It was the viciousness and self-seeking interests of kings, priests, and masters; ignorance and fanaticism determined those forms. But the spirit that filled them was that of right and justice. All past experience proves that this spirit is ever alive and that it is a powerful and dominant factor in the whole scale of human life.

The conditions of our present-day existence weaken and vitiate this noblest trait of man, pervert its manifestation, and turn it into channels of intolerance, persecution, hatred, and strife. But once man is freed from the corrupting influences of material interests, lifted out of ignorance and class antagonism, his innate spirit of right and justice would find new forms of expression, forms that would tend toward greater brotherhood and good will, toward individual peace and social harmony.

Only under Anarchy could this spirit come into its full development. Liberated from the degrading and brutalizing struggle for our daily bread, all sharing in labor and well-being, the best qualities of man's heart and mind would have opportunity for growth and beneficial application. Man would indeed become the noble work of nature that he has till now envisioned himself only in his dreams.

It is for these reasons that Anarchy is the ideal not only of some particular element or class, but of all humanity, because it would benefit, in the largest sense, all of us. For Anarchism is the formulation of a universal and perennial desire of mankind.

Every man and woman, therefore, should be vitally interested in helping to bring Anarchy about. They would surely do so if they but understood the beauty and justice of such a new life. Every human being who is not devoid of feeling and common sense is inclined to Anarchism. Every one who suffers from wrong and injustice, from the evil, corruption, and filth of our present day life, is instinctively sympathetic to Anarchy. Every one whose heart is not dead to kindness, compassion, and fellow-sympathy must be interested in furthering it. Every one who has to endure poverty and misery, tyranny and oppression should welcome the coming of Anarchy. Every liberty and justice-loving man and woman should help realize it.

And foremost and most vitally of all the subjected and submerged of the world must be interested in it. Those who build palaces and live in hovels; who set the table of life but are not permitted to partake of the repast; who create the wealth of the world and are disinherited; who fill life with joy and sunshine, and themselves remain scorned in the depths of darkness; the Samson of life shorn of his strength by the hand of fear and ignorance; the helpless Giant of Labor, the proletariat of brain and brawn, the industrial and agrarian masses—these should most gladly embrace Anarchy.

It is to them that Anarchism makes the strongest appeal; it is they who, first and foremost, must work for the new day that is to give them back their inheritance and bring liberty and well-being, joy and sunshine to the whole of mankind.

"A splendid thing," you remark; "but will it work? And how shall we attain it?"

CHAPTER XXII
WILL COMMUNIST ANARCHISM WORK?

As we have seen in the preceding chapter, no life can be free and secure, harmonious and satisfactory unless it is built on principles of justice and fair play. The first requirement of justice is equal liberty and opportunity.

Under government and exploitation there can be neither equal liberty nor equal opportunity—hence all the evils and troubles of present day society.

Communist Anarchism is based on the understanding of this incontrovertible truth. It is founded on the principle of non-invasiveness and non-coercion; in other words, on liberty and opportunity.

Life on such a basis fully satisfies the demands of justice. You are to be entirely free, and everybody else is to enjoy equal liberty, which means that no one has a right to compel or force another, for coercion of any kind is interference with your liberty.

Similarly equal opportunity is the heritage of all. Monopoly and the private ownership of the means of existence are therefore eliminated as an abridgement of the equal opportunity of all.

If we keep in mind this simple principle of equal liberty and opportunity, we shall be able to solve the questions involved in building a society of Communist Anarchism.

Politically, then, man will recognize no authority which can force or coerce him. Government will be abolished.

Economically he will permit no exclusive possession of the sources of life in order to preserve his opportunity of free access.

Monopoly of land, private ownership of the machinery of production, distribution, and communication can therefore not be tolerated under Anarchy. Opportunity to use what every one needs in order to live must be free to all.

In a nutshell, then, the meaning of Communist Anarchism is this: the abolition of government, of coercive authority and all its agencies, and joint ownership—which means free and equal participation in the general work and welfare.

"You said that Anarchy will secure economic equality," remarks your friend. "Does that mean equal pay for all?"

It does. Or, what amounts to the same, equal participation in the public welfare. As we already know, labor is social. No man can create anything all by himself, by his own efforts. Now, then, if labor is social, it stands to reason that the results of it, the wealth produced, must also be social, belong to the collectivity. No person can therefore justly lay claim to the exclusive ownership of the social wealth. It is to be enjoyed by all alike.

"But why not give each according to the value of his work?" you ask.

Because there is no way by which value can be measured. That is the difference between value and price. Value is what a thing is worth, while price is what it can be sold or bought for in the market. What a thing is worth no one really can tell. Political economists generally claim that the value of a commodity is the amount of labor required to produce it, of "socially necessary labor," as Marx says. But evidently it is not a just standard of measurement. Suppose the carpenter worked three hours to make a kitchen chair, while the surgeon took only half an hour to perform an operation that saved your life. If the amount of labor used determines value, then the chair is worth more than your life. Obvious nonsense, of course. Even if you should count in the years of study and practice the surgeon needed to make him capable of performing the operation, how are you going to decide what "an hour of operating" is worth? The carpenter and mason also had to be trained before they could do their work properly, but you don't figure in those years of apprenticeship when you contract for some work with them. Besides, there is also to be considered the particular ability and aptitude that every worker, writer, artist or physician must exercise in his labors. That is a purely individual, personal factor. How are you going to estimate its value?

That is why value cannot be determined. The same thing may be worth a lot to one person while it is worth nothing or very little to another. It may be worth much or little even to the same person, at different times. A diamond, painting, or a book may be worth a great deal to one man very little to another. A loaf of bread will be worth a great deal to you when you are hungry, and much less when you are not. Therefore the real value of a thing cannot be ascertained; it is an unknown quantity.

But the price is easily found out. If there are five loaves of bread to be had and ten persons want to get a loaf each, the price of bread will rise. If there are ten loaves and only five buyers, then it will fall. Price depends on supply and demand.

The exchange of commodities by means of prices leads to profit making, to taking advantage and exploitation; in short, to some form of capitalism. If you do away with profits, you cannot have any price system, nor any system of wages or payment. That means that exchange must be according to value. But as value is uncertain or not ascertainable, exchange must consequently be free, without "equal" value, since such does not exist. In other words, labor and its products must be exchanged without price, without profit, freely, according to necessity. This logically leads to ownership in common and to joint use. Which is a sensible, just, and equitable system, and is known as Communism.

"But is it just that all should share alike?" you demand. "The man of brains and the dullard, the efficient and the inefficient, all the same? Should there be no distinction, no special recognition for those of ability?"

Let me in turn ask you, my friend, shall we punish the man whom nature has not endowed as generously as his stronger or more talented neighbor? Shall we add injustice to the handicap nature has put upon him? All we can reasonably expect from any man is that he do his best— can any one do more? And if John's best is not as good as his brother Jim's, it is his misfortune, but in no case a fault to be punished.

There is nothing more dangerous than discrimination. The moment you begin discriminating against the less capable, you establish conditions that breed dissatisfaction and resentment: you invite envy, discord, and strife. You would think it brutal to withhold from the less capable the air or water they need. Should not the same principle apply to the other wants of man? After all, the matter of food, clothing, and shelter is the smallest item in the world's economy.

The surest way to get one to do his best is not by discriminating against him, but by treating him on an equal footing with others. That is the most effective encouragement and stimulus. It is just and human.

"But what will you do with the lazy man, the man who does not want to work?" inquires your friend.

That is an interesting question, and you will probably be very much surprised when I say that there is really no such thing as laziness. What we call a lazy man is generally a square man in a round hole. That is, the right man in the wrong place. And you will always find that when a fellow is in the wrong place, he will be inefficient or shiftless. For so-called laziness and a good deal of inefficiency are merely unfitness, misplacement. If you are compelled to do the thing you are unfitted for by your inclinations or temperament, you will be inefficient at it; if you are forced to do work you are not interested in, you will be lazy at it.

Every one who has managed affairs in which large numbers of men were employed can substantiate this. Life in prison is a particularly convincing proof of the truth of it—and, after all, present day existence for most people is but that of a larger jail. Every prison warden will tell you that inmates put to tasks for which they have no ability or interest are always lazy and subject to continuous punishment. But as soon as these "refractory convicts" are assigned to work that appeals to their leanings, they become "model men," as the jailers term them.

Russia has also signally demonstrated the verity of it. It has shown how little we know of human potentialities and of the effect of environment upon them—how we mistake wrong conditions for bad conduct. Russian refugees, leading a miserable and insignificant life in foreign lands, on returning home and finding in the Revolution a proper field for their activities, have accomplished most wonderful work in their right sphere, have developed into brilliant organizers, builders of railroads and creators of industry. Among the Russian names best known abroad today are those of men considered shiftless and inefficient under conditions where their ability and energies could not find proper application.

That is human nature: efficiency in a certain direction means inclination and capability for it; industry and application signify interest. That is why there is so much inefficiency and laziness in the world today. For who indeed is nowadays in his right place? Who works at what he really likes and is interested in?

Under present conditions there is little choice given the average man to devote himself to the tasks that appeal to his leanings and preferences. The accident of your birth and social station generally predetermines your trade or profession. The son of the financier does not, as a rule, become a woodchopper, though he may be more fit to handle logs than bank accounts. The middle classes send their children to colleges which turn them into doctors, lawyers, or engineers. But if your parents were workers who could not afford to let you study, the chances are that you will take any job which is offered you, or enter some trade that happens to afford you an apprenticeship. Your particular situation will decide your work or profession, not your natural preferences, inclinations, or abilities. Is it any wonder, then, that most people, the overwhelming majority, in fact, are misplaced? Ask the first hundred men you meet whether they would have selected the work they are doing, or whether they would continue in it, if they were free to choose, and ninety-nine of them will admit that they would prefer some other occupation. Necessity and material advantages, or the hope of them, keep most people in the wrong place.

It stands to reason that a person can give the best of himself only when his interest is in his work, when he feels a natural attraction to it, when he likes it. Then he will be industrious and efficient. The things the craftsman produced in the days before modern capitalism were objects of joy and beauty, because the artisan loved his work. Can you expect the modern drudge in the ugly huge factory to make beautiful things? He is part of the machine, a cog in the soulless industry, his labor mechanical, forced. Add to this his feeling that he is not working for himself but for the benefit of some one else, and that he hates his job or at best has no interest in it except that it secures his weekly wage. The result is shirking, inefficiency, laziness.

The need of activity is one of the most fundamental urges of man. Watch the child and see how strong is his instinct for action, for movement, for doing something. Strong and continuous. It is the same with the healthy man. His energy and vitality demand expression. Permit him to do the work of his choice, the thing he loves, and his application will know neither weariness nor shirking. You can observe this in the factory worker when he is lucky enough to own a garden or a patch of ground to raise some flowers or vegetables on. Tired from his toil as he is, he enjoys the hardest labor for his own benefit, done from free choice.

Under Anarchism each will have the opportunity of following whatever occupation will appeal to his natural inclinations and aptitude. Work will become a pleasure instead of the deadening drudgery it is today. Laziness will be unknown, and the things created by interest and love will be objects of beauty and joy.

"But can labor ever become a pleasure?" you demand.

Labor is toil today, unpleasant, exhausting, and wearisome. But usually it is not the work itself that is so hard: it is the conditions under which you are compelled to labor that make it so. Particularly the long hours, unsanitary workshops, bad treatment, insufficient pay, and so on. Yet the most unpleasant work could be made lighter by improving the environment. Take gutter cleaning, for instance. It is dirty work and poorly paid for. But suppose, for example, that you should get 20 dollars a day instead of 5 dollars for such work. You will immediately find your job much lighter and pleasanter. The number of applicants for the work would increase at once. Which means that men are not lazy, not afraid of hard and unpleasant labor if it is properly rewarded. But such work is considered menial and is looked down upon. Why is it considered menial? Is it not most useful and absolutely necessary? Would not epidemics sweep our city but for the street and gutter cleaners? Surely, the men who keep our town clean and sanitary are real benefactors, more vital to our health and welfare than the family physician. From the viewpoint of social usefulness the street cleaner is the professional colleague of the doctor: the latter treats us when we are ill, but the former helps us keep well. Yet the physician is looked up to and respected, while the street cleaner is slighted. Why? Is it because the street cleaner's work is dirty? But the surgeon often has much "dirtier" jobs to perform. Then why is the street cleaner scorned? Because he *earns little*.

In our perverse civilization things are valued according to money standards. Persons doing the most useful work are lowest in the social scale when their employment is ill paid. Should something happen, however, that would cause the street cleaner to get 100 dollars a day, while the physician earns 50, the "dirty" street cleaner would immediately rise in estimation and social station, and from the "filthy laborer" he would become the much-sought man of good income.

You see that it is pay, remuneration, *the wage scale*, not worth or merit, that today—under our system of profit—determines the value of work as well as the "worth" of a man. A sensible society—under Anarchist conditions—would have entirely different standards of judging such matters. People will then be appreciated according to their *willingness to be socially useful*.

Can you perceive what great changes such a new attitude would produce? Every one yearns for the respect and admiration of his fellow men; it is a tonic we cannot live without. Even in prison I have seen how the clever pickpocket or safe blower longs for the appreciation of his friends and how hard he tries to earn their good estimate of him. The opinions of our circle rule our behavior. The social atmosphere to a profound degree determines our values and our attitude. Your personal experience will tell you how true this is, and therefore you will not be surprised when I say that in an Anarchist society it will be the most useful and difficult toil that men will seek rather than the lighter job. If you consider this, you will have no more fear of laziness or shirking.

But the hardest and most onerous task could be made easier and cleaner than is the case today. The capitalist employer does not care to spend money, if he can help it, to make the toil of his employees pleasanter and brighter. He will introduce improvements only when he hopes to gain larger profits thereby, but he will not go to extra expense out of purely humanitarian reasons. Though here I must remind you that the more intelligent employers are beginning to see that it pays to improve their factories, make them more sanitary and hygienic, and generally better the conditions of labor. They realize it is a good investment: it results in the increased contentment and consequent greater efficiency of their workers. The principle is sound. Today, of course, it is being exploited for the sole purpose of bigger profits. But under Anarchism it would be applied not for the sake of personal gain, but in the interest of the workers' health, for the lightening of labor. Our progress in mechanics is so great and continually advancing that most of the hard toil could be eliminated by the use of modern machinery and labor-saving devices. In many industries, as in coal mining, for instance, new safety and sanitary appliances are not introduced because of the master's indifference to the welfare of their employees and on account of the expenditure involved. But in a non-profit system technical science would work exclusively with the aim of making labor safer, healthier, lighter, and more pleasant.

"But however light you make work, eight hours a day of it is no pleasure," objects your friend.

You are perfectly right. But did you ever stop to consider why we have to work eight hours a day? Did you know that not so long ago people used to slave twelve and fourteen hours, and that it is still the case in backward countries like China and India?

It can be statistically proven that three hours' work a day, at most, is sufficient to feed, shelter, and clothe the world and supply it not only with necessities but also with all modern comforts of life. The point is that not one man in five today is doing productive work. The entire world is supported by a small number of toilers.

First of all, consider the amount of work done in present day society that would become unnecessary under Anarchist conditions. Take the armies and navies of the world, and how many men would be released for productive effort once war is abolished, as would of course be the case under Anarchy.

In every country today labor supports the millions who contribute nothing to the welfare of the country, who create nothing and perform no useful work whatever. Those millions are only consumers without being producers. In the United States, for instance, out of a population of 120 million there are less than 30 million workers, farmers included.* A similar situation is the rule in every land.

Is it any wonder that labor has to toil long hours, since there are only thirty workers out of every 120 persons? The large business classes with their clerks, assistants, agents, and commercial travelers; the courts with their judges, record keepers, bailiffs, etc.; the legion of attorneys with their staffs; the militia and police forces; the churches and monasteries; the charity institutions and poorhouses; the prisons with their wardens, officers, keepers, and the non-productive convict population; the army of advertisers and their helpers, whose business it is to persuade you to buy what you don't want or need, not to speak of the numerous elements that live luxuriously in entire idleness. All these mount into the millions in every country.

Now, if all those millions would apply themselves to useful labor, would the worker have to drudge eight hours a day? If 30 men have to put in eight hours to perform a certain task, how much less time would it take 120 men to accomplish the same thing? I don't want to burden you with statistics, but there is enough data to prove that less than 3 hours of daily physical effort would be sufficient to do the world's work.

Can you doubt that even the hardest toil would become a pleasure instead of the cursed slavery it is at present, if only three hours a day were required, and that under the most sanitary and hygienic conditions, in an atmosphere of brotherhood and respect for labor?

But it is not difficult to foresee the day when even those short hours would be still further reduced. For we are constantly improving our technical methods, and new labor-saving machinery is being invented all the time. Mechanical progress means less work and greater comforts, as you

* *N.Y. World Almanac*, 1927

can see by comparing life in the United States with that in China or India. In the latter countries they toil long hours to secure the barest necessities of existence, while in America even the average laborer enjoys a much higher standard of living with fewer hours of work. The advance of science and invention signifies more leisure for the pursuits we love.

I have sketched in large, broad outline the possibilities of life under a sensible system where profit is abolished. It is not necessary to go into the minute details of such a social condition: sufficient has been said to show that Communist Anarchism means the greatest material welfare with a life of liberty for each and all.

We can visualize the time when labor will have become pleasant exercise, a joyous application of physical effort to the needs of the world. Man will then look back at our present day and wonder that work could ever have been slavery, and question the sanity of a generation that suffered less than one fifth of its population to earn the bread for the rest by the sweat of their brow while those others idled and waste their time, their health, and the people's wealth. They will wonder that the freest satisfaction of man's needs could have ever been considered as anything but self-evident, or that people naturally seeking the same objects insisted on making life hard and miserable by mutual strife. They will refuse to believe that the whole existence of man was a continuous struggle for food in a world rich with luxuries, a struggle that left the great majority neither time nor strength for the higher quest of the heart and mind.

"But will not life under Anarchy, in economic and social equality mean general leveling?" you ask.

No, my friend, quite the contrary. Because equality does not mean an equal amount but equal *opportunity*. It does not mean, for instance, that if Smith needs five meals a day, Johnson also must have as many. If Johnson wants only three meals while Smith requires five, the quantity each consumes may be unequal, but both men are perfectly equal in the opportunity each has to consume as much as he needs, as much as his particular nature demands.

Do not make the mistake of identifying equality in liberty with the forced equality of the convict camp. True Anarchist equality implies freedom, not quantity. It does not mean that every one must eat, drink, or wear the same things, do the same work, or live in the same manner. Far from it; the very reverse, in fact.

Individual needs and tastes differ, as appetites differ. It is *equal opportunity to satisfy* them that constitutes true equality.

Far from leveling, such equality opens the door for the greatest possible variety of activity and development. For human character is diverse, and only the repression of this diversity results in leveling, in uniformity and sameness. Free opportunity of expressing and acting out your individuality means development of natural dissimilarities and variations.

It is said that no two blades of grass are alike. Much less so are human beings. In the whole wide world no two persons are exactly similar even in physical appearance; still more dissimilar are they in their physiological, mental, and psychical make-up. Yet in spite of this diversity and of a thousand and one differentiations of character we compel people to be alike today. Our life and habits, our behavior and manners, even our thoughts and feelings are pressed into a uniform mold and fashioned into sameness. The spirit of authority, law, written and unwritten, tradition and custom force us into a common groove and make of man a will-less automaton without independence or individuality. This moral and intellectual bondage is more compelling than any physical coercion, more devastating to our manhood and development. All of us are its victims, and only the exceptionally strong succeed in breaking its chains, and that only partly.

The authority of the past and of the present dictates not only our behavior but dominates our very minds and souls, and is continuously at work to stifle every symptom of nonconformity, of independent attitude and unorthodox opinion. The whole weight of social condemnation comes down upon the head of the man or woman who dares defy conventional codes. Ruthless vengeance is wreaked upon the protestant who refuses to follow the beaten track, or upon the heretic who disbelieves in the accepted formulas. In science and art, in literature, poetry, and painting this spirit compels adaptation and adjustment, resulting in imitation of the established and approved, in uniformity and sameness, in stereotype expression. But more terribly still is punished non-conformity in actual life, in our everyday relationships and behavior. The painter and writer may occasionally be forgiven for defiance of custom and precedent because, after all, their rebellion is limited to paper or canvas: it affects only a comparatively small circle. They may be disregarded or labeled cranks who can do little harm, but not so with the man of action who carries his challenge of accepted standards into social life. Not harmless he. He is dangerous by the power of example, by his very presence. His infraction of social canons can be neither ignored nor forgiven. He will be denounced as an enemy of society.

It is for this reason that revolutionary feeling or thought expressed in exotic poetry or masked in high-brow philosophic dissertations may be condoned, may pass the official and unofficial censor, because it is neither accessible to nor understood by the public at large. But give voice to the same dissenting attitude in a popular manner, and immediately you will face the frothing denunciation of all the forces that stand for the preservation of the established.

More vicious and deadening is compulsory compliance than the most virulent poison. Throughout the ages it has been the greatest impediment to man's advance, hedging him in with a thousand prohibitions and taboos, weighting his mind and heart down with outlived canons and codes, thwarting his will with imperatives of thought and feeling, with "thou shalt" and "thou shalt not" of behavior and action. Life, the art of living, has become a dull formula, flat and inert.

Yet so strong is the innate diversity of man's nature that centuries of this stultification have not succeeded in entirely eradicating his originality and uniqueness. True, the great majority have fallen into ruts so deepened by countless feet that they cannot get back to the broad spaces. But some do break away from the beaten track and find the open road where new vistas of beauty and inspiration beckon to heart and spirit. These the world condemns, but little by little it follows their example and lead, and finally it comes up abreast of them. In the meantime those pathfinders have gone much further or died, and then we build monuments to them and glorify the men we have vilified and crucified, as we go on crucifying their brothers in spirit, the pioneers of our own day.

Beneath this spirit of intolerance and persecution is the habit of authority: coercion to conform to dominant standards, compulsion—moral and legal—to be and act as others, according to precedent and rule.

But the general view that conformity is a natural trait is entirely false. On the contrary, given the least chance, unimpeded by the mental habits instilled from the very cradle, man evidences uniqueness and originality. Observe children, for instance, and you will see most varied differentiation in manner and attitude, in mental and psychic expression. You will discover an instinctive tendency to individuality and independence, to non-conformity, manifested in open and secret defiance of the will imposed from the outside, in rebellion against the authority of parent and teacher. The whole training and "education" of the child is a continuous process of stifling and crushing this tendency, the eradication of his distinctive characteristics, of his unlikeness to others, of his personality and originality. Yet even in spite of year-long repression, suppression, and molding, some originality persists in the child when it reaches maturity, which shows how deep are the springs of individuality. Take any two persons, for example, who have witnessed some tragedy, a big fire, let us say, at the same time and place. Each will tell the story in a different manner, each will be original in his way of relating it and in the impression he will produce, because of his naturally different psychology. But talk to the same two persons on some fundamental social matter, about life and government, for instance, and immediately you bear expressed an exactly similar attitude, the accepted view, the dominant mentality.

Why? Because where man is left free to think and feel for himself, unhindered by precept and rule, and not restrained by the fear of being "different" and unorthodox, with the unpleasant consequences it involves, he will be independent and free. But the moment the conversation touches matters within the sphere of our social imperatives, one is in the clutches of the taboos and becomes a copy and a parrot.

Life in freedom, in Anarchy, will do more than liberate man merely from his present political and economic bondage. That will be only the first step, the preliminary to a truly human existence. Far greater and more significant will be the results of such liberty, its effects upon man's mind, upon his personality. The abolition of the coercive external will, and with it of the fear of authority, will loosen the bonds of moral compulsion no less than of economic and physical. Man's spirit will breathe freely, and that mental emancipation will be the birth of a new culture, of a new humanity. Imperatives and taboos will disappear, and man will begin to be himself, to develop and express his individual tendencies and uniqueness. Instead of "thou shalt not," the public conscience will say "thou mayest, taking full responsibility." That will be a training in human dignity and self-reliance, beginning at home and in school, which will produce a new race with a new attitude to life.

The man of the coming day will see and feel existence on an entirely different plane. Living to him will be an art and a joy. He will cease to consider it as a race where every one must try to become as good a runner as the fastest. He will regard leisure as more important than work, and work will fall into its proper, subordinate place as the means to leisure, to the enjoyment of life.

Life will mean the striving for finer cultural values, the penetration of nature's mysteries, the attainment of higher truth. Free to exercise the limitless possibilities of his mind, to pursue his love of knowledge, to apply his inventive genius, to create, and to soar, on the wings of imagination, man will reach his full stature and become man indeed. He will grow and develop according to his nature. He will scorn uniformity, and human diversity will give him increased interest in, and a more satisfying sense of, the richness of being. Life to him will not consist in functioning but in living, and he will attain the greatest kind of freedom man is capable of, freedom in joy.

"That day lies far in the future," you say; "how shall we bring it about?"

Far in the future, maybe; yet perhaps not so far—one cannot tell. At any rate we should always hold our ultimate object in view if we are to remain on the right road. The change I have described will not come over night; nothing ever does. It will be a gradual development, as everything in nature and social life is. But a logical, necessary, and, I dare say, an inevitable development. Inevitable, because the whole trend of man's growth has been in that direction; even if in zigzags, often losing its way, yet always returning to the right path.

How, then, might it be brought about?

CHAPTER XXIII
NON-COMMUNIST ANARCHISTS

Before we proceed let me make a short explanation. I owe it to those Anarchists who are not Communists.

Because you should know that not all Anarchists are Communists: not all of them believe that Communism—social ownership and sharing according to need—would be the best and most just economic arrangement.

I have first explained to you Communist Anarchism because it is, in my estimation, the most desirable and practical form of society. The Communist Anarchists hold that only under Communist conditions could Anarchy prosper, and equal liberty, justice, and well-being be assured to every one without discrimination.

But there are Anarchists who do not believe in Communism. They can be generally classed as Individualists and Mutualists.*

All Anarchists agree on this fundamental position: that government means injustice and oppression, that it is invasive, enslaving, and the greatest hindrance to man's development and growth. They all believe that freedom can exist only in a society where there is no compulsion of any kind. All Anarchists are therefore at one on the basic principle of abolishing government.

They disagree mostly on the following points:

First: the manner in which Anarchy will come about. The Communist Anarchists say that only a social revolution can abolish government and establish Anarchy, while Individualist Anarchists and Mutualists do not believe in revolution. They think that present society will gradually develop out of government into a non-governmental condition.

Second: Individualist Anarchists and Mutualists believe in individual ownership, as against the Communist Anarchists who see in the institution of private property one of the main sources of injustice and inequality, of poverty and misery. The Individualists and Mutualists maintain that liberty means "the right of every one to the product of his toil"; which is true, of course. Liberty does mean that. But the question is not whether one has a right to his product, but whether there is such a thing as an individual

---

* The Mutualists, though not calling themselves Anarchists (probably because the name is so misunderstood), are nevertheless thoroughgoing Anarchists, since they disbelieve in government and political authority of any kind.

product. I have pointed out in preceding chapters that there is no such thing in modern industry: all labor and the products of labor are social. The argument, therefore, about the right of the individual to his product has no practical merit.

I have also shown that exchange of products or commodities cannot be individual or private, unless the profit system is employed. Since the value of a commodity cannot be adequately determined, no barter is equitable. This fact leads, in my opinion, to social ownership and use; that is, to Communism, as the most practicable and just economic system.

But, as stated, Individualist Anarchists and Mutualists disagree with the Communist Anarchists on this point. They assert that the source of economic inequality is monopoly, and they argue that monopoly will disappear with the abolition of government, because it is special privilege—given and protected by government—which makes monopoly possible. Free competition, they claim, would do away with monopoly and its evils.

Individualist Anarchists, followers of Stirner and Tucker, as well as Tolstoyan Anarchists who believe in non-resistance, have no very clear plan of the economic life under Anarchy. The Mutualists, on the other hand, propose a definite new economic system. They believe with their teacher, the French philosopher Proudhon, that mutual banking and credit without interest would be the best economic form of a non-government society. According to their theory, free credit, affording everyone to borrow money without interest, would tend to equalize incomes and reduce profits to a minimum, and would thus eliminate riches as well as poverty. Free credit and compensation in the open market, they say, would result in economic equality, while the abolition of government would secure equal freedom. The social life of the Mutualist community, as well as of the Individualist society, would be based on the sanctity of voluntary agreement, of free contract.

I have given here but the briefest outline of the attitude of Individualist Anarchists and Mutualists. It is not the purpose of this work to treat in detail those Anarchist ideas which the author thinks erroneous and impractical. Being a Communist Anarchist I am interested in submitting to the reader the views that I consider best and soundest. I thought it fair, however, not to leave you in ignorance about the existence of other, non-Communist Anarchist theories. For a closer acquaintance with them I refer you to the appended list of books on Anarchism in general.

PART THREE—

THE SOCIAL REVOLUTION

CHAPTER XXIV
WHY REVOLUTION

Let us return to your question, "How will Anarchy come? Can we help bring it about?"

This is a most important point, because in every problem there are two vital things: first, to know clearly just what you want; second, how to attain it.

We already know what we want. We want social conditions wherein all will be free and where each shall have the fullest opportunity to satisfy his needs and aspirations, on the basis of equal liberty for all. In other words, we are striving for the free cooperative commonwealth of Communist Anarchism.

How will it come about?

We are not prophets, and no one can tell just how a thing will happen. But the world does not exist since yesterday; and man, as a reasonable being, must benefit by the experience of the past.

Now, what is that experience? If you glance over history you will see that the whole life of man has been a struggle for existence. In his primitive state man fought single handed the wild beasts of the forest, and helplessly he faced hunger, cold, darkness, and storm. Because of his ignorance all the forces of nature were his enemies: they worked evil and destruction to him, and he, alone, was powerless to combat them. But little by little man learned to come together with others of his kind; together they sought safety and security. By joint effort they presently began to turn the energies of nature to their service. Mutual help and cooperation gradually multiplied man's strength and ability till he has succeeded in conquering nature, in applying her forces to his use, in chaining the lightning, bridging oceans, and mastering even the air.

Similarly the primitive man's ignorance and fear made life a continuous struggle of man against man, of family against family, of tribe against tribe, until men realized that by getting together, by joint effort and mutual aid, they could accomplish more than by strife and enmity. Modern science shows that even animals had learned that much in the struggle for existence. Certain kinds survived because they quit fighting each other and lived in herds, and in that way were better able to protect themselves against other beasts.* In proportion as men substituted joint

* See *Mutual Aid*, by Peter Kropotkin.

effort and cooperation in place of mutual struggle, they advanced, grew out of barbarism, and became civilized. Families which had formerly fought each other to the death combined and formed one common group; groups joined and became tribes, and tribes federated into nations. The nations still stupidly keep on fighting each other, but gradually they are also learning the same lesson, and now they are beginning to look for a way to stop the international slaughter known as war.

Unfortunately in our social life we are still in a condition of barbarism, destructive and fratricidal: group still combats group, class fights against class. But here also men are beginning to see that it is a senseless and ruinous warfare, that the world is big and rich enough to be enjoyed by all, like the sunshine, and that a united mankind would accomplish more than one divided against itself.

What is called progress is just the realization of this, a step in that direction.

The whole advance of man consists in the striving for greater safety and peace, for more security and welfare. Man's natural impulse is toward mutual help and joint effort, his most instinctive longing is for liberty and joy. These tendencies seek to express and assert themselves in spite of an obstacles and difficulties. The lesson of the entire history of man is that neither hostile natural forces nor human opposition can hold back his onward march. If I were asked to define civilization in a single phrase I should say that it is the triumph of man over the powers of darkness, natural and human. The inimical forces of nature we have conquered, but we still have to fight the dark powers of men.

History fails to show a single important social improvement made without meeting the opposition of the dominant powers—the church, government, and capital. Not a step forward but was achieved by break- ing down the resistance of the masters. Every advance has cost a bitter struggle. It took many long fights to destroy slavery; it required revolts and uprisings to secure the most fundamental rights for the people; it necessitated rebellions and revolutions to abolish feudalism and serfdom. It needed civil warfare to do away with the absolute power of kings and establish democracies, to conquer more freedom and well-being for the masses. There is not a country on earth, not an epoch in history, where any great social evil was eliminated without a bitter struggle with the powers that be. In recent days it again took revolutions to get rid of

Tsardom in Russia, of the Kaiser in Germany, the Sultan in Turkey, the monarchy in China, and so on, in various lands.

There is no record of any government or authority, of any group or class in power having given up its mastery voluntarily. In every instance it required the use of force, or at least the threat of it.

Is it reasonable to assume that authority and wealth will experience a sudden change of heart, and that they will behave differently in the future than they had in the past?

Your common sense will tell you that it is a vain and foolish hope. Government and capital will *fight* to retain power. They do it even today at the least menace to their privileges. They will fight to the death for their existence.

That is why it is no prophecy to foresee that some day it must come to a decisive struggle between the masters of life and the dispossessed classes.

As a matter of fact, that struggle is going on all the time.

There is a continuous warfare between capital and labor. That warfare generally proceeds within so-called legal forms. But even these erupt now and then in violence, as during strikes and lockouts, because the armed fist of government is always at the service of the masters, and that fist gets into action the moment capital feels its profits threatened: then it drops the mask of "mutual interests" and "partnership" with labor and resorts to the final argument of every master, to coercion and force.

It is therefore certain that government and capital will not allow themselves to be quietly abolished if they can help it; nor will they miraculously "disappear" of themselves, as some people pretend to believe. It will require a revolution to get rid of them.

There are those who smile incredulously at the mention of revolution. "Impossible!" they say confidently. So did Louis XVI and Marie Antoinette of France think only a few weeks before they lost their throne together with their heads. So did the nobility at the court of Tsar Nicholas II believe on the very eve of the upheaval that swept them away. "It doesn't look like revolution," the superficial observer argues. But revolutions have a way of breaking out when it "doesn't look like it." The more far-seeing modern capitalists, however, do not seem willing to take any chances. They know that uprisings and revolutions are possible at any time. That is why the great corporations and big employers of labor, particularly in

America, are beginning to introduce new methods calculated to serve as lightning rods against popular disaffection and revolt. They initiate bonuses for their employees, profit sharing, and similar methods designed to make the worker more satisfied and financially interested in the prosperity of his industry. These means may temporarily blind the proletarian to his true interests, but do not believe that the worker will forever remain content with his wage slavery even if his cage be slightly gilded from time to time. Improving material conditions is no insurance against revolution. On the contrary, the satisfaction of our wants creates new needs, gives birth to new desires and aspirations. That is human nature, and that's what makes improvement and progress possible. Labor's discontent is not to be choked down with an extra piece of bread, even if it be buttered. That is why there is more conscious and active revolt in the industrial centers of better-situated Europe than in backward Asia and Africa. The spirit of man forever yearns for greater comfort and freedom, and it is the masses who are the truest bearers of this incentive to further advancement. The hope of modern plutocracy to forestall revolution by throwing a fatter bone to the toiler now and then is illusory and baseless. The new policies of capital may seem to appease labor for a while, but its onward march cannot be stopped by such makeshifts. The abolition of capitalism is inevitable, in spite of all schemes and resistance, and it will be accomplished only by revolution.

A revolution is similar to the struggle of man against nature. Single-handed he is powerless and cannot succeed; by the aid of his fellow men he triumphs over all obstacles.

Can the individual worker accomplish anything against the big corporation? Can a small labor union compel the large employer to grant its demands? The capitalist class is organized in its fight against labor. It stands to reason that a revolution can be fought successfully only when the workers are United, when they are organized throughout the land; when the proletariat of all countries will make a joint effort, for capital is international and the masters always combine against labor in every big issue. That is why, for instance, the plutocracy of the whole world turned against the Russian Revolution. As long as the people of Russia meant only to abolish the Tsar, international capital did not interfere: it did not care what political form Russia would have, as long as the government would be bourgeois and capitalistic. But as soon as the Revolution attempted to do away with the system of capitalism, the governments and the bourgeoisie of every land combined to crush it. They saw in it a menace to the continuance of their own mastery.

Keep that well in mind, my friend. Because there are revolutions and revolutions. Some revolutions change only the governmental form by putting in a new set of rulers in place of the old. These are political revolutions, and as such they often meet with little resistance. But a revolution that aims to abolish the entire system of wage slavery must also do away with the power of one class to oppress another. That is, it is not any more a mere change of rulers, of government, not a political revolution, but one that seeks to alter the whole character of society. That would be a *social* revolution. As such it would have to fight not only government and capitalism, but it would also meet with the opposition of popular ignorance and prejudice, of those who believe in government and capitalism.

How is it then to come about?

CHAPTER XXV
THE IDEA IS THE THING

Did you ever ask yourself how it happens that government and capitalism continue to exist in spite of all the evil and trouble they are causing in the world?

If you did, then your answer must have been that it is because the people support those institutions, and that they support them because they *believe* in them.

That is the crux of the whole matter: present day society rests on the belief of the people that it is good and useful. It is founded on the idea of authority and private ownership. It is *ideas* that maintain conditions. Government and capitalism are the forms in which the popular ideas express themselves. Ideas are the foundation; the institutions are the house built upon it.

A new social structure must have a new foundation, new ideas at its base. However you may change the form of an institution, its character and meaning will remain the same as the foundation on which it is built. Look closely at life and you will perceive the truth of this. There are all kinds and forms of government in the world, but their real nature is the same everywhere, as their effects are the same: it always means authority and obedience.

Now, what makes governments exist? The armies and navies? Yes, but only apparently so. What supports the armies and navies? It is the belief of the people, of the masses, that government is necessary; it is the generally accepted idea of the *need* of government. That is its real and solid foundation. Take that idea or belief away, and no government could last another day.

The same applies to private ownership. The idea that it is right and necessary is the pillar that supports it and gives it security.

Not a single institution exists today but is founded on the popular belief that it is good and beneficial.

Let us take an illustration; the United States, for instance. Ask yourself why revolutionary propaganda has been of so little effect in that country in spite of fifty years of Socialist and Anarchist effort. Is the American worker not exploited more intensely than labor in other countries? Is political corruption as rampant in any other land? Is the capitalist class in America not the most arbitrary and despotic in the world? True, the worker in the United States is better situated materially than in Europe, but is he not at the same time treated with the utmost brutality and terrorism the moment he shows the least dissatisfaction? Yet the American worker remains loyal to the government and is the first to defend it against criticism. He is still the most devoted champion of the "grand and noble institutions of the greatest country on earth." Why? Because he believes that they are *his* institutions, that *he*, as sovereign and free citizen, is running them and that he could change them if he so wished. It is his *faith* in the existing order that constitutes its greatest security against revolution. His faith is stupid and unjustified, and some day it will break down and with it American capitalism and despotism. But as long as that faith persists, American plutocracy is safe against revolution.

As men's minds broaden and develop, as they advance to new ideas and lose faith in their former beliefs, institutions begin to change and are ultimately done away with. The people grow to understand that their former views were false, that they were not truth but prejudice and superstition.

In this way many ideas, once held to be true, have come to be regarded as wrong and evil. Thus the ideas of the divine right of kings, of slavery and serfdom. There was a time when the whole world believed those institutions to be right, just, and unchangeable. In the measure that those superstitions and false beliefs were fought by advanced thinkers, they become discredited and lost their hold upon the people, and finally the institutions that incorporated those ideas were abolished. Highbrows will tell you that they had "outlived their usefulness" and that therefore they "died." But how did they "outlive" their "usefulness"? To whom were they useful, and how did they "die"?

We know already that they were useful only to the master class, and that they were done away with by popular uprisings and revolutions.

Why did not old and effete institutions "disappear" and die off in a peaceful manner?

For two reasons: first, because some people think faster than others. So that it happens that a minority in a given place advance in their views quicker than the rest. The more that minority will become imbued with the new ideas, the more convinced of their truth, and the stronger they will feel themselves, the sooner they will try to realize their ideas; and that is usually before the majority have come to see the new light. So that the minority have to struggle against the majority who still cling to the old views and conditions.

Second, the resistance of those who hold power. It makes no difference whether it is the church, the king, or the kaiser, a democratic government or a dictatorship, a republic or an autocracy—those in authority will fight desperately to retain it as long as they can hope for the least chance of success. And the more aid they get from the slower-thinking majority the better the fight they can put up. Hence the fury of revolt and revolution.

The desperation of the masses, their hatred of those responsible for their misery, and the determination of the lords of life to hold on to their privileges and rule combine to produce the violence of popular uprisings and rebellions.

But blind rebellion without definite object and purpose is not revolution. Revolution is rebellion become conscious of its aims. Revolution is *social* when it strives for a *fundamental* change. As the foundation of life is economics, the social revolution means the reorganization of the industrial, economic life of the country and consequently also of the entire structure of society.

But we have seen that the social structure rests on the basis of *ideas*, which implies that changing the structure presupposes changed ideas. In other words, social ideas must change first before a new social structure can be built.

The social revolution, therefore, is not an accident, not a sudden happening. There is nothing sudden about it, for ideas don't change suddenly. They grow slowly, gradually, like the plant or flower. Hence the social revolution is a result, a development, which means that it is revolutionary. It develops to the point when considerable numbers of people have embraced the new ideas and are determined to put them into practice. When they attempt to do so and meet with opposition, then the slow, quiet, and peaceful social evolution becomes quick, militant, and violent. Evolution becomes revolution.

Bear in mind, then, that evolution and revolution are not two separate and different things. Still less are they opposites, as some people wrongly believe. Revolution is merely the boiling point of evolution.

Because revolution is evolution at its boiling point you cannot "make" a real revolution any more than you can hasten the boiling of a tea kettle.

It is the fire underneath that makes it boil: how quickly it will come to the boiling point will depend on how strong the fire is.

The economic and political conditions of a country are the fire under the evolutionary pot. The worse the oppression, the greater the dissatisfaction of the people, the stronger the flame. This explains why the fires of social revolution swept Russia, the most tyrannous and backward country, instead of America where industrial development has almost reached its highest point—and that in spite of all the learned demonstrations of Karl Marx to the contrary.

We see, then, that revolutions, though they cannot be made, can be hastened by certain factors; namely, by pressure from above: by more intense political and economical oppression; and by pressure from below: by greater enlightenment and agitation. These spread the ideas; they further evolution and thereby also the coming of revolution.

But pressure from above, though hastening revolution, may also cause its failure, because such revolution is apt to break out before the evolutionary process has been sufficiently advanced. Coming prematurely, as it were, it will fizzle out in mere rebellion; that is, without clear, conscious aim and purpose. At best, rebellion can secure only some temporary alleviation; the real causes of the strife, however, remain intact and continue to operate to the same effect, to cause further dissatisfaction and rebellion.

Summing up what I have said about revolution, we must come to the conclusion that

(*1*) a social revolution is one that entirely changes the foundation of society, its political, economic, and social character;

(*2*) such a change must *first* take place in the ideas and opinions of the people, in the minds of men;

(*3*) oppression and misery may hasten revolution, but may *thereby* also turn it into failure, because lack of evolutionary preparation will make real accomplishment impossible;

(*4*) only that revolution can be fundamental, social, and successful which will be the expression of a basic change of ideas and opinions.

From this it obviously follows that the social revolution must be *prepared*. Prepared in the sense of furthering the evolutionary process, of enlightening the people about the evils of present day society and convincing them of the desirability and possibility, of the justice and practicability of a social life based on liberty; prepared, moreover, by making the masses realize very clearly just what they need and how to bring it about.

Such preparation is not only an absolutely necessary preliminary step. Therein lies also the safety of the revolution, the only guarantee of its accomplishing its objects.

It has been the fate of most revolutions—as a result of lack of preparation—to be sidetracked from their main purpose, to be misused and led into blind alleys. Russia is the best recent illustration of it. The February Revolution, which sought to do away with the autocracy, was entirely successful. The people knew exactly what they wanted; namely the abolition of Tsardom. All the machinations of politicians, all the oratory and schemes of the Lvovs and Miliukovs—the "liberal" leaders of those days—could not save the Romanov regime in the face of the intelligent and conscious will of the people. It was this clear understanding of its aims which made the February Revolution a complete success, with, mind you, almost no bloodshed.

Furthermore, neither appeals nor threats by the provisional government could avail against the determination of the people to end the war. The armies left the fronts and thus terminated the matter by their own direct action. The will of a people conscious of their objects always conquers.

It was the will of the people again, their resolute aim to get hold of the soil, which secured for the peasant the land he needed. Similarly the city workers, as repeatedly mentioned before, possessed themselves of the factories and the machinery of production.

So far the Russian Revolution was a complete success. But at the point where the masses lacked the consciousness of definite purpose, defeat began. That is always the moment when politicians and political parties step in to exploit the revolution for their own uses or to experiment their theories upon it. This happened in Russia, as in many previous revolutions. The people fought the good fight—the political parties fought over the spoils to the detriment of the revolution and to the ruin of the people.

This is, then, what took place in Russia. The peasant, having secured the land, did not have the tools and machinery he needed. The worker, having taken possession of the machinery and factories, did not know how to handle them to accomplish his aims. In other words, he did not have the experience necessary to organize production and he could not manage the distribution of the things he was producing.

His own efforts—the worker's, the peasants, the soldier's—had done away with Tsardom, paralyzed the government, stopped the war, and abolished private ownership of land and machinery. For *that* he was prepared by years of revolutionary education and agitation. But for no more than that. And because he was prepared for no more, where his knowledge ceased and definite purpose was lacking, there stepped in the political party and took affairs out of the hands of the masses who had made the revolution. Politics replaced economic reconstruction and thereby sounded the death knell of the social revolution; for people live by bread and economics, not by politics.

Food and supplies are not created by decree of party or government. Legislative edicts don't till the soil; laws can't turn the wheels of industry. Dissatisfaction, strife, and famine came upon the heels of government coercion and dictatorship. Again, as always, politics and authority proved the swamp in which the revolutionary fires became extinguished.

Let us learn this most vital lesson: thorough understanding by the masses of the true aims of revolution means success. Carrying out their conscious will by their own efforts guarantees the right development of the new life. On the other hand, lack of this understanding and of preparation means certain defeat, either at the hands of reaction or by the experimental theories of would be political party friends.

Let us prepare, then.

What and how?

"Prepare for revolution!" exclaims your friend; "is that possible?"

Yes. Not only is it possible but absolutely necessary.

"Do you refer to secret preparations, armed bands, and men to lead the fight?" you ask.

No, my friend, not that at all.

If the social revolution meant only street battles and barricades, then the preparations you have in mind would be the thing. But revolution does not signify that; at least the fighting phase of it is the smallest and least important part.

The truth is, in modern times revolution does not mean barricades any more. These belong to the past. The social revolution is a far different and more essential matter: it involves the reorganization of the entire life of society. You will agree that this is certainly not to be accomplished by mere fighting.

Of course, the obstacles in the path of the social reconstruction have to be removed. That is to say the means of that reconstruction must be secured by the masses. Those means are at present in the hands of government and capitalism, and these will resist every effort to deprive them of their power and possessions. That resistance will involve a fight. But remember that the fight is not the main thing, is not the object, not the revolution. It is only the preface, the preliminary to it.

It is very necessary that you get this straight. Most people have very confused notions about revolution. To them it means just fighting, smashing things, destroying. It is the same as if rolling up your sleeves for work should be considered as the work itself that you have to do. The fighting part of revolution is merely the rolling up of your sleeves. The real, actual task is ahead.

What is that task?

"The destruction of the existing conditions," you reply.

True. But *conditions* are not destroyed by breaking and smashing things. You can't destroy wage slavery by wrecking the machinery in mills and factories, can you? You won't destroy government by setting fire to the White House.

To think of revolution in terms of violence and destruction is to misinterpret and falsify the whole idea of it. In practical application such a conception is bound to lead to disastrous results.

When a great thinker, like the famous Anarchist Bakunin, speaks of revolution as destruction, he has in mind the ideas of authority and obedience which are to be destroyed. It is for this reason that he said that destruction means construction, for to destroy a false belief is indeed most constructive work.

But the average man, and too often even the revolutionist, thoughtlessly talks of revolution as being exclusively destructive in the physical sense of the word. That is a wrong and dangerous view. The sooner we get rid of it the better.

Revolution, and particularly the social revolution, is *not destruction but construction*. This cannot be sufficiently emphasized, and unless we clearly realize it, revolution will remain only destructive and thereby always a failure. Naturally revolution is accompanied by violence, but you might as well say that building a new house in place of an old one is destructive because you have first to tear down the old one. Revolution is the culminating point of a certain evolutionary process: it *begins* with a violent upheaval. It is the rolling up of your sleeves preparatory to *starting the actual work*.

Indeed, consider what the social revolution is to do, what it is to accomplish, and you will perceive that it comes not to destroy but to build.

What, really, is there to destroy?

The wealth of the rich? Nay, that is something we want the whole of society to enjoy.

The land, the fields, the coal mines, the railroads, factories, mills, and shops? These we want not to destroy but to make useful to the entire people.

The telegraphs, telephones, the means of communication and distribution—do we want to destroy them? No, we want them to serve the needs of all.

What, then, is the social revolution to destroy? It is to *take over* things for the general benefit, not to destroy them. It is to reorganize conditions for the public welfare.

Not to destroy is the aim of the revolution, but to reconstruct and rebuild.

It is for this that preparation is needed, because the social revolution is not the Biblical Messiah who is to accomplish his mission by simple edict or order. Revolution works with the hands and brains of men. And these have to understand the objects of the revolution so as to be able to carry them out. They will have to know what they want and how to achieve it. The way to achieve it will be pointed by the objects to be attained. For the end determines the means, just as you have to sow a particular seed to grow the thing you need.

What, then, must the preparation for the social revolution be?

If your object is to secure liberty, you must learn to do without authority and compulsion. If you intend to live in peace and harmony with your fellow men, you and they should cultivate brotherhood and respect for each other. If you want to work together with them for your mutual benefit, you must practice cooperation. The social revolution means much more than the reorganization of conditions only: it means the establishment of new human values and social relationships, a changed attitude of man to man, as of one free and independent to his equal; it means a different spirit in individual and collective life, and that spirit cannot be born overnight. It is a spirit to be cultivated, to be nurtured and reared, as the most delicate flower is, for indeed it is the flower of a new and beautiful existence.

Do not dupe yourself with the silly notion that "things will arrange themselves." Nothing ever arranges itself, least of all in human relations. It is men who do the arranging, and they do it according to their attitude and understanding of things.

New situations and changed conditions make us feel, think, and act in a different manner. But the new conditions themselves come about only as a result of new feelings and ideas. The social revolution is such a new condition. We must learn to think differently before the revolution can come. That alone can bring the revolution.

We must learn to think differently about government and authority, for as long as we think and act as we do today, there will be intolerance, persecution, and oppression, even when organized government is abolished. We must learn to respect the humanity of our fellow man, not to invade him or coerce him, to consider his liberty as sacred as our own; to respect his freedom and his personality, to foreswear compulsion in any form: to understand that the cure for the evils of liberty is more liberty, that liberty is the mother of order.

And furthermore we must learn that equality means equal opportunity, that monopoly is the denial of it, and that only brotherhood secures equality. We can learn this only by freeing ourselves from the false ideas of capitalism and of property, of mine and thine, of the narrow conception of ownership.

By learning this we shall grow into the spirit of true liberty and solidarity, and know that free association is the soul of every achievement. We shall then realize that the social revolution is the work of cooperation, of solidaric purpose, of mutual effort.

Maybe you think this too slow a process, a work that will take too long. Yes, I must admit that it is a difficult task. But ask yourself if it is better to build your new house quickly and badly and have it break down over your head, rather than to do it efficiently, even if it requires longer and harder work.

Remember that the social revolution represents the liberty and welfare of the whole of mankind, that the complete and final emancipation of labor depends upon it. Consider also that if the work is badly done, all the effort and suffering involved in it will be for nothing and perhaps even worse than for nothing, because making a botch job of revolution means putting a new tyranny in place of the old, and new tyrannies, because they are new, have a new lease on life. It means forging new chains which are stronger than the old.

Consider also that the social revolution we have in mind is to accomplish the work that many generations of men have been laboring to achieve, for the whole history of man has been a struggle of liberty against servitude, of social well-being against poverty and wretchedness, of justice against inequity. What we call progress has been a painful but continuous march in the direction of limiting authority and the power of government and increasing the rights and liberties of the individual, of the masses. It has been a struggle that has taken thousands of years. The reason that it took such a long time—and is not ended yet—is because people did not know what the real trouble was: they fought against this and for that, they changed kings and formed new governments, they put out one ruler only to set up another, they drove away a "foreign" oppressor only to suffer the yoke of a native one, they abolished one form of tyranny, such as the Tsar's, and submitted to that of a party dictatorship, and always and ever they shed their blood and heroically sacrificed their lives in the hope of securing liberty and welfare.

But they secured only new masters, because however desperately and nobly they fought, they never touched the *real source* of trouble, the *principle* of *authority* and *government*. They did not know that *that* was the fountainhead of enslavement and oppression, and therefore they never succeeded in gaining liberty.

But now we understand that true liberty is not a matter of changing kings or rulers. We know that the whole system of master and slave must go, that the entire social scheme is wrong, that government and compulsion must be abolished, that the very foundations of authority and monopoly must be uprooted. Do you still think any kind of preparation for such a great task can be too difficult?

Let us, then, fully realize how important it is to prepare for the social revolution, and to prepare for it in the right way.

"But what is the right way?" you demand. "And who is to prepare?"

Who is to prepare? First of all, you and I—those who are interested in the success of the revolution, those who want to help bring it about. And you and I means every man and woman; at least every decent man and woman, every one who hates oppression and loves liberty, every one who cannot endure the misery and injustice which fill the world today.

"The workers, of course," you say.

Yes, the workers. As the worst victims of present institutions, it is to their own interest to abolish them. It has been truly said that "the emancipation of he workers must be accomplished by the workers themselves," for no other social class will do it for them. Yet labor's emancipation means at the same time the redemption of the whole of society, and that is why some people speak of labor's "historic mission" to bring about the better day.

But "mission" is the wrong word. It suggest a duty or task imposed on one from the outside, by some external power. It is a false and misleading conception, essentially a religious, metaphysical sentiment. Indeed, if the emancipation of labor is a "historic mission," then history will see to it that it is carried out no matter what we may think, feel, or do about it. This attitude makes human effort unnecessary, superfluous; because "what must be will be." Such a fatalistic notion is destructive to all initiative and the exercise of one's mind and will.

It is a dangerous and harmful idea. There is no power outside of man which can free him, none which can charge him with any "mission." Neither heaven nor history can do it. History is the story of what has happened. It can teach a lesson but not impose a task. It is not the "mission" but *the interest* of the proletariat to emancipate itself from bondage. If labor does not consciously and actively strive for it, it will never "happen." It is necessary to free ourselves from the stupid and false notion of "historic missions." It is only by growing to a true realization of their present position, by visualizing their possibilities and powers, by learning unity and cooperation, and practicing them, that the masses can attain freedom. In achieving that they will also have liberated the rest of mankind.

Because of this the proletarian struggle is the concern of every one, and all sincere men and women should therefore be at the service of labor in its great task. Indeed, though only the toilers can accomplish the work of emancipation, they need the aid of other social groups. For you must remember that the revolution faces the difficult problem of reorganizing the world and building a new civilization—a work that will require the greatest revolutionary integrity and the intelligent cooperation of all well-meaning and liberty-loving elements. We already know that the social revolution is not a matter of abolishing capitalism only. We might turn out capitalism, as feudalism was got rid of, and still remain slaves as before. Instead of being, as now, the bondmen of private monopoly we might become the servants of State capitalism, as has happened to the people in Russia, for instance, and as conditions are developing in Italy and other lands.

The social revolution, it must never be forgotten, is not to alter one form of subjection for another, but is to do away with everything that can enslave and oppress you.

A political revolution may be carried to a successful issue by a conspirative minority, putting one ruling faction in place of another. But the social revolution is not a mere political change: it is a fundamental economic, ethical, and cultural transformation. A conspirative minority or political party undertaking such a work must meet with the active and passive opposition of the great majority and therefore degenerate into a system of dictatorship and terror.

In the face of a hostile majority the social revolution is doomed to failure from its very beginning. It means, then, that the first preparatory work of the revolution consists in winning over the masses at large in favor of the revolution and its objects, winning them over, at least, to the extent of neutralizing them, of turning them from active enemies to passive sympathizers, so that they may not fight against the revolution even if they do not fight for it.

The actual, positive work of the social revolution must, of course, be carried on by the toilers themselves, by the laboring people. And here let us bear in mind that it is not only the factory hand who belongs to labor but the farm worker as well. Some radicals are inclined to lay too much stress on the industrial proletariat, almost ignoring the existence of the agricultural toiler. Yet what could the factory worker accomplish without the farmer? Agriculture is the *primal* source of life, and the city would starve but for the country. It is idle to compare the industrial worker with the farm laborer or discuss their relative value. Neither can do without the other; both are equally important in the scheme of life and equally so in the revolution and the building of a new society.

It is true that revolution first breaks out in industrial localities rather than in agricultural. This is natural, since these are greater centers of laboring population and therefore also of popular dissatisfaction. But if the industrial proletariat is the advance-guard of revolution, then the farm laborer is its backbone. If the latter is weak or broken, the advance-guard, the revolution itself, is lost.

Therefore, the work of the social revolution lies in the hands of *both* the industrial worker and the farm laborer. Unfortunately it must be admitted that there is too little understanding and almost no friendship or direct cooperation between the two. Worse than that—and no doubt the result of it—there is a certain dislike and antagonism between the proletarians of field and factory. The city man has too little appreciation of the hard and exhausting toil of the farmer. The latter instinctively resents it; moreover, unfamiliar with the strenuous and often dangerous labor of the factory, the farmer is apt to look upon the city worker as an idler. A closer approach and better understanding between the two is absolutely vital. Capitalism thrives not so much on division of work as on the division of the workers. It seeks to incite race against race, the factory hand against the farmer, the laborer against the skilled man, the workers of one country against those of another. The strength of the exploiting class lies in disunited, divided labor. But the social revolution requires the *unity* of the toiling masses, and first of all the cooperation of the factory proletarian with his brother in the field.

A nearer approach between the two is an important step in preparation for the social revolution. Actual contact between them is of prime necessity. Joint councils, exchange of delegates, a system of cooperatives, and other similar methods, would tend to form a closer bond and better understanding between the worker and farmer.

But it is not only the cooperation of the factory proletarian with the farm laborer which is necessary for the revolution. There is another element absolutely needed in its constructive work. It is the trained mind of the professional man.

Do not make the mistake of thinking that the world has been built with hands only. It has also required brains. Similarly does the revolution need *both* the man of brawn and the man of brain. Many people imagine that the manual worker alone can do the entire work of society. It is a false idea, a very grave error that can bring no end of harm. In fact, this conception has worked great evil on previous occasions, and there is good reason to fear that it may defeat the best efforts of the revolution.

The working class consists of the industrial wage earners and the agricultural toilers. But the workers require the services of the professional elements, of the industrial organizer, the electrical and mechanical engineer, the technical specialist, the scientist, inventor, chemist, the educator, doctor, and surgeon. In short, the proletariat absolutely needs the aid of certain professional elements without whose cooperation no productive labor is possible.

Most of those professional men in reality also belong to the proletariat. They are the intellectual proletariat, the proletariat of brain. It is clear that it makes no difference whether one earns his living with his hands or with his head. As a matter of fact, no work is done *only* with the hands or only with the brain. The application of both is required in every kind of effort. The carpenter, for instance, must estimate, measure, and figure in the course of his task: he must use both hand and brain. Similarly the architect must think out his plan before it can be drawn on paper and put to practical use.

"But only labor can produce," your friend objects; "brain work is not productive."

Wrong, my friend. Neither manual labor nor brain work can produce anything *alone*. It requires both, working together, to create something. The bricklayer and mason can't build the factory without the architect's plans, nor can the architect erect a bridge without the iron and steel worker. Neither can produce alone. But both together can accomplish wonders.

Furthermore, do not fall into the error of believing that only productive labor counts. There is much work that is not directly productive, but which is useful and even absolutely necessary to our existence and comfort, and therefore just as important as productive labor.

Take the railroad engineer and conductor, for instance. They are not producers, but they are essential factors in the system of production. Without the railroads and other means of transport and communication we could manage neither production nor distribution.

Production and distribution are the two points of the same life pole. The labor required for the one is as important as that needed for the other.

What I said above applies to numerous phases of human effort which, though themselves not directly productive, play a vital part in the manifold processes of our economic and social life. The man of science, the educator, the physician and surgeon are not productive in the industrial sense of the word. But their work is absolutely necessary to our life and welfare. Civilized society could not exist without them.

It is therefore evident that useful work is equally important whether it be that of brain or of brawn, manual or mental. Nor does it matter whether it is a salary or wages which one receives, whether he is paid much or little, or what his political or other opinions might be.

All the elements that can contribute useful work to the general welfare are needed in the revolution for the building of the new life. No revolution can succeed without their solidaric cooperation, and the sooner we understand this the better. The reconstruction of society involves the reorganization of industry, the proper functioning of production, the management of distribution, and numerous other social, educational and cultural efforts to transform present day wage slavery and servitude into a life of liberty and well-being. Only by working hand in hand will the proletariat of brain and brawn be able to solve those problems.

It is most regrettable that there exists a spirit of unfriendliness, even of enmity, between the manual and intellectual workers. That feeling is rooted in lack of understanding, in prejudice and narrow-mindedness on both sides. It is sad to admit that there is a tendency in certain labor circles, even among some Socialists and Anarchists, to antagonize the workers against the members of the intellectual proletariat. Such an attitude is stupid and criminal, because it can only work evil to the growth and development of the social revolution. It was one of the fatal mistakes of the Bolsheviki during the first phases of the Russian Revolution that they deliberately set the wage earners against the professional classes, to such an extent indeed that friendly cooperation became impossible. A direct result of that policy was the breaking down of industry for lack of intelligent direction, as well as the almost total suspension of railroad communication because there was no trained management. Seeing Russia facing economic shipwreck, Lenin decided that the factory worker and farmer alone could not carry on the industrial and agricultural life of the country, and that the aid of the professional elements was necessary. He introduced a new system to induce the technical men to help in the work of reconstruction. But almost too late came the change, for the years of mutual hating and hounding had created such a gulf between the manual worker and his intellectual brother that common understanding and cooperation were made exceptionally difficult. It has taken Russia years of heroic effort to undo, to some extent, the effects of that fratricidal war.

Let us learn this valuable lesson from the Russian experiment.

"But professional men belong to the middle classes," you object, "and they are bourgeois-minded."

True, men of the professions generally have a bourgeois attitude toward things; but are not most workingmen also bourgeois-minded? It merely means that both are steeped in authoritarian and capitalistic prejudices. It is just these that must be eradicated by enlightening and educating the people, be they manual or brain workers. That is the first step in preparation for the social revolution.

But it is not true that professional men, as such, necessarily belong to the middle classes.

The real interests of the so-called intellectuals are with the workers rather than with the masters. To be sure, most of them do not realize that. But no more does the comparatively highly-paid railroad conductor or locomotive engineer feel himself a member of the working class. By his income and attitude he also belongs to the bourgeoisie. But it is not income or feeling that determines to what social class a person belongs. If the street beggar should fancy himself a millionaire, would he thereby be one? What one imagines himself to be does not alter his actual situation. And the actual situation is that whoever has to sell his labor is an employee, a salaried dependent, a wage earner, and as such his true interests are those of employees and he belongs to the working class.

As a matter of fact, the intellectual proletarian is even more subject to his capitalistic master than the man with pick and shovel. The latter can easily change his place of employment. If he does not care to work for a certain boss he can look for another. The intellectual proletarian, on the other hand, is much more dependent on his particular job. His sphere of exertion is more limited. Not skilled in any trade and physically incapable of serving as a day laborer, he is (as a rule) confined to the comparatively narrow field of architecture, engineering, journalism, or similar work. This puts him more at the mercy of his employer and therefore also inclines him to side with the latter as against his more independent fellow worker at the bench.

But whatever the attitude of the salaried and dependent intellectual, he belongs to the proletarian class. Yet it is entirely false to maintain that the intellectuals always side with the masters as against the workers. "Generally they do," I hear some radical fanatic interject. And the workers? Do *they* not, generally, support the masters and the system of capitalism? Could that system continue but for their support? It would be wrong to argue from that, however, that the workers consciously join hands with their exploiters. No more is it true of the intellectuals. If the majority of the latter stand by the ruling class it is because of social ignorance, because they do not understand their own best interests, for all their "intellectuality." Just so the great masses of labor, similarly unaware of their true interests, aid the masters against their fellow workers, sometimes even in the same trade and factory, not to speak of their lack of national and international solidarity. It merely proves that the one as the other, the manual worker no less than the brain proletarian, needs enlightenment.

In justice to the intellectuals let us not forget that their best representatives have always sided with the oppressed. They have advocated liberty and emancipation, and often they were the first to voice the deepest aspirations of the toiling masses. In the struggle for freedom they have frequently fought on the barricades shoulder to shoulder with the workers and died championing their cause.

We need not look far for proof of this. It is a familiar fact that every progressive, radical, and revolutionary movement within the past hundred years has been inspired, mentally and spiritually, by the efforts of the finest element of the intellectual classes. The initiators and organizers of the revolutionary movement in Russia, for instance, dating back a century, were intellectuals, men and women of non-proletarian origin and station. Nor was their love of freedom merely theoretical. Literally thousands of them consecrated their knowledge and experience, and dedicated their lives, to the service of the masses. Not a land exists but where such noble men and women have testified to their solidarity with the disinherited by exposing themselves to the wrath and persecution of their own class and joining hands with the downtrodden. Recent history, as well as the past, is full of such examples. Who were the Garibaldis, the Kossuths, the Liebknechts, Rosa Luxemburgs, the Landauers, the Lenins, and Trotskys but intellectuals of the middle classes who gave themselves to the proletariat? The history of every country and of every revolution shines with their unselfish devotion to liberty and labor.

Let us bear these facts in mind and not be blinded by fanatical prejudice and baseless antagonism. The intellectual has done labor great service in the past. It will depend on the attitude of the workers toward him as to what share he will be able and willing to contribute to the preparation and realization of the social revolution.

CHAPTER XXVII
ORGANIZATION OF LABOR FOR
THE SOCIAL REVOLUTION

Proper preparation, as suggested in the preceding pages, will greatly lighten the task of the social revolution and assure its healthy development and functioning.

Now, what will be the main functions of the revolution?

Every country has its specific conditions, its own psychology, habits, and traditions, and the process of revolution will naturally reflect the peculiarities of every land and its people. But fundamentally all countries are alike in their social (rather anti-social) character; whatever the political forms or economic conditions, they are all built on invasive authority, on monopoly, on the exploitation of labor. The main task of the social revolution is therefore essentially the same everywhere: the abolition of government and of economic inequality, and the socialization of the means of production and distribution.

Production, distribution, and communication are the basic sources of existence; upon them rests the power of coercive authority and capital. Deprived of that power, governors and rulers become just ordinary men, like you and me, common citizens among millions of others. To accomplish that is consequently the most primal and most vital function of the social revolution.

We know that revolution begins with street disturbances and outbreaks: it is the initial phase that involves force and violence. But that is merely the spectacular prologue of the real revolution. The age long misery and indignity suffered by the masses burst into disorder and tumult, the humiliation and injustice meekly borne for decades find vent in acts of fury and destruction. That is inevitable, and it is solely the master class which is responsible for this preliminary character of revolution. For it is even more true socially than individually that "whoever sows the wind will reap the whirlwind": the greater the oppression and wretchedness to which the masses had been made to submit, the fiercer will rage the social storm. All history proves it, but the lords of life have never harkened to its warning voice.

This phase of the revolution is of short duration. It is usually followed by the more conscious, yet still spontaneous, destruction of the citadels of authority, the visible symbols of organized violence and brutality: jails, police stations, and other government buildings are attacked, the prisoners liberated, legal documents destroyed. It is the manifestation of instinctive popular justice. Thus one of the first gestures of the French Revolution was the demolition of the Bastille. Similarly in Russia prisons were stormed and the prisoners released at the very outset of the Revolution.* The wholesome intuition of the people justly sees in prisoners social unfortunates, victims of conditions, and sympathizes with them as such. The masses regard the courts and their records as instruments of class injustice, and these are destroyed at the beginning of the revolution, and quite properly so.

But this stage passes quickly: the people's ire is soon spent. Simultaneously the revolution begins its constructive work.

"Do you really think that reconstruction could start so soon?" you ask.

My friend, it must begin immediately. In fact, the more enlightened the masses have become, the clearer the workers realize their aims, and the better they are prepared to carry them out, the less destructive the revolution will be, and the quicker and more effectively will begin the work of reconstruction.

"Are you not too hopeful?"

No, I don't think so. I am convinced that the social revolution will not "just happen." It will have to be prepared, organized. Yes, indeed, organized—just as a strike is organized. In truth, it will be a strike, the strike of the united workers of an entire country— a *general strike*.

Let us pause and consider this.

How do you imagine a revolution could be fought in these days of armored tanks, poison gas, and military planes? Do you believe that the unarmed masses and their barricades could withstand high-power artillery and bombs thrown upon them from flying machines? Could labor fight the military forces of government and capital?

It's ridiculous on the face of it, isn't it? And no less ridiculous is the suggestion that the workers should form their own regiments, "shock troops," or a "red front," as the Communist parties advise you to do.

* The official liberation of political prisoners in Russia took place subsequently, *after* the revolutionary masses had wrecked prisons in Petrograd, Moscow, and other cities.

Will such proletarian bodies ever be able to stand up against the trained armies of the government and the private troops of capital? Will they have the least chance?

Such a proposition needs only to be stated to be seen in all its impossible folly. It would simply mean sending thousands of workers to certain death.

It is time to have done with this obsolete idea of revolution. Nowadays government and capital are too well organized in a military way for the workers ever to be able to cope with them. It would be criminal to attempt it, insanity even to think of it.

The strength of labor is not on the field of battle. It is in the shop, in the mine and factory. There lies its power that no army in the world can defeat, no human agency conquer.

In other words, the social revolution can take place only by means of the *General Strike*. The General Strike, rightly understood and thoroughly carried out, is the social revolution. Of this the British government became aware much quicker than the workers when the General Strike was declared in England in May, 1926. "It means revolution," the government said, in effect, to the strike leaders. With all their armies and navies the authorities were powerless in the face of the situation. You can shoot people to death but you can't shoot them to work. The labor leaders themselves were frightened of the thought that the General Strike actually implied revolution.

British capital and government won the strike—not by their strength of arms, but because of the lack of intelligence and courage on the part of the labor leaders and because the English workers were not prepared for the consequences of the General Strike. As a matter of fact, the idea was quite new to them. They had never before been interested in it, never studied its significance and potentialities. It is safe to say that a similar situation in France would have developed quite differently, because in that country the toilers have for years been familiar with the General Strike as a revolutionary proletarian weapon.

It is important that we realize that the General Strike is the only possibility of social revolution. In the past the General Strike has been propagated in various countries without sufficient emphasis that its real meaning is revolution, that it is the only practical way to it. It is time for us to learn this, and when we do so the social revolution will cease to be a vague, unknown quantity. It will become an actuality, a definite method and aim, a program whose first step is taking over of the industries by organized labor.

"I understand now why you said that the social revolution means construction rather than destruction," your friend remarks.

I am glad you do. And if you have followed me so far, you will agree that the taking over of industries is not something that can be left to chance, nor can it be carried out in a haphazard manner. It can be accomplished only in a well planned, *systemic*, and organized way. You alone can't do it, nor can I, nor any other man, be he worker, Ford, or the Pope of Rome. There is no man nor any body of men that can manage it except for the *workers themselves*, for it takes the workers to operate the industries. But even the workers can't do it unless they are organized and *organized just for such an undertaking*.

"But I thought you were an Anarchist," interrupts your friend.

I am.

"I've heard that Anarchists don't believe in organization."

I imagine you have, but that's an old argument. Any one who tells you that Anarchists don't believe in organization is talking nonsense. Organization is everything, and everything is organization. The whole of life is organization, conscious or unconscious. Every nation, every family, why, even every individual is an organization or organism. Every part of every living thing is organized in such a manner that the whole works in harmony. Otherwise the different organs could not function properly and life could not exist.

But there is organization and organization. Capitalist society is so badly organized that its various members suffer: just as when you have pain in some part of you, your whole body aches and you are ill.

There is organization that is painful because it is ill and there is organization that is joyous because it means health and strength. An organization is ill or evil when it neglects or suppresses any of its organs or members. In the healthy organism all parts are equally valuable and none is discriminated against. The organization built on compulsion, which coerces and forces, is bad and unhealthy. The libertarian organization, formed voluntarily and in which every member is free and equal, is a sound body and can work well. Such organization is a free union of equal parts. It is the kind of organization the Anarchists believe in.

Such must be the organization of the workers if labor is to have a healthy body, one that can operate effectively.

It means, first of all, that not a single member of the organization or union may with impunity be discriminated against, suppressed or ignored. To do so would be the same as to ignore an aching tooth: you would be sick all over.

In other words, the labor union must be built on the principle of the equal liberty of all its members.

Only when each is a free and independent unit, cooperating with the others from his own choice because of mutual interests, can the whole work successfully and become powerful.

This equality means that it makes no difference what or who the particular worker is: whether he is skilled or unskilled, whether he is mason, carpenter, engineer or day laborer, whether he earn much or little. The interests of all are the same; all belong together, and only by standing together can they accomplish their purpose.

It means that the workers in the factory, mill, or mine must be organized as one body; for it is not a question of what particular jobs they hold, what craft or trade they follow, but what their interests are. And their interests are identical, as against the employer and the system of exploitation.

Consider yourself how foolish and inefficient is the present form of labor organization in which one trade or craft may be on strike while the other branches of the same industry continue at work. Is it not ridiculous that when the street car workers of New York, for instance, quit work, the employees of the subway, the cab and omnibus drivers remain on the job? The main purpose of a strike is to bring about a situation that will compel the employer to give in to the demands of labor. Such a situation can be created only by a complete tie-up of the industry in question, so that a partial strike is merely a waste of labor's time and energy, not to speak of the harmful moral effect of the inevitable defeat.

Think over the strikes in which you yourself have taken part and of others you know of. Did your union ever win a fight unless it was able to compel the employer to give in? But *when* was it able to do so? Only when the boss knew that the workers meant business, that there was no dissent among them, that there was no hesitation and dallying, that they were determined to win, at whatever cost. But particularly when the employer felt himself at the mercy of the union, when he could not operate his factory or mine in the face of the workers' resolute stand, when he could not get scabs or strikebreakers, and when he saw that his interests would suffer more by defying his employees than by granting their demands.

It is clear, then, that you can compel compliance only when you are determined, when your union is strong, when you are well organized, when you are united in such a manner that the boss cannot run his factory against your will. But the employer is usually some big manufacturer or a company that has mills or mines in various places. Suppose it is a coal combine. If it cannot operate its mines in Pennsylvania because of a strike, it will try to make good its losses by continuing mining in Virginia or Colorado and increasing production there. Now, if the miners in those States keep on working while you in Pennsylvania are on strike, the company loses nothing. It may even welcome the strike in order to raise the price of coal on the ground that the supply is short because of your strike. In that way the company not only breaks your strike, but it also influences public opinion against you, because the people foolishly believe that the higher price of coal is really the result of your strike while in fact it is due to the greed of the mine owners. You will lose your strike, and for some time to come you and the workers everywhere will have to pay more for coal, and not only for coal but for all the other necessities of life, because together with the price of coal the general cost of living will go up.

Reflect, then, how stupid is the present union policy to permit the other mines to operate while your mine is on strike. The others remain at work and give financial support to your strike, but don't you see that their aid only helps to break your strike, because they have to keep on working, really scabbing on you, in order to contribute to your strike fund? Can anything be more senseless and criminal?

This holds true of every industry and every strike. Can you wonder that most strikes are lost? That is the case in America as well as in other countries. I have before me the Blue Book just published in England under the title of *Labor Statistics*. The data proves that strikes do not lead to labor victories. The figures for the last eight years are as follows:

Results in Favor of:	Working People	Employers
1920	390	507
1921	152	315
1922	111	222
1923	187	183
1924	163	235
1925	154	189
1926	67	126
1927	61	118

Actually, then, almost 60% of the strikes were lost. Incidentally, consider also the loss of working days resulting from strikes, which means no wages. The total number of workdays lost by English labor in 1912 was 40,890,000, which is almost equal to the lives of 2,000 men, allotting to each 60 years. In 1919 the number of workdays lost was 34,969,000; in 1920, 26,568,000; in 1921, 85,872,000; in 1926, as a result of the general strike, 162,233,000 days. These figures do not include time and wages lost through unemployment.

It doesn't take much arithmetic to see that strikes as at present conducted don't pay, that the labor unions are not the winners in industrial disputes.

This does not mean, however, that strikes serve no purpose. On the contrary, they are of great value: they teach the worker the vital need of cooperation, of standing shoulder to shoulder with his fellows and united fighting in the common cause. Strikes train him in the class struggle and develop his spirit of joint effort, of resistance to the masters, of solidarity and responsibility. In this sense even an unsuccessful strike is not a complete loss. Through it the toilers learn that "an injury to one is the concern of all," the practical wisdom that embodies the deepest meaning of the proletarian struggle. This does not relate only to the daily battle for material betterment, but equally so to everything pertaining to the worker and his existence, and particularly to matters where justice and liberty are involved.

It is one of the most inspiring things to see the masses roused in behalf of social justice, whomever the case at issue may concern. For, indeed, it is the concern of all of us, in the truest and deepest sense. The more labor becomes enlightened and aware of its larger interests, the broader and more universal grow its sympathies, the more world-wide its defense of justice and liberty. It was a manifestation of this understanding when the workers in every country protested against the judicial murder of Sacco and Vanzetti in Massachusetts. Instinctively and consciously the masses throughout the world felt, as did all decent men and women, that it is *their* concern when such a crime is being perpetrated. Unfortunately that protest, as many similar ones, contented itself with mere resolutions. Had organized labor resorted to action, such as a general strike, its demands would not have been ignored, and two of the workers' best friends and noblest of men would not have been sacrificed to the forces of reaction.

Equally important, it would have served as a valuable demonstration of the tremendous power of the proletariat, the power that always conquers when it is unified and resolute. This has been proven on numerous occasions in the past when the determined stand of labor prevented planned legal outrages, as in the case of Haywood, Moyer, and Pettibone, officials of the Western Federation of Miners, whom the coal barons of the state of Idaho had conspired to send to the gallows during the miners' strike of 1905. Again, in 1917, it was the solidarity of the toilers which thwarted the execution of Tom Mooney, in California. The sympathetic attitude of organized labor in America toward Mexico has also till now been an obstacle to the military occupation of that country by the United States government in behalf of the American oil interests. Similarly in Europe united action by the workers has been successful in repeatedly forcing the authorities to grant amnesty to political prisoners. The government of England so feared the expressed sympathy of British labor for the Russian Revolution that it was compelled to pretend neutrality. It did not dare openly to aid the counter-revolution in Russia. When the dock workers refused to load food and ammunition intended for the White armies, the English government resorted to deception. It solemnly assured the workers that the shipments were intended for France. In the course of my work collecting historic material in Russia, in 1920 and 1921, I came into possession of official British documents proving that the shipments had been immediately forwarded from France, by direct orders of the British government, to the counter-revolutionary generals in the North of Russia who had established there the so-called Tchaikovsky-Miller government—this incident—one out of many—demonstrates the wholesome fear the powers that be have of the awakening class-consciousness and solidarity of the international proletariat.

The stronger the workers grow in this spirit the more effective will be their struggle for emancipation. Class-consciousness and solidarity must assume national and international proportions before labor can attain its full strength. Wherever there is injustice, wherever persecution and suppression—be it the subjugation of the Philippines, the invasion of Nicaragua, the enslavement of the toilers in the Congo by Belgian exploiters, the oppression of the masses in Egypt, China, Morocco, or India—it is the business of the workers everywhere to raise their voice against all such outrages and demonstrate their solidarity in the common cause of the despoiled and disinherited throughout the world.

Labor is slowly advancing to this social consciousness: strikes and other sympathetic expressions are a valuable manifestation of this spirit. If the greater number of strikes are lost at present, it is because the proletariat is not yet fully aware of its national and international interests, it is not organized on the right principles, and does not sufficiently realize the need of world-wide cooperation.

Your daily struggles for better conditions would quickly assume a different character if you were organized in such a manner that when your factory or mine goes on strike, the whole industry should quit work; not gradually but at once, all at the same time. Then the employer would be at your mercy, for what could he do when not a wheel turns in the whole industry? He can get enough strikebreakers for one or a few mills, but an entire industry can not be supplied with them, nor would he consider it safe or advisable. Moreover, suspension of work in any one industry would immediately affect a large number of others, because modern industry is interwoven. The situation would become the direct concern of the whole country, the public would become aroused and demand a settlement. (At present, when your single factory strikes, no one cares and you may starve as long as you remain quiet). That settlement would again depend on yourself, on the strength of your organization. When the bosses would see that you know your power and that you are determined, they'd give in quickly enough or seek a compromise. They would be losing millions everyday, the strikers may even sabotage the works and machinery, and the employers would only be too anxious to "settle," while in a strike of one factory or district they usually welcome the situation, knowing as they do that the chances are well against you.

Reflect therefore how important it is *what manner and on what principles your union is built*, and how vital labor solidarity and cooperation are in your everyday struggle for better conditions. In unity is your strength, but that unity is non-existent and impossible as long as you are organized on craft lines instead of by industries.

There is nothing more important and urgent than that you and your fellow workers see to it immediately that you change the form of your organization.

But it is not only the form that must be changed. Your union must become clear about its aims and purposes. The worker should most earnestly consider what he really wants, how he means to achieve it, by what methods. He must learn what his union should be, how it should function, and what it should try to accomplish.

Now, what is the union to accomplish? What should be the aims of a real labor union?

First of all, the purpose of the union is to serve the interests of its members. That is its primary duty. There is no quarrel about that; every workingman understands it. If some refuse to join a labor body it is because they are too ignorant to appreciate its great value, in which case they must be enlightened. But generally they decline to belong to the union because they have no faith or are disappointed in it. Most of those who remain away from the union do so because they hear much boasting about the strength of organized labor while they know, often from bitter experience, that it is defeated in almost every important struggle. "Oh, the union," they say scornfully, "it don't amount to anything." To speak quite truthfully, to a certain extent they are right. They see organized capital proclaim the open shop policy and defeat the unions; they see labor leaders sell out strikes and betray the workers; they see the membership, the rank and file, helpless in the political machinations in and out of the union. To be sure, they don't understand why it is so; but they do see the facts, and they turn against the union.

Some again refuse to have anything to do with the union because they had at one time belonged to it, and they know what an insignificant role the individual member, the average worker, plays in the affairs of the organization. The local leaders, the district and central bodies, the national and international officers, and the chiefs of the American Federation of Labor, in the United States, "run the whole show," they will tell you; "you have nothing to do but vote, and if you object you'll fly out."

Unfortunately they are right. You know how the union is managed. The rank and file have little to say. They have delegated the whole power to the leaders, and these have become the bosses, just as in the larger life of society the people are made to submit to the orders of those who were originally meant to serve them—the government and its agents. Once you do that, the power you have delegated will be used against you and your own interests every time. And then you complain that your leaders "misuse their power." No, my friend, they don't misuse it; they only use it, for it is the *use* of power which is itself the worst misuse.

All this has to be changed if you really want to achieve results. In society it has to be changed by taking political power away from your governors, abolishing it altogether. I have shown that political power means authority, oppression, and tyranny, and that it is not political government that we need but rational management of our collective affairs.

Just so in your union you need sensible administration of your business. We know what tremendous power labor has as the creator of all wealth and the supporter of the world. If properly organized and united, the workers could control the situation, be the masters of it. But the strength of the worker is not in the union meeting-hall; it is in the shop and factory, in the mill and mine. It is *there* that he must organize; there, on the job. There he knows what he wants, what his needs are, and it is there that he must concentrate his efforts and his will. Every shop and factory should have its special committee to attend to the wants and requirements of the men, not leaders, but members of the rank and file, from the bench and furnace, to look after the demands and complaints of their fellow employees. Such a committee, being on the spot and constantly under the direction and supervision of the workers, wields no power: it merely carries out instructions. Its members are recalled at will and others selected in their place, according to the need of the moment and the ability required for the task in hand. It is the workers who decide the matters at issue and carry their decisions out through the shop committees.

That is the character and form of organization that labor needs. Only this form can express its real purpose and will, be its adequate spokesman, and serve its true interests.

These shop and factory committees, combined with similar bodies in other mills and mines, associated locally, regionally, and nationally, would constitute a new type of labor organization which would be the virile voice of toil and its effective agency. It would have the whole weight and energy of the united workers back of it and would represent a power tremendous in its scope and potentialities.

In the daily struggle of the proletariat such an organization would be able to achieve victories about which the conservative union, as at present built, cannot even dream. It would enjoy the respect and confidence of the masses, would attract the unorganized and unite the labor forces on the basis of the equality of all workers and their joint interests and aims. It would face the masters with the whole might of the working class back of it, in a new attitude of consciousness and strength. Only then would labor acquire dignity and the expression of it assume real significance.

Such a union would soon become something more than a mere defender and protector of the worker. It would gain a vital realization of the meaning of unity and consequent power, of labor solidarity. The factory and shop would serve as a training camp to develop the worker's understanding of his proper role in life, to cultivate his self-reliance and independence, teach him mutual help and cooperation, and make him conscious of his responsibility. He will learn to decide and act on his own judgment, not leaving it to leaders or politicians to attend to his affairs and look out for his welfare. It will be he who will determine, together with his fellows at the bench, what they want and what methods will best serve their aims, and his committee on the spot would merely carry out instructions. The shop and factory would become the worker's school and college. There he will learn his place in society, his function in industry, and his purpose in life. He will mature as a workingman and as a man, and the giant of labor will attain his full stature. He will know and be strong thereby.

Not long will he then be satisfied to remain a wage slave, an employee and dependent on the good will of his master whom his toil supports. He will grow to understand that present economic and social arrangements are wrong and criminal, and he will determine to change them. The shop committee and union will become the field of preparation for a new economic system, for a new social life.

You see, then, how necessary it is that you and I, and every man and woman who has the interests of labor at heart, work toward these objects.

And right here I want to emphasize that it is particularly urgent that the more advanced proletarian, the radical and the revolutionary, reflect upon this more earnestly, for to most of them, even to some Anarchists, this is only a pious wish, a distant hope. They fail to realize the transcending importance of efforts in that direction. Yet it is no mere dream. Large numbers of progressive workingmen are coming to this understanding: the Industrial Workers of the World and the revolutionary Anarchist-syndicalists in every country are devoting themselves to this end. It is the most pressing need of the present. It cannot be stressed too much that *only the right organization of the workers* can accomplish what we are striving for. In it lies the salvation of labor and of the future. Organization from the bottom up, beginning with the shop and factory, on the foundation of the joint interests of the workers everywhere, irrespective of trade, race, or country, by means of mutual effort and united will, alone can solve the labor question and serve the true emancipation of man.

"You were speaking of the workers taking over the industries," your friend reminds me. "How are they going to do it?"

Yes, I was on the subject when you made that remark about organization. But it is well that the matter was discussed, because there is nothing more vital in the problems we are examining.

To return to the taking over of the industries. It means not only taking them over, but the running of them by labor. As concerns the taking over, you must consider that the workers are actually now *in* the industries. The taking over consists in the workers *remaining* where they are, yet remaining not as employees but as the rightful collective possessors.

Grasp this point, my friend. The expropriation of the capitalist class during the social revolution—the taking over of the industries—requires tactics directly the reverse of those you now use in a strike. In the latter you quit work and leave the boss in full possession of the mill, factory, or mine. It is an idiotic proceeding, of course, for you give the master the entire advantage: he can put scabs in your place, and you remain out in the cold.

In expropriating, on the contrary, you *stay* on the job and you put the boss out. He may remain only on equal terms with the rest: a worker among workers.

The labor organizations of a given place take charge of the public utilities, of the means of communication, of production and distribution in their particular locality. That is, the telegraphers, the telephone and electrical workers, the railroad men, and so on, take possession (by means of their revolutionary shop committees) of the workshop, factory, or other establishment. The capitalistic foremen, overseers, and managers are removed from the premises if they resist the change and refuse to cooperate. If willing to participate, they are made to understand that henceforth there are neither masters nor owners: that the factory becomes public property in charge of the union of workers engaged in the industry, all equal partners in the general undertaking.

It is to be expected that the higher officials of large industrial and manufacturing concerns will refuse to cooperate. Thus they eliminate themselves. Their place must be taken by workers previously prepared for the job. That is why I have emphasized the utmost importance of industrial preparation. This is a primal necessity in a situation that will inevitably develop and on it will depend, more than on any other factor, the success of the social revolution. Industrial preparation is the most essential point, for without it the revolution is doomed to collapse.

The engineers and other technical specialists are more likely to join hands with labor when the social revolution comes, particularly if a closer bond and better understanding have in the meantime been established between the manual and mental workers.

Should they refuse and should the workers have failed to prepare themselves industrially and technically, then production would depend on *compelling* the willfully obstinate to cooperate—an experiment tried in the Russian Revolution and proved a complete failure.

The grave mistake of the Bolsheviki in this connection was their hostile treatment of the whole class of the intelligentsia on account of the opposition of some members of it. It was the spirit of intolerance, inherent in fanatical dogma, which caused them to persecute an entire social group because of the fault of a few. This manifested itself in the policy of wholesale vengeance upon the professional elements, the technical specialists, the cooperative organizations, and all cultured persons in general. Most of them, at first friendly to the Revolution, some even enthusiastic in its favor, were alienated by these Bolshevik tactics, and their cooperation was made impossible. As a result of their dictatorial attitude the Communists were led to resort to increased oppression and tyranny till they finally introduced purely martial methods in the industrial life of the country. It was the era of compulsory labor, the militarization of factory and mill, which unavoidably ended in disaster, because forced labor is, by the very nature of coercion, bad and inefficient; moreover, those so compelled react upon the situation by willful sabotage, by systematic delay and spoilage of work, which an intelligent enemy can practice in a way that cannot be detected in due time and which results in greater harm to machinery and product than direct refusal to work. In spite of the most drastic measures against this kind of sabotage, in spite even of the death penalty, the government was powerless to overcome the evil. The placing of a Bolshevik, of a political commissar, over every technician in the more responsible positions did not help matters. It merely created a legion of parasitic officials who, ignorant of industrial matters, only interfered with the work of those friendly to the Revolution and willing to aid, while their unfamiliarity with the task in no way prevented continued sabotage. The system of forced labor finally developed in what practically became economic counter-revolution, and no efforts of the dictatorship could alter the situation. It was this that caused the Bolsheviki to change from compulsory labor to a policy of winning over the specialists and technicians by returning them to authority in the industries and rewarding them with high pay and special emoluments.

It would be stupid and criminal to try again the methods which have so signally failed in the Russian Revolution and which, by their very character, are bound to fail every time, both industrially and morally.

The only solution of this problem is the already suggested preparation and training of the workers in the art of organizing and managing industry, as well as closer contact between the manual and technical men. Every factory, mine, and mill should have its special workers' council, separate from and independent of the shop committee, for the purpose of familiarizing the workers with the various phases of their particular industry, including the sources of raw material, the consecutive processes of manufacture, by-products, and manner of distribution. This industrial council should be permanent, but its membership must rotate in such a manner as to take in practically all the employees of a given factory or mill. To illustrate: suppose the industrial council in a certain establishment consists of five members or of twenty-five, as the case may be, according to the complexity of the industry and the size of the particular factory. The members of the council, after having thoroughly acquainted themselves with their industry, publish what they had learned for the information of their fellow workers, and new council members are chosen to continue the industrial studies. In this manner the whole factory or mill can consecutively acquire the necessary knowledge about the organization and management of their trade and keep step with its development. These councils would serve as industrial colleges where the workers would become familiar with the technique of their industry in all its phases.

At the same time the larger organization, the union, must use every effort to compel capital to permit greater labor participation in the actual management. But this, even at best, can benefit only a small minority of the workers. The plan suggested above, on the other hand, opens the possibility of industrial training to practically every worker in shop, mill, and factory.

It is true, of course, that there are certain kinds of work—such as engineering: civil, electrical, mechanical—which the industrial councils will not be able to acquire by actual practice. But what they will learn of the general processes of industry will be of inestimable value as preparation. For the rest, the closer bond of friendship and cooperation between worker and technician is a paramount necessity.

The taking over of the industries is therefore the first great object of the social revolution. It is to be accomplished by the proletariat, by the part of it organized and prepared for the task. Considerable numbers of workers are already beginning to realize the importance of this and to understand the task before them. But understanding what is necessary to be done is not sufficient. Learning how to do it is the next step. It is up to the organized working class to enter at once upon this preparatory work.

CHAPTER XXVIII
PRINCIPLES AND PRACTICE

The main purpose of the social revolution must be the *immediate* betterment of conditions for the masses. The success of the revolution fundamentally depends on it. This can be achieved only by organizing consumption and production so as to be of real benefit to the populace. In that lies the greatest—in fact, the only—security of the social revolution. It was not the Red army which conquered counter-revolution in Russia: it was the peasants holding on for dear life to the land they had taken during the upheaval. The social revolution must be of material gain to the masses if it is to live and grow. The people at large must be sure of actual advantage from their efforts, or at least entertain the hope of such advantage in the near future. The revolution is doomed if it relies for its existence and its defense on *mechanical* means, such as war and armies. The real safety of the revolution is *organic*; that is, it lies in industry and production.

The object of revolution is to secure greater freedom, to increase the material welfare of the people. The aim of the social revolution, in particular, is to enable the masses by *their own efforts* to bring about conditions of material and social well-being, to rise to higher moral and spiritual levels.

In other words, it is liberty which is to be established by the social revolution. For true liberty is based on economic opportunity. Without it all liberty is a sham and a lie, a mask for exploitation and oppression. In the profoundest sense liberty is the daughter of economic equality.

The main aim of the social revolution is therefore to establish equality on the basis of equal opportunity. The revolutionary reorganization of life must immediately proceed to secure the equality of all, economically, politically, and socially.

That reorganization will depend, first and foremost, on the thorough familiarity of labor with the economic situation of the country: on a complete inventory of the supply, on exact knowledge of the sources of raw material, and on the proper organization of the labor forces for efficient management.

It means that statistics and intelligent workers' associations are vital needs of the revolution, on the day after the upheaval. The entire problem of production and distribution—the life of the revolution—

is based on it. It is obvious, as pointed out before, that this knowledge must be acquired by the workers *before* the revolution if the latter is to accomplish its purposes.

That is why the shop and factory committee, dealt with in the previous chapter, are so important and will play such a decisive role in the revolutionary reconstruction.

For a new society is not born suddenly, any more than a child is. New social life gestates in the body of the old just as new individual life does in the mother's womb. Time and certain processes are required to develop it till it becomes a complete organism capable of functioning. When that stage has been reached birth takes place in agony and pain, socially as individually. Revolution, to use a trite but expressive saying, is the midwife of the new social being. This is true in the most literal sense. Capitalism is the parent of the new society; the shop and factory committee, the union of class-conscious labor and revolutionary aims, is the germ of the new life. In that shop committee and union the worker must acquire the knowledge of how to manage his affairs: in the process he will grow to the perception that social life is a matter of proper organization, of united effort, of solidarity. He will come to understand that it is not the bossing and ruling of men but free association and harmonious working together which accomplish things; that it is not government and laws which produce and create, make the wheat grow and the wheels turn, but concord and cooperation. Experience will teach him to substitute the management of things in place of the government of men. In the daily life and struggles of his shop-committee the worker must learn how to conduct the revolution.

Shop and factory committees, organized locally, by district, region, and state, and federated nationally, will be the bodies best suited to carry on revolutionary production.

Local and State labor councils, federated nationally, will be the form of organization most adapted to manage distribution by means of the people's cooperatives.

These committees, elected by the workers on the job, connect their shop and factory with other shops and factories of the same industry. The Joint Council of an entire industry links that industry with other industries, and thus is formed a federation of labor councils for the entire country.

Cooperative associations are the mediums of exchange between the country and city. The farmers, organized locally and federated regionally and nationally, supply the needs of the cities by means of the cooperatives and receive through the latter in exchange the products of the city industries.

Every revolution is accompanied by a great outburst of popular enthusiasm full of hope and aspiration. It is the spring-board of revolution. This high tide, spontaneous and powerful, opens up the human sources of initiative and activity. The sense of equality liberates the best there is in man and makes him consciously creative. These are the great motors of the social revolution, its moving forces. Their free and unhindered expression signifies the development and deepening of the revolution. Their suppression means decay and death. The revolution is safe, it grows and becomes strong, as long as the masses feel that they are direct participants in it, that they are fashioning their own lives, that *they* are making the revolution, that they *are* the revolution. But the moment their activities are usurped by a political party or are centered in some special organization, revolutionary effort becomes limited to a comparatively small circle from which the large masses are practically excluded. The natural result is that popular enthusiasm is dampened, interest gradually weakens, initiative languishes, creativeness wanes, and the revolution becomes the monopoly of a clique which presently turns dictator.

This is fatal to the revolution. The sole prevention of such a catastrophe lies in the continued active interest of the workers through their everyday participation in all matters pertaining to the revolution. The source of this interest and activity is the shop and the union.

The interest of the masses and their loyalty to the revolution depend furthermore on their feeling that the revolution represents justice and fair play. This explains why revolutions have the power of rousing the people to acts of great heroism and devotion. As already pointed out, the masses instinctively see in revolution the enemy of wrong and iniquity and the harbinger of justice. In this sense revolution is a highly ethical factor and an inspiration. Fundamentally it is only great moral principles which can fire the masses and lift them to spiritual heights.

All popular upheavals have shown this to be true; particularly so the Russian Revolution. It was because of that spirit that the Russian masses so strikingly triumphed over all obstacles in the days of February and October. No opposition could conquer their devotion inspired by a great and noble cause. But the Revolution began to decline when it had become emasculated of its high moral values, when it was denuded of its elements of justice, equality, and liberty. Their loss was the doom of the Revolution.

It cannot be emphasized too strongly how essential spiritual values are to the social revolution. These, and the consciousness of the masses that the revolution also means material betterment, are dynamic influences in the life and growth of the new society. Of the two factors the spiritual values are foremost. The history of previous revolutions proves that the masses were ever willing to suffer and to sacrifice material well-being for the sake of greater liberty and justice. Thus in Russia neither cold nor starvation could induce the peasants and workers to aid counter-revolution. All privation and misery notwithstanding they served heroically the interests of the great cause. It was only when they saw the Revolution monopolized by a political party, the new-won liberties curtailed, a dictatorship established, and injustice and inequality dominant again that they became indifferent to the Revolution, declined to participate in the sham, refused to cooperate, and even turned against it.

To forget ethical values, to introduce practices and methods inconsistent with or opposed to the high moral purposes of the revolution means to invite counter-revolution and disaster.

It is therefore clear that the success of the social revolution primarily depends on liberty and equality. Any deviation from them can only be harmful; indeed, is sure to prove destructive. It follows that *all* the activities of the revolution must be based on freedom and equal rights. This applies to small things as to great. Any acts or methods tending to limit liberty, to create inequality and injustice, can result only in a popular attitude inimical to the revolution and its best interests.

It is from this angle that all the problems of the revolutionary period must be considered and solved. Among those problems the most important are consumption and housing, production and exchange.

CHAPTER XXIX
CONSUMPTION AND EXCHANGE

Let us take up the organization of consumption first, because people have to eat before they can work and produce.

"What do you mean by the organization of consumption?" your friend asks.

"He means rationing, I suppose," you remark.

I do. Of course, when the social revolution has become thoroughly organized and production is functioning normally there will be enough for everybody. But in the first stages of the revolution, during the process of reconstruction, we must take care to supply the people as best we can, and equally, which means rationing.

"The Bolsheviki did not have equal rationing," your friend interrupts; "they had different kinds of rations for different people."

They did, and that was one of the greatest mistakes they made. It was resented by the people as a wrong and it provoked irritation and discontent. The Bolsheviki had one kind of ration for the sailor, another of lower quality and quantity for the soldier, a third for the skilled worker, a fourth for the unskilled one; another ration again for the average citizen, and yet another for the bourgeois. The best rations were for the Bolsheviki, the members of the Party, and special rations for the Communist officials and commissars. At one time they had as many as fourteen different food rations. Your own common sense will tell you that it was all wrong. Was it fair to discriminate against people because they happened to be laborers, mechanics, or intellectuals rather than soldiers or sailors? Such methods were unjust and vicious: they immediately created material inequality and opened the door to misuse of position and opportunity, to speculation, graft, and swindle. They also stimulated counter-revolution, for those indifferent or unfriendly to the Revolution were embittered by the discrimination and therefore became an easy prey to counter-revolutionary influences.

This initial discrimination and the many others which followed were not dictated by the needs of the situation but solely by political party considerations. Having usurped the reins of government and fearing the opposition of the people, the Bolsheviki sought to strengthen themselves in the government seat by currying favor with the sailors, soldiers, and workers. But by these means they succeeded only in creating indignation and antagonizing the masses, for the injustice of the system was too crying and obvious. Furthermore, even the "favored class," the proletariat, felt discriminated against because the soldiers were given better rations. Was the worker not as good as the soldier? Could the soldier fight for the Revolution—the factory man argued—if the worker would not supply him with ammunition? The soldier, in his turn, protested against the sailor getting more. Was he not as valuable as the sailor? And all condemned the special rations and privileges bestowed on the Bolshevik members of the Party, and particularly the comforts and even luxuries enjoyed by the higher officials and commissars, while the masses suffered privation.

Popular resentment of such practices was strikingly expressed by the Kronstadt sailors. It was in the midst of an extremely severe and hungry winter, in March, 1921, that a public mass-meeting of the sailors unanimously resolved voluntarily to give up their extra rations in behalf of the less favored population of Kronstadt, and to equalize the rations in the entire city.* This truly ethical revolutionary action voiced the general feeling against discrimination and favoritism, and gave convincing proof of the deep sense of justice inherent in the masses.

All experience teaches that the just and square thing is at the same time also the most sensible and practical in the long run. This holds equally true of the individual as of collective life. Discrimination and injustice are particularly destructive to revolution, because the very spirit of revolution is born of the hunger for equity and justice.

I have already mentioned that when the social revolution attains the stage where it can produce sufficient for all, then is adopted the Anarchist principle of "to each according to his needs." In the more industrially developed and efficient countries that stage would naturally be reached sooner than in backward lands. But until it is reached, the system of equal sharing, equal distribution per capita, is imperative as the only just method. It goes without saying, of course, that special consideration must be given to the sick and the old, to children, and to women during and after pregnancy, as was also the practice in the Russian Revolution.

"Let me get this straight," you remark. "There is to be equal sharing, you say. Then you won't be able to buy anything?"

* See *The Kronstadt Rebellion*, by the author.

No. There will be no buying or selling. The revolution abolishes private ownership of the means of production, distribution, and with it goes capitalistic business. Personal possession remains only in the things you use. Thus, your watch is your own, but the watch factory belongs to the people. Land, machinery, and all other public utilities will be collective property, neither to be bought nor sold. Actual use will be considered the only title—not to ownership but to possession. The organization of the coal miners, for example, will be in charge of the coal mines, not as owners but as the operating agency. Similarly will the railroad brotherhoods run the railroads, and so on. Collective possession, cooperatively managed in the interests of the community, will take the place of personal ownership privately conducted for profit.

"But if you can't buy anything, then what's the use of money?" you ask.

None whatever; money becomes useless. You can't get anything for it. When the sources of supply, the land, factories, and products become public property, socialized, you can neither buy nor sell. As money is only a medium for such transactions, it loses its usefulness.

"But how will you exchange things?"

Exchange will be free. The coal miners, for instance, will deliver the coal they mined to the public coal yards for the use of the community. In their turn the miners will receive from the community's warehouses the machinery, tools, and the other commodities they need. That means free exchange without the medium of money and without profit, on the basis of requirement and the supply on hand.

"But if there is no machinery or food to be given to miners?"

If there is none, money will not help matters. The miners couldn't feed on banknotes. Consider how such things are managed today. You trade coal for money, and for the money you get food. The free community we are speaking of will exchange the coal for food *directly*, without the medium of money.

"But on what basis? Today you know what a dollar is worth, more or less, but how much coal will you give for a sack of flour?"

You mean, how will value or price be determined. But we have seen already in preceding chapters that there is no real measure of value, and that price depends on supply and demand and varies accordingly. The price of coal rises if there is a scarcity of it; it becomes cheaper if the supply is greater than the demand. To make bigger profits the coal own-ers artificially limit the output, and the same methods obtain throughout the capitalistic system. With the abolition of capitalism no one will be interested in raising the price of coal or limiting its supply. As much coal will be mined as will be necessary to satisfy the need. Similarly will as much food be raised as the country needs. It will be the *requirements* of the community and the supply obtainable which will determine the amount it is to receive. This applies to coal and food as to all other needs of the people.

"But suppose there is not enough of a certain product to go around. What will you do then?"

Then we'll do what is done even in capitalistic society in time of war and scarcity: the people are rationed, with the difference that in the free community rationing will be managed on principles of equality.

"But suppose the farmer refuses to supply the city with his products unless he gets money?"

The farmer, like any one else, wants money only if he can buy with it the things he needs. He will quickly see that money is useless to him. In Russia during the Revolution you could not get a peasant to sell you a pound of flour for a bag full of money. But he was eager to give you a barrel of the finest grain for an old pair of boots. It is plows, spades, rakes, agricultural machinery, and clothing which the farmer wants, not money. For these he will let you have his wheat, barley, and corn. In other words, the city will exchange with the farm the products each requires, on the basis of need.

It has been suggested by some that exchange during the period of revolutionary reconstruction should be based on some definite standard. It is proposed, for example, that every community issue its own money, as is often done in time of revolution; or that a day's work should be considered the unit of value and so-called labor notes serve as medium of exchange. But neither of these proposals is of practical help. Money issued by communities in revolution would quickly depreciate to the point of no value, since such money would have no secure guarantees behind it, without which money is worth nothing. Similarly labor notes would not represent any definite and measurable value as a means of exchange. What would, for instance, an hour's work of the coal miner be worth? Or fifteen minutes' consultation with the physician? Even if all effort should be considered equal in value and an hour's labor be made the unit, could the house painter's hour of work or the surgeon's operation be equitably measured in terms of wheat?

Common sense will solve this problem on the basis of human equality and the right of everyone to life.

"Such a system might work among decent people," you friend objects; "but how about shirkers? Were not the Bolsheviki right in establishing the principle that whoever doesn't work, doesn't eat?'"

No, my friend, you are mistaken. At first sight it may appear as if that was a just and sensible idea. But in reality it proved impractical, not to speak of the injustice and harm it worked all around.

"How so?"

It was impractical because it required an army of officials to keep tab on the people who worked or didn't work. It led to incrimination and recrimination and endless disputes about official decisions. So that in a short time the number of those who didn't work was doubled and even tripled by the effort to force people to work and to guard against their dodging or doing bad work. It was the system of compulsory labor which soon proved such a failure that the Bolsheviki were compelled to give it up.

Moreover, the system caused even greater evils in other directions. Its injustice lay in the fact that you cannot break in to a person's heart or mind and decide which particular physical or mental condition makes it temporarily impossible for him to work. Consider further the precedent you establish by introducing a false principle and thereby rousing the opposition of those who feel it wrong and oppressive and therefore refuse cooperation.

A rational community will find it more practical and beneficial to treat all alike, whether one happens to work at the time or not, rather than create more non-workers to watch those already on hand, or to build prisons for their punishment and support. For if you refuse to feed a man, for whatever cause, you drive him to theft and other crimes—and thus you yourself create the necessity for courts, lawyers, judges, jails, and warders, the upkeep of whom is far more burdensome than to feed the offenders. And these you have to feed, anyhow, even if you put them in prison.

The revolutionary community will depend more on awakening the social consciousness and solidarity of its delinquents than on punishment.

It will rely on the example set by its working members, and it will be right in doing so. For the natural attitude of the industrious man to the shirker is such that the latter will find the social atmosphere so unpleasant that he will prefer to work and enjoy the respect and good will of his fellows rather than to be despised in idleness.

Bear in mind that it is more important, and in the end more practical and useful, to do the square thing rather than to gain a seeming immediate advantage. That is, to do justice is more vital than to punish. For punishment is never just and always harmful to both sides, the punished and the punisher; harmful even more spiritually than physically, and there is no greater harm than that, for it hardens and corrupts you. This is unqualifiedly true of your individual life and with the same force it applies to the collective social existence.

On the foundations of liberty, justice, and equality, as also on understanding and sympathy, must be built every phase of life in the social revolution. Only so it can endure. This applies to the problems of shelter, food, and the security of your district or city, as well as to the defense of the revolution.

As regards housing and local safety Russia has shown the way in the first months of the October Revolution. House committees, chosen by the tenants, and city federations of such committees, take the problem in hand. They gather statistics of the facilities of a given district and of the number of applicants requiring quarters. The latter are assigned according to personal or family need on the basis of equal rights.

Similar house and district committees have charge of the provisioning of the city. Individual application for rations at the distributing centers is a stupendous waste of time and energy. Equally false is the system, practiced in Russia in the first years of the Revolution, of issuing rations in the institutions of one's employment, in shops, factories, and offices. The better and more efficient way, which at the same time insures more equitable distribution and closes the door to favoritism and misuse, is rationing by houses or streets. The authorized house or street committee procures at the local distributing center the provisions, clothing, etc., apportioned to the number of tenants represented by the committee. Equal rationing has the added advantage of eradicating food speculation, the vicious practice which grew to enormous proportions in Russia because of the system of inequality and privilege. Party members or persons with a political pull could freely bring to the cities carloads of flour while some old peasant woman was severely punished for selling a loaf of bread. No wonder speculation flourished, and to such an extent, indeed, that the Bolsheviki had to form special regiments to cope with the evil.* The prisons were filled with offenders; capital punishment was resorted to; but even the most drastic measures of the government failed to stop speculation, for the latter was the direct consequence of the system of discrimination and favoritism. Only equality and freedom of exchange can obviate such evils or at least reduce them to a minimum.

Taking care of the sanitary and kindred needs of street and district by voluntary committees of house and locality affords the best results, since such bodies, themselves tenants of the given district, are personally interested in the health and safety of their families and friends. This system worked much better in Russia than the subsequently established regular police force. The latter consisting mostly of the worst city elements, proved corrupt, brutal, and oppressive.

The hope of material betterment is, as already mentioned, a powerful factor in the forward movement of humanity. But that incentive alone is not sufficient to inspire the masses, to give them the vision of a new and better world, and cause them to face danger and privation for its sake. For that an ideal is needed, an ideal which appeals not only to the stomach but even more to the heart and imagination, which rouses our dormant longing for what is fine and beautiful, for the spiritual and cultural values of life. An ideal, in short, which wakens the inherent social instincts of man, feeds his sympathies and fellow feeling, fires his love of liberty and justice, and imbues even the lowest with nobility of thought and deed, as we frequently witness in the catastrophic events of life. Let a great tragedy happen anywhere—an earthquake, flood, or railroad accident—and the compassion of the whole world goes out to the sufferers. Acts of heroic self-sacrifice, of brave rescue, and of unstinted aid demonstrate the real nature of man and his deep-felt brotherhood and unity.

This is true of mankind in all times, climes, and social strata. The story of Amundsen is a striking illustration of it. After decades of

---

* Those special police and military bodies, known as *zagriaditelniye otriadi*, were most bitterly hated and popularly known as "robber regiments" because of their irresponsible thievery, incredible depravity and cruelty. They were abolished by the introduction of the "new economic policy."

arduous and dangerous work the famous Norwegian explorer resolves to enjoy his remaining years in peaceful literary pursuits. He is announcing his decision at a banquet given in his honor, and almost at the same moment comes the news that the Nobile expedition to the North Pole had met with disaster. On the instant Amundsen renounces all his plans of a quiet life and prepares to fly to the aid of the lost aviators, fully aware of the peril of such an undertaking. Human sympathy and the compelling impulse to help those in distress overcome all considerations of personal safety, and Amundsen sacrifices his life in an attempt to rescue the Nobile party.

Deep in all of us lives the spirit of Amundsen. How many men of science have given up their lives in seeking knowledge by which to benefit their fellow men—how many physicians and nurses have perished in the work of ministering to people stricken with contagious diseases—how many men and women have voluntarily faced certain death in the effort to check an epidemic which was decimating their country or even some foreign land—how many men, common workingmen, miners, sailors, railroad employees—unknown to fame and unsung—have given themselves in the spirit of Amundsen? Their name is legion.

It is *this* human nature, this idealism which must be roused by the social revolution. Without it the revolution cannot be, without it, it cannot live. Without it man is forever doomed to remain a slave and a weakling.

It is the work of the Anarchist, of the revolutionist, of the intelligent, class-conscious proletarian to exemplify and cultivate this spirit and instill it in others. It alone can conquer the powers of evil and darkness, and build a new world of humanity, liberty, and justice.

CHAPTER XXX
PRODUCTION

"What about production," you ask; "how is it to be managed?"

We have already seen what principles must underlie the activities of the revolution if it is to be social and accomplish its aims. The same principles of freedom and voluntary cooperation must also direct the reorganization of the industries.

The first effect of the revolution is reduced production. The general strike, which I have forecast as the starting point of the social revolution, itself constitutes a suspension of industry. The workers lay down their tools, demonstrate in the streets, and thus temporarily stop production.

But life goes on. The essential needs of the people must be satisfied. In that stage the revolution lives on the supplies, already on hand. But to exhaust those supplies would be disastrous. The situation rests in the hands of labor: the immediate resumption of industry is imperative. The organized agricultural and industrial proletariat takes possession of the land, factories, shops, mines and mills. Most energetic application is now the order of the day.

It should be clearly understood that *the social revolution necessitates more intensive production* than under capitalism in order to supply the needs of the large masses who till then had lived in penury. This greater production can be achieved only by the workers having previously prepared themselves for the new situation. Familiarity with the processes of industry, knowledge of the sources of supply, and determination to succeed will accomplish the task. The enthusiasm generated by the revolution, the energies liberated, and the inventiveness stimulated by it must be given full freedom and scope to find creative channels. Revolution always wakens a high degree of responsibility. Together with the new atmosphere of liberty and brotherhood it creates the realization that hard work and severe self-discipline are necessary to bring production up to the requirements of consumption.

On the other hand, the new situation will greatly simplify the present very complex problems of industry. For you must consider that capitalism, because of its competitive character and contradictory financial and commercial interests, involves many intricate and perplexing issues which would be entirely eliminated by the abolition of the conditions of today. Questions of wage scales and selling prices; the requirements of the existing markets and the hunt for new ones; the scarcity of capital for large operations and the heavy interest to be paid on it; new investments, the effects of speculation and monopoly, and a score of related problems which worry the capitalist and make industry such a difficult and cumbersome network today would all disappear. At present these require diverse departments of study and highly trained men to keep unraveling the tangled skein of plutocratic cross purposes, many specialists to calculate the actualities and possibilities of profit and loss, and a large force of aids to help steer the industrial ship between the perilous rocks which beset the chaotic course of capitalist competition, national and international.

All this would be automatically done away with by the socialization of industry and the termination of the competitive system; and thereby the problems of production will be immensely lightened. The knotted complexity of capitalist industry need therefore inspire no undue fear for the future. Those who talk of labor not being equal to manage "modern" industry fail to take into account the factors referred to above. The industrial labyrinth will turn out to be far less formidable on the day of the social reconstruction.

In passing it may be mentioned that all the other phases of life would also be very much simplified as a result of the indicated changes: various present day habits, customs, compulsory and unwholesome modes of living will naturally fall into disuse.

Furthermore it must be considered that the task of increased production would be enormously facilitated by the addition to the ranks of labor of vast numbers whom the altered economic conditions will liberate for work.

Recent statistics show that in 1920 there were in the United States over 41 million persons of both sexes engaged in gainful occupations out of a total population of over 105 million.* Out of those 41 million only 26 million were actually employed in the industries, including transportation and agriculture, the balance of 15 million consisting mostly of persons engaged in trade, of commercial travelers, advertisers, and various other middlemen of the present system. in other words, 15 million persons**

---

* *N.Y. World Almanac*, 1927

** Exclusive of the army, militia, and navy, and the great numbers employed in unnecessary and harmful occupations, such as the building of warships, the manufacture of ammunition and other military equipment, etc.

would be released for useful work by a revolution in the United States. A similar situation, proportionate to population, would develop in other countries.

The greater production necessitated by the social revolution would therefore have an additional army of many million persons at its disposal. The systematic incorporation of those millions into industry and agriculture, aided by modern scientific methods of organization and production, will go a long way toward helping to solve the problems of supply.

Capitalist production is for profit; more labor is used today to sell things than to produce them. The social revolution reorganizes the industries on the basis of the *needs* of the populace. Essential needs come first, naturally. Food, clothing, shelter—these are the primal requirements of man. The first step in this direction is the ascertaining of the available supply of provisions and other commodities. The labor associations in every city and community take this work in hand for the purpose of equitable distribution. Workers Committees in every street and district assume charge cooperating with similar committees in the city and state, and federating their efforts throughout the country by means of general councils of producers and consumers.

Great events and upheavals bring to the fore the most active and energetic elements. The social revolution will crystallize the class-conscious labor ranks. By whatever name they will be known—as industrial unions, revolutionary syndicalist bodies, cooperative associations, leagues of producers and consumers—they will represent the most enlightened and advanced part of labor, the organized workers aware of their aims and how to attain them. It is they who will be the moving spirit of the revolution.

With the aid of industrial machinery and by scientific cultivation of the land freed from monopoly the revolution must first of all supply the elemental wants of society. In farming and gardening intensive cultivation and modern methods have made us practically independent of natural soil quality and climate. To a very considerable extent man now makes his own soil and his own climate, thanks to the achievements of chemistry. Exotic fruits can be raised in the north to be supplied to the warm south, as is being done in France. Science is the wizard who enables man to master all difficulties and overcome all obstacles. The future, liberated from the incubus of the profit system and enriched by the work of the millions of non-producers of today, holds the greatest welfare for society. That future must be the objective point of the social revolution; its motto: bread and well-being for all. First bread, then well-being and luxury. Even luxury, for luxury is a deep-felt need of man, a need of his physical as of his spiritual being.

Intense application to this purpose must be the continuous effort of the revolution: not something to be postponed for a distant day but of immediate practice. The revolution must strive to enable every community to sustain itself, to become materially independent. No country should have to rely on outside help or exploit colonies for its support. That is the way of capitalism. The aim of Anarchism, on the contrary, is material independence, not only for the individual, but for every community.

This means gradual decentralization instead of centralization. Even under capitalism we see the decentralization tendency manifest itself in spite of the essentially centralistic character of the present day industrial system. Countries which were before entirely dependent on foreign manufactures, as Germany in the last quarter of the nineteenth century, later Italy and Japan, and now Hungary, Czechoslovakia, etc., are gradually emancipating themselves industrially, working their own natural resources, building their own factories and mills, and attaining economic independence from other lands. International finance does not welcome this development and tries its utmost to retard its progress, because it is more profitable for the Morgans and Rockefellers to keep such countries as Mexico, China, India, Ireland, or Egypt industrially backward, in order to exploit their natural resources and at the same time be assured of foreign markets for "overproduction" at home. The governments of the great financiers and lords of industry help them secure those foreign natural resources and markets, even at the point of the bayonet. Thus Great Britain by force of arms compels China to permit English opium to poison the Chinese, at a good profit, and exploits every means to dispose in that country of the greater part of its textile products. For the same reason Egypt, India, Ireland, and other dependencies and colonies are not permitted to develop their home industries.

In short, capitalism seeks centralization. But a free country needs decentralization, independence not only political but also industrial, economic.

Russia strikingly illustrates how imperative economic independence is, particularly to the social revolution. For years following the October upheaval the Bolshevik government concentrated its efforts on currying favor with bourgeois governments for "recognition" and inviting foreign capitalists to help exploit the resources of Russia. But capital, afraid to make large investments under the insecure conditions of the dictatorship, failed to respond with any degree of enthusiasm. Meanwhile Russia was approaching economic breakdown. The situation finally compelled the Bolsheviki to understand that the country must depend on its own efforts for maintenance. Russia began to look around for means to help itself; and thereby it acquired greater confidence in its own abilities, learned to exercise self-reliance and initiative, and started to develop its own industries; a slow and painful process, but a wholesome necessity which will ultimately make Russia economically self-supporting and independent.

The social revolution in any given country must from the very first determine to make itself self-supporting. *It must help itself.* This principle of self-help is not to be understood as a lack of solidarity with other lands. On the contrary, mutual aid and cooperation between countries, as among individuals, can exist only on the basis of equality, among equals. *Dependence* is the very reverse of it.

Should the social revolution take place in several countries at the same time—France and Germany, for instance—then joint effort would be a matter of course and would make the task of revolutionary reorganization much easier.

Fortunately, the workers are learning to understand that their cause is international: the organization of labor is now developing beyond national boundaries. It is to be hoped that the time is not far away when the entire proletariat of Europe may combine in a General Strike, which is to be the prelude to the social revolution. That is emphatically a consummation to be striven for with the greatest earnestness. But at the same time the probability is not to be discounted that the revolution may break out in one country sooner than in another—let us say in France earlier than in Germany—and in such a case it would become imperative for France not to wait for possible aid from outside but immediately to exert all her energies to help herself, to supply the most essential needs of her people by her own efforts.

Every country in revolution must seek to achieve agricultural independence no less than political, industrial self-help no less than agricultural.

This process is going on to a certain extent even under capitalism. It should be one of the main objects of the social revolution. Modern methods make it possible. The manufacture of watches and clocks, for example, which was formerly a monopoly of Switzerland, is now carried on in every country. Production of silk, previously limited to France, is among the great industries of various countries today. Italy, without sources of coal or iron, constructs steel-clad ships. Switzerland, no richer, also makes them.

Decentralization will cure society of many evils of the centralized principle. Politically decentralization means freedom; industrially, material independence; socially it implies security and well-being for the small communities; individually it results in manhood and liberty.

Equally important to the social revolution as independence from foreign lands is decentralization within the country itself. Internal decentralization means making the larger regions, even every community, so far as possible, self-supporting. In his very illuminating and suggestive work, *Fields, Factories, and Workshops,* Peter Kropotkin has convincingly shown how a city like Paris even, now almost exclusively commercial, could raise enough food in its own environs to support its population abundantly. By using modern agricultural machinery and intensive cultivation London and New York could subsist upon the products raised in their own immediate vicinity. It is a fact that "our means of obtaining from the soil whatever we want, under *any* climate and upon any *soil,* have lately been improved at such a rate that we cannot foresee yet what is the limit of productivity of a few acres of land. The limit vanishes in proportion to our better study of the subject, and every year makes it vanish further and further from our sight."

When the social revolution begins in any land, its foreign commerce stops: the importation of raw materials and finished products is suspended. The country may even be blockaded by the bourgeois governments, as was the case with Russia. Thus the revolution is *compelled* to become self-supporting and provide for its own wants. Even various parts of the same country may have to face such an eventuality. They would have to produce what they need within their own area, by their own efforts. Only decentralization could solve this problem. The country would have to reorganize its activities in such a manner as to be able to feed itself. It would have to resort to production on a small scale, to home industry, and to intensive agriculture and horticulture. Man's initiative freed by the revolution and his wits sharpened by necessity will rise to the situation.

It must therefore be clearly understood that it would be disastrous to the interests of the revolution to suppress or interfere with the small-scale industries which are even now practiced to such a great extent in various European countries. Numerous articles of everyday use are produced by the peasants of Continental Europe during their leisure winter hours. Those home manufactures total up tremendous figures and fill a great need. It would be most harmful to the revolution to destroy them, as Russia so foolishly did in her mad Bolshevik passion for centralization. When a country in revolution is attacked by foreign governments, when it is blockaded and deprived of imports, when its large-scale industries threaten to break down or the railroads actually do break down, then it is just the small home industries which become the vital nerve of economic life: they alone can feed and save the revolution.

Moreover, such home industries are not only a potent economic factor; they are also of the greatest social value. They serve to cultivate friendly intercourse between the farm and the city, bringing the two into closer and more solidaric contact. In fact, the home industries are themselves an expression of a most wholesome social spirit which from earliest times has manifested itself in village gatherings, in communal efforts, in folk dance and song. This normal and healthy tendency, in its various aspects, should be encouraged and stimulated by the revolution for the greater weal of the community.

The role of industrial decentralization in the revolution is unfortunately too little appreciated. Even in progressive labor ranks there is a dangerous tendency to ignore or minimize its importance. Most people are still in the thralldom of the Marxian dogma that centralization is "more efficient and economical." They close their eyes to the fact that the alleged "economy" is achieved at the cost of the worker's limb and life, that the "efficiency" degrades him to a mere industrial cog, deadens his soul, and kills his body. Furthermore, in a system of centralization the administration of industry becomes constantly merged in fewer hands, producing a powerful bureaucracy of industrial overlords. It would indeed be the sheerest irony if the revolution were to aim at such a result. It would mean the creation of a new master class.

The revolution can accomplish the emancipation of labor only by gradual decentralization, by developing the individual worker into a more conscious and determining factor in the processes of industry, by making him the impulse whence proceeds all industrial and social activity. The deep significance of the social revolution lies in the abolition of the mastery of man over man, putting in its place the management of things. Only thus can be achieved industrial and social freedom.

"Are you sure it would work?" you demand.

I am sure of this: if that will not work, nothing else will. The plan I have outlined is a free communism, a life of voluntary cooperation and equal sharing. There is no other way of securing economic equality which alone is liberty. Any other system must lead back to capitalism.

It is likely, of course, that a country in social revolution may try various economic experiments. A limited capitalism might be introduced in one part of the land or collectivism in another. But collectivism is only another form of the wage system and it would speedily tend to become the capitalism of the present day. For collectivism begins by abolishing private ownership of the means of production and immediately reverses itself by returning to the system of remuneration according to work performed; which means the reintroduction of inequality.

Man learns by doing. The social revolution in different countries and regions will probably try out various methods, and by practical experience learn the best way. The revolution is at the same time the opportunity and justification for it. I am not attempting to prophesy what this or that country is going to do, what particular course it will follow. Nor do I presume to dictate to the future, to prescribe its mode of conduct. My purpose is to suggest, in broad outline, the principles which must animate the revolution, the general lines of action it should follow if it is to accomplish its aim—the reconstruction of society on a foundation of freedom and equality.

We know that previous revolutions for the most part failed of their objects; they degenerated into dictatorship and despotism, and thus re-established the old institutions of oppression and exploitation. We know it from past and recent history. We therefore draw the conclusion that the old way will not do. A new way must be tried in the coming social revolution. What new way? The only one so far known to man: the way of liberty and equality, the way of free communism, of Anarchy.

CHAPTER XXXI
DEFENSE OF THE REVOLUTION

"Suppose your system is tried, would you have any means of defending the revolution?" you ask.

Certainly.

"Even by armed force?"

Yes, if necessary.

"But armed force is organized violence. Didn't you say Anarchism was against it?"

Anarchism is opposed to any interference with your liberty, be it by force and violence or by any other means. It is against all invasion and compulsion. But if any one attacks *you* then it is *he* who is invading you, he who is employing violence against you. You have a right to defend yourself. More than that, it is your duty, as an Anarchist, to protect your liberty, to resist coercion and compulsion. Otherwise you are a slave, not a free man. In other words, the social revolution will attack no one, but it will defend itself against invasion from any quarter.

Besides, you must not confuse the social revolution with Anarchy. Revolution, in some of its stages, is a violent upheaval; Anarchy is a social condition of freedom and peace. The revolution is the *means* of bringing Anarchy about but it is not Anarchy itself. It is to pave the road for Anarchy, to establish conditions which will make a life of liberty possible.

But to achieve its purpose the revolution must be imbued with and directed by the Anarchist spirit and ideas. The end shapes the means, just as the tool you use must be fit to do the work you want to accomplish. That is to say, the social revolution must be Anarchistic in method as in aim.

Revolutionary defense must be in consonance with this spirit. Self-defense excludes all acts of coercion, of persecution or revenge. It is concerned only with repelling attack and depriving the enemy of opportunity to invade you.

"How would you repel foreign invasion?"

By the strength of the revolution. In what does that strength consist? First and foremost, in the support of the people, in the devotion of the industrial and agricultural masses. If they feel that they themselves are making the revolution, that they have become the masters of their lives, that they have gained freedom and are building up their welfare, then in that very sentiment you have the greatest strength of the revolution. The masses fight today for king, capitalist, or president because they believe them worth fighting for. Let them believe in the revolution, and they will defend it to the death.

They will fight for the revolution with heart and soul, as the half-starved working men, women, and even children of Petrograd defended their city, almost with bare hands, against the White army of General Yudenitch. Take that faith away, deprive the people of power by setting up some authority over them, be it a political party or military organization, and you have dealt a fatal blow to the revolution. You will have robbed it of its main source of strength, the masses. You will have made it defenseless.

The armed workers and peasants are the only effective defense of the revolution. By means of their unions and syndicates they must always be on guard against counter-revolutionary attack. The worker in factory and mill, in mine and field, is the soldier of the revolution. He is at his bench and plow or on the battlefield, according to need. But in his factory as in his regiment he is the soul of the revolution, and it is *his* will that decides its fate. In industry the shop committees, in the barracks the soldiers' committees—these are the fountain-head of all revolutionary strength and activity.

It was the *volunteer* Red Guard, made up of toilers, that successfully defended the Russian Revolution in its most critical initial stages. Later on it was again volunteer peasant regiments who defeated the White armies. The regular Red army, organized later, was powerless without the volunteer workers' and peasants' divisions. Siberia was freed from Kolchak and his hordes by such peasant volunteers. In the North of Russia it was also workers' and peasants' detachments that drove out the foreign armies which came to impose the yoke of native reactionaries upon the people.* In the Ukraine the volunteer peasant armies—known as povstantsi—saved the Revolution from numerous counter-revolutionary generals and particularly from Denikin when the latter was already at the very gates of Moscow. It was the revolutionary povstantsi who freed southern Russia from the invading armies of Germany, France, Italy, and Greece, and subsequently also routed the White forces of General Wrangel.

* The Tchaikovsky-Miller government

The military defense of the revolution may demand a supreme command, coordination of activities, discipline, and obedience to orders. But these must proceed from the devotion of the workers and peasants, and must be based on their voluntary cooperation through their own local, regional, and federal organizations. In the matter of defense against foreign attack, as in all other problems of the social revolution, the active interest of the masses, their autonomy and self determination are the best guarantee of success.

Understand well that the only really effective defense of the revolution lies in the attitude of the people. Popular discontent is the worst enemy of the revolution and its greatest danger. We must always bear in mind that the strength of the social revolution is organic, not mechanistic: not in mechanical, military measures lies its might, but in its industry, in its ability to reconstruct life, to establish liberty and justice. Let the people feel that it is indeed their own cause which is at stake, and the last man of them will fight like a lion on its behalf.

The same applies to internal as to external defense. What chance would any White general or counter-revolutionist have if he could not exploit oppression and injustice to incite the people against the revolution? Counter-revolution can feed only on popular discontent. Where the masses are conscious that the revolution and all its activities are in their own hands, that they themselves are managing things and are free to change their methods when they consider it necessary, counter-revolution can find no support and is harmless.

"But would you let counter-revolutionists incite the people if they tried to?"

By all means. Let them talk all they like. To restrain them would serve only to create a persecuted class and thereby enlist popular sympathy for them and their cause. To suppress speech and press is not only a theoretic offense against liberty: it is a direct blow at the very foundations of the revolution. It would, first of all, raise problems where none had existed before. It would introduce methods which must lead to discontent and opposition, to bitterness and strife, to prison, Tcheka, and civil war. It would generate fear and distrust, would hatch conspiracies, and culminate in a reign of terror which has always killed revolutions in the past.

The social revolution must from the very start be based on entirely different principles, on a new conception and attitude. Full freedom is the very breath of its existence; and be it never forgotten that the cure for evil and disorder is *more* liberty, not suppression. Suppression leads only to violence and destruction.

"Will you not defend the revolution then?" your friend demands.

Certainly we will. But not against mere talk, not against an expression of opinion. The revolution must be big enough to welcome even the severest criticism, and profit by it if it is justified. The revolution will defend itself most determinedly against real counter-revolution, against all active enemies, against any attempt to defeat or sabotage it by forcible invasion or violence. That is the right of the revolution and its duty. But it will not persecute the conquered foe, nor wreak vengeance upon an entire social class because of the fault of individual members of it. The sins of the fathers shall not be visited upon their children.

"What will you do with counter-revolutionists?"

Actual combat and armed resistance involve human sacrifices, and the counter-revolutionists who lose their lives under such circumstances suffer the unavoidable consequences of their deeds. But the revolutionary people are not savages. The wounded are not slaughtered nor those taken prisoners executed. Neither is practiced the barbarous system of shooting hostages, as the Bolsheviki did.

"How will you treat counter-revolutionists taken prisoners during an engagement?"

The revolution must find new ways, some sensible method of dealing with them. The old method is to imprison them, support them in idleness, and employ numerous men to guard and punish them. And while the culprit remains in prison, incarceration and brutal treatment still further embitter him against the revolution, strengthen his opposition, and nurse thoughts of vengeance and new conspiracies. The revolution will regard such methods as stupid and detrimental to its best interests. It will try instead by humane treatment to convince the defeated enemy of the error and uselessness of his resistance. It will apply liberty instead of revenge. It will take into consideration that most of the counter-revolutionists are dupes rather than enemies, deluded victims of some individuals seeking power and authority. It will know that they need enlightenment rather than punishment, and that the former will accomplish more than the latter. Even today this perception is gaining ground. The Bolsheviki defeated the Allied armies in Russia more effectively by revolutionary propaganda among the enemy soldiers than by the strength of their artillery. These new methods have been recognized as practical even by the United States government which is making use of them now in its Nicaraguan campaign. American aeroplanes scatter proclamations and appeals to the Nicaraguan people to persuade them to desert Sandino and his cause, and the American army chiefs expect the best results from these tactics. But the Sandino patriots are fighting for home and country against a foreign invader, while counter-revolutionists wage war against their own people. The work of their enlightenment is much simpler and promises better results.

"Do you think that would really be the best way to deal with counter-revolution?"

By all means. Humane treatment and kindness are more effective than cruelty and vengeance. The new attitude in this regard would suggest also a number of other methods of similar character. Various modes of dealing with conspirators and active enemies of the revolution would develop as soon as you begin to practice the new policy. The plan might be developed, for instance, of scattering them, individually or in small groups, over districts removed from the counter-revolutionary influences, among communities of revolutionary spirit and consciousness. Consider also that counter-revolutionists must eat; which means that they would find themselves in a situation that would claim their thoughts and time for other things than the hatching of conspiracies. The defeated counter-revolutionist, left at liberty instead of being imprisoned, would have to seek means of existence. He would not be denied his livelihood, of course, since the revolution would be generous enough to feed even its enemies. But the man in question would have to join some community, secure lodgings, and so forth, in order to enjoy the hospitality of the distributing center. In other words, the counter-revolutionary "prisoners in freedom" would depend on the community and the good will of its members for their means of existence. They would live in its atmosphere and be influenced by its revolutionary environment. Surely they will be safer and more contented than in prison, and presently they would cease to be a danger to the revolution. We have repeatedly seen such examples in Russia, in cases where counter-revolutionists had escaped the Tcheka and settled down in some village or city , where as a result of considerate and decent treatment they became useful members of the community, often more zealous in behalf of the public welfare than the average citizen, while hundreds of their fellow conspirators, who had not been lucky enough to avoid arrest, were busy in prison with thoughts of revenge and new plots.

Various plans of treating such "prisoners in freedom" will no doubt be tried by the revolutionary people. But whatever the methods, they will be more satisfactory than the present system of revenge and punishment, the complete failure of which has been demonstrated throughout human experience. Among the new ways might also be tried that of free colonization. The revolution will offer its enemies an opportunity to settle in some part of the country and there establish the form of social life that will suit them best. It is no vain speculation to foresee that it would not be long before most of them would prefer the brotherhood and liberty of the revolutionary community to the reactionary regime of their colony. But even if they did not, nothing would be lost. On the contrary, the revolution would itself be the greatest gainer, spiritually, by forsaking methods of revenge and persecution and practicing humanity and magnanimity. Revolutionary self-defense, inspired by such methods, will be the more effective because of the very freedom it will guarantee even to its enemies. Its appeal to the masses and to the world at large will thereby be the more irresistible and universal. In its justice and humanity lies the invincible strength of the social revolution.

No revolution has yet tried the true way of liberty. None has had sufficient faith in it. Force and suppression, persecution, revenge, and terror have characterized all revolutions in the past and have thereby defeated their original aims. The time has come to try new methods, new ways. The social revolution is to achieve the emancipation of man through liberty, but if we have no faith in the latter, revolution becomes a denial and betrayal of itself. Let us then have the courage of freedom: let it replace suppression and terror. Let liberty become our faith and our *deed* and we shall grow strong therein.

Only liberty can make the social revolution effective and wholesome. It alone can pave the way to greater heights and prepare a society where well-being and joy shall be the heritage of all. Then will dawn the day when man shall for the first time have full opportunity to grow and expand in the free and generous sunshine of Anarchy.

Pacifism and Pathology in the American Left
CHURCHILL, Ward
AK Press/Alternative Tentacles
ISBN: 1 902593 58 8
CD: $14.98 / £10.00

Liberal activism often embraces non-violent resistance in response to state-sponsored terrorism at home and abroad. In this emotional critique, Churchill urges activists to support any and all tactics in order to stop the tyranny of the state. Churchill argues that the terrorist attack of 9/11 disrupted U.S. global capitalism more radically than any peaceful protest the Left has been able to organize. Recorded at a packed and fired up AK Press warehouse in Oakland.

Mob Action Against the State: Collected Speeches from the Bay Area Anarchist Book Fair
VARIOUS
AK Press/Alternative Tentacles
ISBN: 1 902593 51 0
2 x CD: $19.98 / £10.00

The Bay Area is rich in local radicals, and most of them have taken a turn at the microphone of the Bay Area Anarchist Bookfair. Here's an all-star collection from the speakers' corner of the bookfair: Jello Biafra, spoken word artist and ex-frontman for punk band Dead Kennedys; Beat poet Lawrence Ferlinghetti; author Christian Parenti (*Lockdown America*); author and punk rocker Craig O'Hara (*The Philosophy of Punk*); anti-prison activist and author Ruth Wilson Gilmore (*Golden Gulag*); and Emma Goldman Papers Project curator Barry Pateman cut loose on anarchism, art, prisons, politics and more, in a relaxed setting.

Distorted Morality: America's War On Terror?
CHOMSKY, Noam
AK Press
ISBN: 1 902593 76 6
DVD: $25.00

Chomsky offers a devastating critique of America's current War on Terror—arguing that it is a logical impossibility for such a war to be taking place. Chomsky presents his reasoning with refreshing clarity, drawing from a wealth of historic knowledge and analysis. The DVD also includes a shorter, more recent talk on the danger, cruelty, and stupidity of the US and Israel's policy of Pre-emptive War and a lively Q&A session. All in an easily searchable user friendly format.

Anarchism: Arguments For and Against

MELTZER, Albert
AK Press/AntiTheses
ISBN: 1 873176 57 0
pb: $5.95 / £3.95

Everything you wanted to know about anarchism. A new, revised and updated edition of the definitive pocket primer on anarchism. From the historical background and justification of anarchism to the class struggle, organization and the role of the anarchist in authoritarian society, this slim tome walks the reader through both with a set of questions and objections from a variety of political positions: Leninist, Fascist, Social-Democrat, and apolitical Christ on the corner. The perfect introduction for those who wish they were better informed, the mildly curious, and especially for those looking for a place to start their new anarchist life. Albert Meltzer is the author of *I Couldn't Paint Golden Angels: Sixty Years of Commonplace Life and Anarchist Agitation*. He was described by Emma Goldman as a "hooligan and rascal who knows nothing of anarchism." Judge for yourself.

Reinventing Anarchy, Again

EHRLICH Ed., Howard J.
AK Press
ISBN: 1 873176 88 0
pb: $24.95 / £13.95

RECENTLY REPRINTED. This book brings together the major currents of social anarchist theory in a collection of some of the most important writers from the United States, Canada, England and Australia The book is organized into eight sections: What is Anarchism?, The State and Social Organization, Moving Toward Anarchist Society, Anarchafeminism, Work, The Culture of Anarchy, The Liberation of Self, and, finally, Reinventing Anarchist Tactics.

AK PRESS:

EDINBURGH   LONDON   OAKLAND

A New World In Our Hearts: 8 Years of Writings from the Love and Rage Revolutionary Anarchist Federation

SAN FILIPPO, Roy (ed)
AK Press
ISBN: 1 902593 61 8
pb: $11.95 / £9.00

The Love and Rage Federation was perhaps the most visible revolutionary anarchist organization in North America in the last few decades. This book keeps alive the many key political contributions Love and Rage made to debates around anarchism and organization, race, white supremacy and the national question, as well as documenting the rise and fall of an important political movement.

Facing the Enemy: A History Of Anarchist Organisation From Proudhon To May 1968

SKIRDA, Alexandre
AK Press
ISBN: 1 902593 19 7
pb: $17.95 / £12.00

The finest single volume history of European Anarchism is finally available in English in Paul Sharkey's elegant translation. Drawing on decades of research, Alexandre Skirda traces anarchism as a major political movement and ideology across the 19th and 20th centuries. Critical and engaged, he offers biting and incisive portraits of the major thinkers, and more crucially, the organizations they inspired, influenced, came out of and were spurned by. Opinionated and witty, he is equally at home skewering the actions of the early anarchist Victor Serge as he is the Paris chief of police who organized undercover "anarchist bombers" in an attempt to infiltrate and discredit the movement. Skirda argues that the core problem for anarchists has been to create a revolutionary movement and envision a future society in which the autonomy of the individual is not compromised by the need to take collective action. How anarchists have grappled with that question in theory and practice make up the core of the book. Bakuninist secret societies; the Internationals and the clash with Marx; the Illegalists, bombers and assassins; the mass trade unions and insurrections; and, of course, the Russian and Spanish Revolutions are all discussed through the prism of working people battling fiercely for a new world free of the shackles of Capital and the State.

Orgasms of History:
3000 Years of Spontaneous Revolt

FREMION, Yves and VOLNY
AK Press
ISBN: 1 902593 34 0
pb: $18.95 / £12.00

Every now and then, things explode. Riots, uprisings, revolutions, new and bizarre social groups spring up seemingly from nowhere. Our standard histories tend to treat these as oddities, if treated at all, or as misguided responses to hard times, limited by lack of responsible leadership. For the first time in English, here's a People's History to puncture that balloon. From the Cynics & Spartacus through the Levelers, Diggers & Ranters to the Revolution of the Carnation, the San Francisco Diggers, Red Guard of Shenwulian, Brethren of the Free Spirit, Guevara, the Provos & the Metropolitan Indians. Nearly 100 episodes of revolt and utopia which popped up without a plan or a leader from the ancient Greeks to the present. Includes Volny's original artwork and sketches throughout of the characters involved in the greatest, most inspiring events of all time. Yves Fremion lives in Paris where he participated in the May '68 orgasm.

Obsolete Communism:
The Left-Wing
Alternative

COHN-BENDIT, Daniel & Gabriel
AK Press
ISBN: 1 902593 25 1
pb: $17.95 / £12.00

"Their nightmares are our dreams." In May 68 a student protest at Nanterre University spread to other universities, to Paris factories and in a few weeks to most of France. On May 13 a million Parisians marched. Ten million workers went out on strike. At the center of the fray from the beginning was Daniel Cohn-Bendit, expelled from Nanterre for his agitation. Obsolete Communism was written in 5 weeks immediately after the French state regained control, and no account of May 68 or indeed of any rebellion can match its immediacy or urgency. Daniel's gripping account of the revolt is complemented by brother Gabriel's biting criticism of the collaboration of the state, the union leadership and the French Communist Party in restoring order, defusing revolutionary energy & handing the factories back to the capitalists. Leninism & the unions come under fire as top-down bureaucracies whose need to manage and control are always at odds with revolutionary action. "Daniel Cohn-Bendit is the most dangerous scoundrel in France."
—President Charles deGaulle

No Gods No Masters: Book One

DANIEL GUERIN (ed)
AK Press
ISBN: 1 873176 64 3
pb: $18.95 / £11.95

This is the first English translation of Guerin's monumental anthology of Anarchism. It details, through a vast array of hitherto unpublished documents, writings, letters and reports, the history, organization and practice of the anarchist movement—its theorists, advocates and activists. Book 1 includes the writings of Max Stirner, Pierre-Joseph Proudhon, Mikhail Bakunin, James Guillaume, Max Nettlau, Peter Kropotkin, Emma Goldman and Cesar de Paepe amongst others—traversing through 'The Ego And His Own', 'Property Is Theft', 'God And The State', 'The International Revolutionary Society Or Brotherhood', the controversy with Marx and the First International, The Paris Commune, Worker Self-Management, The Jura Federation and more...

No Gods No Masters: Book Two

DANIEL GUERIN (ed)
AK Press
ISBN: 1 873176 69 4
pb: $16.95 / £11.95

Book 2 includes work from the likes of Malatesta, Emile Henry, Emile Pouget, Augustin Souchy, Gaston Leval, Voline, Nestor Makhno, the Kronstadt sailors, Luigi Fabbri, Buenaventura Durruti and Emma Goldman—covering such momentous events as the Anarchist International, French 'propaganda by the deed', the General Strike, collectivization, The Russian Revolution, the Nabat, The Insurgent Peasant Army of the Ukraine, the Kronstadt Uprising, and the Spanish Civil War and Revolution.

Quiet Rumours:
An Anarcha-Feminist Reader

DARK STAR COLLECTIVE (ed.)
AK Press
ISBN: 1 902593 40 5
pb: $15.00 / £10.00

From consciousness-raising groups to hair-razing punk rockers, here's a fascinating window into the development of the women's movement, in the words of the women who moved it. These classic essays span the century, providing welcome context for feminism as part of a larger politics of liberation and equality. Critical analysis and biting polemic, whether it's Emma Goldman's attack on the suffrage movement or the debates of Second Wave feminists of the 1970s, connect the dots to show not just how anarchism influenced feminism, but how feminism changed the political landscape around it.

Moving Forward: Program for a Participatory Economy

ALBERT, Michael
AK Press
ISBN: 1 902593 41 3
pb: $11.95 / £8.00

If not capitalism, then what? Something's not working here, and it's pretty clear what's wrong. But there's a dearth of material on what could be right—and more important, how to do it. Albert breaks through the stranglehold on this debate and lays out the vision and strategy for his revolutionary "participatory economy" idea. He argues that we have to change how we conceive of work and wages, rewarding effort and sacrifice rather than output, and restructuring work so that everyone can become involved in controlling their workplaces. From here he moves to a proposal for how we might organize the larger functions of the economy in workers' councils and a general discussion of how our society might look with a participatory economy. The third in Albert's series of *"Forward"* books is written in clear language for anyone from those just beginning to question the (il)logic of capitalism to experienced activists. With its dialogue format and real-world examples, *Moving Forward* gives you all the tools you need to smartly rebut anyone who tries to tell you the system is working. School yourself on self-management, balanced job complexes, just rewards, participatory allocation and other weighty concepts made easy. Michael Albert is a founder of *Z Magazine* and South End Press. He is a lifelong activist and prolific writer, and currently works full time on ZNet, the Z website (*www.zmag.org*). "Michael Albert's work has been noteworthy for its broad vision, thoughtful concern and detailed analysis of the real problems that arise in implementing social and economic arrangements that might bring such far-reaching goals closer to reality."—Noam Chomsky

The Spanish Anarchists: The Heroic Years 1868-1936

MURRAY BOOKCHIN
AK Press
ISBN: 1 873176 04 X
pb: $19.95 / £13.95

A long-awaited new edition of the seminal history of Spanish Anarchism. Hailed as a masterpiece, it includes a new prefatory essay by the author. "I've read *The Spanish Anarchists* with the excitement of learning something new. It's solidly researched, lucidly written and admirably fair-minded...Murray Bookchin is that rare bird today, a historian."—DWIGHT MACDONALD "I have learned a great deal from this book. It is a rich and fascinating account...Most important, it has a wonderful spirit of revolutionary optimism that connects the Spanish Anarchists with our own time."—HOWARD ZINN. Murray Bookchin has written widely on politics, history and ecology. His books *'To Remember Spain: The Anarchist And Syndicalist Revolution Of 1936'* and *'Social Anarchism Or Lifestyle Anarchism: An Unbridgeable Chasm'* are both published by AK Press.

The Struggle Against The State And Other Essays

MAKHNO, Nestor
AK Press
ISBN: 1 873176 78 3
pb: $9.95 / £7.95

A collection of essays and articles written by the Ukrainian Anarchist militant while in exile in Paris in the 1920s. Sheds valuable insight onto the man, and the movement that bore his name while fighting both the White Army and the counter-revolutionist Bolsheviki. He responds to all sorts of accusations, including his alleged anti-semitism, and continues his exhortation for an organised, relevant, revolutionary anarchist movement. Needless to say, this is a crucial text.

Reading Capital Politically

CLEAVER, Harry
AK Press/AntiTheses
ISBN: 1 902593 29 4
pb: $15.00 / £8.00

As social movements waned in the late 70s, the study of Marx seemed to take on a life of its own. Structuralist, post-structuralist, deconstructed Marxes bloomed in journals and seminar rooms across the United States and Europe. These Marxes and their interpreters struggled to interpret the world, and sometimes to interpret Marx himself, losing sight at times of his dictum that the challenge is not to interpret the world but to change it. In 1979 Harry Cleaver tossed an incendiary device called *Reading Capital Politically* into those seminar rooms. Through a close reading of the first chapter, he shows that *Das Kapital* was written for the workers, not for academics, and that we need to expand our idea of workers to include housewives, students, the unemployed and other non-waged workers. *Reading Capital Politically* provides a theoretical and historical bridge between struggles in Europe in the 60s & 70s, and particularly the Autonomia of Italy to the Zapatistas of the 90s. His introduction provides a brilliant and succinct overview of working class struggles in the century since Capital was published. Cleaver adds a new preface to the AK Press/Anti-Theses edition.

AK PRESS:

PO Box 12766 / Edinburgh Scotland / EH89YE /
www.akuk.com / *ak@akedin.demon.uk* / (0131) 555.5165

674A 23rd St. / Oakland, Ca. / 94612 /
www.akpress.org / *akpress@akpress.org* / (510) 208.1700

Social Anarchism or Lifestyle Anarchism: An Unbridgeable Chasm

BOOKCHIN, Murray
AK Press
ISBN: 1 873176 83 X
pb: $9.95 / £5.95

RECENTLY REPRINTED. This book asks—and tries to answer— several basic questions that affect all Leftists today. Will anarchism remain a revolutionary social movement or become a chic boutique lifestyle subculture? Will its primary goals be the complete transformation of a hierarchical, class, and irrational society into a libertarian communist one? Or will it become an ideology focused on personal well-being, spiritual redemption, and self-realization within the existing society? In an era of privatism, kicks, introversion, and post-modernist nihilism, Murray Bookchin forcefully examines the growing nihilistic trends that threaten to undermine the revolutionary tradition of anarchism and co-opt its fragments into a harmless personalistic, yuppie ideology of social accommodation that presents no threat to the existing powers that be. Includes the essay, *"The Left That Was."*

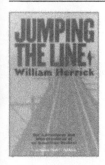

Jumping the Line: The Adventures and Misadventures of an American Radical

HERRICK, William
AK Press
ISBN: 1 902593 42 1
pb: $14.95 / £10.00

Jumping the Line offers a vivid first-hand account of Left culture in America in the heady days of the 20s through the 40s. William Herrick grew up in New York City with pictures of Lenin above his crib. He provides colorful reminiscences of riding the rails with other hobos during the Depression, of organizing Black sharecroppers in the South, of his time on the anarchist collective Sunrise Farm, where his political ideals of communal living and self-sufficiency were tested by the very real demands of agricultural work on a city boy, up through his tumultuous relationship with his employer Orson Welles. The bulk of the book focuses on Herrick's involvement during the Spanish Civil War. Like many of his communist comrades, Herrick went to Spain to fight for freedom. His experiences as part of the Abraham Lincoln Brigade shattered his political world forever. Herrick saw in Spain that the Brigades and their Stalinist masters were fighting not for freedom, but against it by executing the freedom fighting Anarchists. His accounts of Spain provoked great controversy when the Village Voice ran an interview in 1986. This full account of this wartime in Spain provoked Paul Berman to call him "our American Orwell."